Hans-Hellmut Nagel
Francisco J. Perales López (Eds.)

T0259904

Articulated Motion
and Deformable Objects

First International Workshop, AMDO 2000
Palma de Mallorca, Spain, September 7-9, 2000
Proceedings

Series Editors

Gerhard Goos, Karlsruhe University, Germany
Juris Hartmanis, Cornell University, NY, USA
Jan van Leeuwen, Utrecht University, The Netherlands

Volume Editors

Hans-Hellmut Nagel
Technical University of Karlsruhe
Institute for Algorithms and Cognitive Systems
Am Fasanengarten 5, 76132 Karlsruhe, Germany
E-mail: hhn@iitb.fgh.de

Francisco J. Perales López
Computer Graphics Vision Group
Department of Mathematics and Computer Science
Palma de Mallorca, 07071 (Balears), Spain
E-mail: paco.perales@uib.es

Cataloging-in-Publication Data applied for

Die Deutsche Bibliothek - CIP-Einheitsaufnahme

Articulated motion and deformable objects : first international
workshop ; proceedings / AMDO 2000, Palma de Mallorca, Spain,
September 7 - 9, 2000. Hans-Hellmut Nagel ; Francisco J. Perales López
(ed.). - Berlin ; Heidelberg ; New York ; Barcelona ; Hong Kong ;
London ; Milan ; Paris ; Singapore ; Tokyo : Springer, 2000
   (Lecture notes in computer science ; Vol. 1899)
   ISBN 3-540-67912-X

CR Subject Classification (1998): I.4, I.3, I.5, I.2.10

ISSN 0302-9743
ISBN 3-540-67912-X Springer-Verlag Berlin Heidelberg New York

Springer-Verlag Berlin Heidelberg New York
a member of BertelsmannSpringer Science+Business Media GmbH
© Springer-Verlag Berlin Heidelberg 2000
Printed in Germany

Typesetting: Camera-ready by author, data conversion by DA-TeX Gerd Blumenstein
Printed on acid-free paper   SPIN: 10722604   06/3142   5 4 3 2 1 0

Preface

The AMDO 2000 workshop took place at the Universitat de les Illes Balears (UIB) on 7–9 September 2000, sponsored by the International Association for Pattern Recognition Technical Committee, the European Commission by Human Potential Program: High Level Scientific Conferences and the Mathematics and Computer Science Department of UIB. The subject of the workshop was ongoing research in articulated motion on the sequence of images and sophisticated models for deformable objects. The goals of these areas are to understand and interpret object motion around complex objects that we can find in sequences of images in the real world. These topics (geometry and physics of deformable models, motion analysis, articulated models and animation, visualization of deformable models, 3D recovery from motion, single or multiple human motion analysis and synthesis, applications of deformable models and motion analysis, etc.) are interesting examples of how research can be used to solve more general problems. Another objective of this workshop was to relate fields using computer graphics, computer animation or applications in several disciplines combining synthetic and analytical images. In this regard it is of particular interest to encourage links between researchers in areas of computer vision and computer graphics who have common problems and frequently use similar techniques. The workshop included four sessions of presented papers and two tutorials. Invited speakers treating various aspects of the topics were: Y. Aloimonos from the Computer Vision Laboratory, Center for Automation Research, University of Maryland, USA, G. Medioni from the Institute for Robotics and Intelligent Systems, University of Southern California, USA, and R. Boulic, Adjoint scientifique from the Swiss Federal Institute of Technology Lausanne, Switzerland.

September 2000

H.-H. Nagel and F. J. Perales
Program Co-Chairs
AMDO 2000

Organization

AMDO 2000 is organized by the department of Math and Computer Science, Universitat de les Illes Balears (UIB) in cooperation with IAPR (International Association for Pattern Recognition).

Program Committee

General Workshop Co-Chairs:	H.-H. Nagel, Institut für Algorithmen und Kognitive System, Karlsruhe (Germany)
	F. J. Perales, Computer and Math Science Department UIB (Spain)
IAPR TC4 Chair:	E. R. Hancock, Department of Computer Science, University of York (UK)
Organizing Chairs:	M. Gonzalez, A. Igelmo, R. Mas, P. M. Mascaró, A. Mir, P. Palmer, F. J. Perales, J. Rocha, UIB (Spain)
Tutorial Chairs:	R. Mas, F. Perales UIB, (Spain)

Referees

Aloimonos, Y.	University Mariland, USA
Aggarwal, J. K.	University of Texas, USA
Amengual, A.	Universitat Illes Balears, UIB, Spain
Badler, N. I.	University of Pennsylvania, USA
Boulic, R.	EPFL, Switzerland
Cipolla, R.	Univ. of Cambrige, UK
Crowley, J.	INRIA Rhone Alpes, France
Davis, L. S.	Univ. of Maryland, USA
Del Bimbo, A.	Univ. di Firenze, Italy
Gong, S.	QM & Westfield Coll, UK
Hancock, E. R.	University of York UK
Igelmo, A.	Universitat Illes Balears, UIB, Spain
Kittler, J.	Univ. Surrey, UK
Kunii, T. L.	University of Hosei, Japan
Metaxas, D.	Univ. of Pennsylvania, USA
Nagel, H.-H.	Institut für Algorithmen und Kognitive System, Karlsruhe, Germany
Nastar, C.	INRIA Roquercourt, France
Navazo, I.	UPC, Spain
Poggio, T.	MIT, USA
Sanfeliu, A.	IRI, CSIC-UPC, Spain
Seron, F.	Univ. of Zaragoza, Spain
Shirai, Y.	Univ of Osaka, Japan
Terzopoulos, D.	Univ. of Toronto, Canada
Teixeira, J. C.	FCTUC, Portugal
Thalmann, D.	EPFL, Switzerland
Thalmann, Nadia	M. Univ. of Geneve, Switzerland
Villanueva, J. J.	UAB-CVC, Spain

Sponsoring Institutions

IAPR (International Association for Pattern Recognition)

European Commission by Human Potential Program: High Level Scientific Conferences

Mathematics and Computer Science Department, Universitat de les Illes Balears (UIB)

Table of Contents

Robust Manipulation of Deformable Objects Using Model Based Technique

T. Wada[1], S. Hirai[2], H. Mori[2], and S. Kawamura[2]

[1] Kagawa University, Faculty of Engineering,
2217-20, Hayashi-cho, Takamatsu, 761-0396, Kagawa, Japan
wachan@robot.club.ne.jp
http://www.eng.kagawa-u.ac.jp/~wada/
[2] Ritsumeikan University, Department of Robotics,
1-1-1, Noji-higashi, Kusatsu, 525-8577, Shiga, Japan
{hirai,rm141954,kawamura}@se.ritsumei.ac.jp

Abstract. Manipulation of deformable objects will be discussed. Manipulation of deformable objects is defined as controlling deformation of objects as well as their positions and orientations. The manipulation is a fundamental and important task in many industrial fields. In fact, there exist many operations of deformable objects such as textile fabrics, rubber parts, paper sheets, strings, and foods. In order to realize the manipulation of deformable objects by mechanical systems, an object model is indispensable. It is, however, difficult to build exact model of the deformable objects due to their strong nonlinearity such as friction, hysteresis and parameter variations. Thus, such operations strongly depend on skilled human workers. To overcome this problem, we will propose a robust control strategy using a model based technique. We will build a coarse model of an object for the manipulation and will develop a control method robust to the discrepancy between the object and its model. Experimental results will show the robustness of the proposed method.

1   Introduction

There exist many manipulative tasks that deal with deformable objects such as textile fabrics, rubber parts, paper sheets, and food products. Most these operations strongly depend on skilled human workers. We define manipulation of deformable objects as controlling of deformation of deformable objects as well as their positions and orientations in this paper. For example, a positioning operation called *linking* is involved in the manufacturing of seamless knitted products [ ]. In linking of fabrics, knitted loops at the end of a fabric must be matched to those of another fabric so that the two fabrics can be sewed seamlessly. This operation is now done by skillful humans and automatic linking is required in manufacturing of knitted products. In this research, we describe the manipulations of deformable objects including linking by positioning of multiple points on the objects. Then, we regard the manipulations as the operations in which multiple points on a deformable object should be guided to the final

H. H. Nagel and F. J. Perales (Eds.): AMDO 2000, LNCS 1899, pp. 1– , 2000.
© Springer-Verlag Berlin Heidelberg 2000

locations simultaneously as shown in Fig. . In many cases these points cannot be, however, manipulated directly. Thus, the guidance of positioned points must be performed by controlling some points except the positioned points. This operation is referred to as *indirect simultaneous positioning* [ ]. In this paper, we will focus on indirect simultaneous positioning as an example of manipulation of deformable objects.

Some researches on manipulations of deformable objects have been conducted. For automated manufacturing of textile fabrics, many researches have been done [ ]. Ono et al. [ ] have derived a strategy for unfolding a fabric piece based on cooperative sensing of touch and vision. In these researches, since their approaches are for a specific task, thus it is difficult to apply the results to other different tasks with a systematic manner. In addition, some researches have tried to deal with on more general deformable object with systematic manners as follows. Hirai et al. [ ] have proposed a method for modeling linear objects based on their potential energy and analyzed their static deformation. Wakamatsu et al. [ ] have analyzed grasping of deformable objects and introduced bounded force closure. Their approach is static, control of manipulative operations is out of consideration. Howard et al. [ ] have proposed a method to model elastic objects by the connections of springs and dampers. A method to estimate the coefficients of the springs and dampers has been developed by recursive learning method for grasping. This study has focused on model building. Thus, control problems for manipulative operations have not been investigated. Sun et al. [ ] have studied on the positioning operation of deformable objects using two manipulators. They have focused on the control of the object position while deformation control is not discussed.

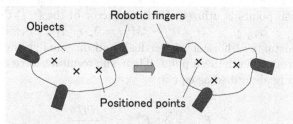

Fig. 1. Indirect positioning of deformable object

In order to realize indirect simultaneous positioning, object model is indispensable. However, it is difficult to build exact model of the deformable objects in general due to nonlinear elasticity, friction, hysteresis, parameter variations, and other uncertainties. These are main difficulties in manipulating deformable objects. To solve this dilemma, we propose to utilize a coarse object model to derive task strategies with a vision sensor. In our approach, we first build a coarse model of a manipulated object. Then, the task is analyzed based on the proposed coarse model. One of the advantages using the coarse object model is that we can analyze the task and may realize its essence relatively easily. Based on the results of the analysis, we can derive a control law robust to discrepancy between the object and its coarse model.

In this article, we will firstly propose a coarse model of deformable objects. Next, indirect positioning will be analyzed based on the coarse model. As the result, we will derive conditions to examine whether the given positioning is feasible or not. Then, we will propose a control method robust to model errors based on the coarse model. Experimental results show the validity of the proposed method and the effects of the parameter errors on the convergence.

2   Formulation of Indirect Positioning

2.1   Modeling of Extensible Deformable Objects

First of all, a model of deformable objects is proposed. On modelling of deformable objects, many researches have been conducted. For example in the area of computer graphics, cloth deformation is animated by Terzopoulos [ ] or Louchet, Provot and Crochemore [   ] and other many researchers. Our research goal is to realize robust manipulation of deformable objects. Therefore, we employ more simple deformation model. We model the object by connection of simple springs similar with Naster and Ayache [   ]. For simplicity, we deal with two dimensional deformable objects such as textile fabrics. We discretize the object by mesh points. Each mesh point is connected by vertical, horizontal, and diagonal springs as shown in Fig. . In the model, we assume that the object deforms in a two-dimensional plane. In order to formulate the manipulation of deformable objects, object model must have the ability to describe translation, orientation, and deformation of the object simultaneously. Thus, position vector of the mesh points is utilized. Position vector of the (i,j)-th mesh point is defined as $\boldsymbol{p}_{i,j} = [x_{i,j}, y_{i,j}]^{\mathrm{T}}$ $(i = 0, \cdots, M; j = 0, \cdots, N)$. Coefficients k_x, k_y, k_θ are spring constants of horizontal, vertical, and diagonal springs. Assume that no moment exert on each mesh point. Then, the resultant force exerted on mesh point $\boldsymbol{p}_{i,j}$ can be described as eq.( ).

$$\boldsymbol{F}_{i,j} = \sum_{k=1}^{8} \boldsymbol{F}_{i,j}^{k} = -\frac{\partial U}{\partial \boldsymbol{p}_{i,j}} \tag{1}$$

U denotes whole potential energy of the object. Then, function U can be calculated by sum of all energies of springs [ ]. Here, we assume that the shape of the object is dominated by eq.( ). Then, we can calculate the deformation of the object by solving eq.( ) under given constraints. Note that the following discussions are valid even if the object has an arbitrary three-dimensional shape by modeling the object similarly. Details have been reported in [ ].

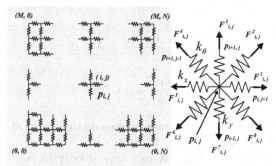

Fig. 2. Spring model of deformable object

2.2 Problem Description

Here, we classify mesh points $p_{i,j}$ into the following three categories(see Fig.4) in order to formulate indirect simultaneous positioning.

manipulated points: are defined as the points that can be manipulated directly by robotic fingers. ($\triangle$)

positioned points: are defined as the points that should be positioned indirectly by controlling manipulated points appropriately. ($\bigcirc$)

non-target points: are defined as the all points except the above two points. (others in Fig.4)

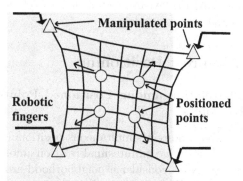

Fig. 3. Classification of mesh point

Let the number of manipulated points and of positioned points be m and p, respectively. The number of non-target points is $n = (M+1) \times (N+1) - m - p$. Then, r_m is defined as a vector that consists of coordinate values of the manipulated points. Vectors r_p and r_n are also defined for positioned and non-target points in the similar way. Eq.( ) can be rewritten as eqs.( ),( ) using r_m, r_p, and r_n.

$$\frac{\partial U(\boldsymbol{r}_m, \boldsymbol{r}_n, \boldsymbol{r}_p)}{\partial \boldsymbol{r}_m} - \boldsymbol{\lambda} = \boldsymbol{0}, \tag{2}$$

$$\begin{bmatrix} \frac{\partial U(\boldsymbol{r}_m, \boldsymbol{r}_n, \boldsymbol{r}_p)}{\partial \boldsymbol{r}_p} \\ \frac{\partial U(\boldsymbol{r}_m, \boldsymbol{r}_n, \boldsymbol{r}_p)}{\partial \boldsymbol{r}_n} \end{bmatrix} = \boldsymbol{0} \tag{3}$$

where a vector $\boldsymbol{\lambda}$ denotes a set of forces exerted on the object at the manipulated points $\boldsymbol{r}_m$ by robotic fingers.

Note that the external forces $\boldsymbol{\lambda}$ can appear only in eq.( ), not in eq.( ). This implies that no external forces are exerted on positioned points and non-target points. These equations represent characteristics of indirect simultaneous positioning of deformable objects.

Let us consider the following task:

[Task]   *Assume that the configuration of robotic fingers and the positioned points on an object are given in advance. Then, the positioned points $\boldsymbol{r}_p$ are guided to their desired location $\boldsymbol{r}_p^d$ by controlling manipulated points $\boldsymbol{r}_m$ appropriately.*

In order to realize the given task, an object model is indispensable since we have to predict directions of displacements of positioned points during the positioning. Then, the proposed model is useful for this purpose. However, in general, the model errors cannot be ignored in modeling deformable objects due to many uncertainties. Thus, a model inversion approach is not effective. Therefore, it is important to develop a control method that is robust to the error between the object and its model.

3   Analysis of Indirect Positioning

3.1   Infinitesimal Relation among Positioned Points and Manipulated Points

In this section, we analyze indirect simultaneous positioning based on the proposed coarse model. Let us derive infinitesimal relation among positioned points and manipulated points. Now, consider a neighborhood around an equilibrium point $\boldsymbol{r}_0 = [\boldsymbol{r}_{m0}^{\mathrm{T}}, \boldsymbol{r}_{p0}^{\mathrm{T}}, \ \boldsymbol{r}_{n0}^{\mathrm{T}}]^{\mathrm{T}}$. We can obtain the following equation by linearlizing eq.( ) around the equilibrium point.

$$A\delta \boldsymbol{r}_m + B\delta \boldsymbol{r}_n + C\delta \boldsymbol{r}_p = 0 \tag{4}$$

where

$$A \triangleq \begin{bmatrix} \frac{\partial^2 U}{\partial r_m \, \partial r_p} \\ \frac{\partial^2 U}{\partial r_m \, \partial r_n} \end{bmatrix} \bigg|_{r0} \in R^{(2p+2n)\times 2m},$$

$$B \triangleq \left[\begin{array}{c} \frac{\partial^2 U}{\partial r_n \, \partial r_p} \\ \frac{\partial^2 U}{\partial r_n \, \partial r_n} \end{array} \right] \Bigg|_{r0} \in R^{(2p+2n) \times 2n},$$

$$C \triangleq \left[\begin{array}{c} \frac{\partial^2 U}{\partial r_p \, \partial r_p} \\ \frac{\partial^2 U}{\partial r_p \, \partial r_n} \end{array} \right] \Bigg|_{r0} \in R^{(2p+2n) \times 2p}.$$

Vector δr_m is defined as an infinitesimal deviation of the manipulated points from their equilibrium points. Vectors δr_n and δr_p are defined in the similar way. By transforming eq.( ), eq.( ) is obtained.

$$F \left[\begin{array}{c} \delta r_m \\ \delta r_n \end{array} \right] = -C \delta r_p \tag{5}$$

where $F = [A \ B]$.

3.2   Feasibility of Indirect Positioning

We can obtain the following theorems. The proof of these theorems have been reported in [ ].

Theorem 1. There exist infinitesimal displacements of manipulated points δr_m corresponding to arbitrary infinitesimal displacements δr_p, if and only if, rank$[A \ B] = 2p + 2n$ is satisfied.

In addition, Theorem 1 needs the following result.

Result 1 *The number of the manipulated points must be greater than or equal to that of the positioned points in order to realize any arbitrary displacement δr_p , that is, $m \geq p$.*

In the case that the number of the manipulated points is equal to that of the positioned points, that is, $m = p$ is satisfied, Theorem 1 can be rewritten as follows:

Theorem 2. *In the case of $m = p$, there exist displacements of the manipulated points δr_m corresponding to any displacements of positioned points δr_p and these are determined uniquely, if and only if, $\det[A \ B] \neq 0$.*

4 Iterative Control Law of Indirect Simultaneous Positioning

In this section, we propose a novel control method to achieve an indirect simultaneous positioning. An iterative control law is derived based on a linearized model of the object eq.( ).

In the control of indirect simultaneous positioning of deformable objects, a vision system is utilized to measure current positions of positioned points. Positions of the manipulated points can be computed from the locations of the robotic fingers because the fingers pinch an object firmly. On the other hand, it is difficult to measure positions of non-target points due to their number.

Now, let us derive an iterative control law for indirect simultaneous positioning based on linearized equations ( ). Fig. shows a flow of our proposed control method. Assume that the number of positioned points is equal to the number of manipulated points, that is, $m = p$. In this case, F is a square matrix. This article deals with only the case that the matrix F is non-singular during operations, for simplicity. Then, eq.( ) can be rewritten as the following two equations:

$$\delta r_m = -S_U F^{-1} C \delta r_p \tag{6}$$

$$\delta r_n = -S_L F^{-1} C \delta r_p \tag{7}$$

where $S_U = [I_m \quad 0_{m \times n}] \quad S_L = [0_{n \times m} \quad I_n]$. Let r_m^k, r_n^k and r_p^k be positions of manipulated points, those of non-target points, and those of positioned points at k-th iteration, respectively. In eq.( ), replacing deviation δr_m with difference $^d r_m^{k+1} - r_m^k$ and deviation δr_p with error $r_p^d - r_p^k$, we obtain the following equation:

$$^d r_m^{k+1} = r_m^k - d S_U F_k^{-1} C_k (r_p^d - r_p^k) \tag{8}$$

where F_k and C_k are functions of r_m^k, r_n^k, and r_p^k. Superscript and subscript k on variables denote their values at k-th iteration. A scalar d denotes a scaling factor. The right hand side of this equation can be evaluated at the k-th iteration. Thus, desired locations of manipulated points at the k-th iteration can be updated into those at the $(k+1)$-th iteration by this equation. Note that matrix F_k^{-1} depends not only r_m and r_p but also r_n. Thus, non-target points r_n^k is estimated by eq.( ).

$$r_n^k = r_n^{k-1} - d S_L F_{k-1}^{-1} C_{k-1} (r_p^{k-1} - r_p^{k-2}) \tag{9}$$

As a result, the proposed iterative control method is summarized as follows: First, a vision system senses current positions of positioned points. Second, locations of manipulated points and those of non-target points are updated using eq.( ) and ( ), respectively. Then, robot fingers are controlled with respect to task oriented coordinates using $^d r_m^{k+1}$ as their desired positions in $(k + 1)$-th iteration with an appropriate controller. For example, we can utilize linear PID feedback. After robot fingers converged to $^d r_m^{k+1}$, positions of positioned points r_p^{k+1} are measured again by the image sensor. Then, the same procedure is iterated.

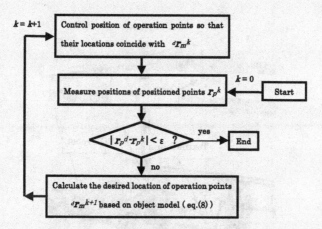

Fig. 4. Flow of proposed control method

We can show that the positioned points r_p can be converged to the desired ones by control law ( ) even if the model includes some errors. The details have been reported in [ ].

5   Experiments

5.1   Textile Fabric

In this section, we will show experimental results in order to illustrate the validity of the proposed control method and to investigate the effect of model errors on the convergence quantitatively. Fig. illustrates the experimental setup. Three 2DOF robots with stepping motors are utilized as robotic fingers. A CCD camera is utilized as a vision sensor. A deformable object is laid on a table. In the experiments, knitted fabrics of the acrylic 85[%] and wool 15[%] (100[mm]×100[mm]) are utilized. The fabric is descritized into 4×4 meshes. Both of the numbers of the manipulated and positioned points are three. Their initial locations on the object are shown in Fig. . Markers are put on the positioned points of the fabric. Their positions are measured by the CCD camera. The configurations of the manipulated and positioned points are as follows:

$$r_m = [x_{0,3}, y_{0,3} , \ \ x_{1,0}, y_{1,0} , \ \ x_{3,2}, y_{3,2}]^T,$$

$$r_p = [x_{1,1}, y_{1,1} , \ \ x_{1,2}, y_{1,2} , \ \ x_{2,2}, y_{2,2}]^T.$$

The desired positioned points used in the experiments are

$$r_p^d = [30, 40, \ 65, 50, \ 53.6, 90]^T.$$

We have identified spring constants $(k_x, k_y, k_\theta) = (4.17, 13.2, 3.32)$ [gf/mm] coarsely for the control method, through tensile tests. Note that the ratio of the

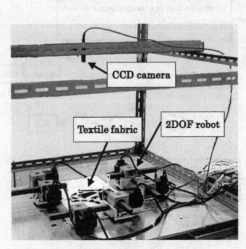

Fig. 5. Experimental setup

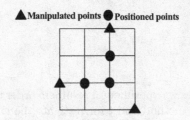

Fig. 6. Configuration of points in experiments

spring constants is important in our control method. Then, we define $\alpha = k_x/k_\theta$ and $\beta = k_y/k_\theta$. From coarsely identified spring constants, $\alpha = 1.256$ and $\beta = 3.976$ are obtained. In experiments, various values of β including errors were utilized in the control method in order to investigate the effects of model errors. Moreover, values 0.1 and 0.5 of scaling factor d are used in eq.( ) to show the effects of the scaling factors. Fig. -(a) and (b) illustrate the experimental results of $d = 0.1$ and 0.5, respectively.

In these figures, we can find that the positioned points can converge to the desired positions if the coefficients (α, β) is near their identified values, while they are gradually oscillatory or diverge if spring constant is far from the identified values. Fig. -(a) shows that the positioned points converge to the desired ones despite of 100 times or 0.01 times of deviations of parameters α and β. Fig. -(b) shows that the positioned points diverge for 10 times and 0.1 times deviations of the parameters. On the other hand, the speed of convergence is higher with $d = 0.5$. As an example, Fig. shows behaviors of manipulated and positioned

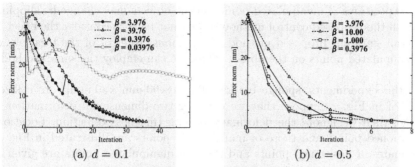

(a) $d = 0.1$ (b) $d = 0.5$

Fig. 7. Experimental results

points with $d = 0.5$, $(\alpha, \beta) = (1.256, 3.976)$. The accuracy of convergence to the desired ones can be reached to a resolution level of the visual sensor (about $1[\mathrm{mm}]$).

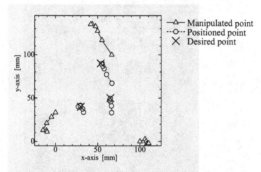

Fig. 8. Behavior of positioned and manipulated points in experiments

According to the experimental results, we can conclude that very coarsely estimated parameters can be utilized in the proposed control method. Scaling factor d should be chosen carefully.

5.2   Sponge Block

In this section, we apply the proposed control method to compressing deformation of sponge blocks. In these operations, we have to consider the following items:

1. In section 5.1, the robots pinch the object firmly. In the operation of sponge blocks, we cannot pinch the objects. Thus, we have to realize manipulations with grasping the object stably. In this paper, we do not deal with this matter, and apply the same control law. We will investigate the effect experimentally with various desired locations.

2. The positions of manipulated points on the objects may change by slipping. With the proposed control method, we do not have to consider the effect in detail since our proposed method is also robust to error of the locations of manipulated points on the object. Thus, we can employ the same method.

   In this experiments, sponge blocks ($90[\mathrm{mm}] \times 90[\mathrm{mm}] \times 30[\mathrm{mm}]$) are utilized as shown in Fig. . Suppose that we consider two-dimensional deformation in a plane, then we ignore the deformation along thickness direction. Locations of positioned points and those of manipulated points are illustrated in Fig. . Coordinates of positioned points and those of manipulated points are given as follows:

$$\boldsymbol{r}_p = [30, 30, \quad 60, 30, \quad 60, 60]^T , \quad \boldsymbol{r}_m = [60, 0, \quad 0, 30, \quad 90, 60]^T \quad (10)$$

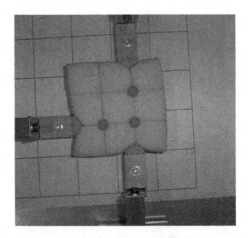

Fig. 9. Manipulation of sponge block

   As shown in Fig. , experiments performed for 6 patterns of desired positions. Desired location of each pattern is given as follows:

Pattern 1: $\boldsymbol{r}_p^d = [35, 30, \quad 65, 30, \quad 65, 60]^T$ (translation)
Pattern 2: $\boldsymbol{r}_p^d = [35, 30, \quad 62, 30, \quad 62, 60]^T$ (compression with translation)
Pattern 3: $\boldsymbol{r}_p^d = [32, 30, \quad 65, 30, \quad 65, 60]^T$ (stretching with translation)
Pattern 4: $\boldsymbol{r}_p^d = [27.6, 32.8, \quad 57.2, 27.6, \quad 62.4, 57.2]^T$ (rotation)
Pattern 5: $\boldsymbol{r}_p^d = [32, 32, \quad 58, 32, \quad 58, 58]^T$ (compression)
Pattern 6: $\boldsymbol{r}_p^d = [32.6, 37.8, \quad 62.2, 32.6, \quad 67.4, 62.2]^T$ (orientation and translation)

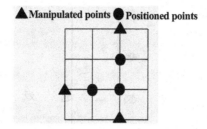

Fig. 10. Location of positioned and manipulated points

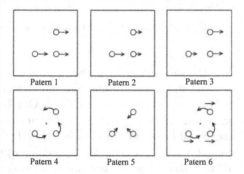

Fig. 11. Motion pattern of positioned points

Table 1. Experimental results for sponge block

	1	2	3	4	5	6	7	8	9	10
Pattern 1	O	O	O	O	O	O	O	O	O	O
	5	9	4	10	3	4	4	5	5	4
	3	4		4				4	4	
Pattern 2	O	Δ	O	Δ	Δ	Δ	Δ	Δ	O	Δ
	4		16						12	
		3	4	4	3	4	3	3	4	4
Pattern 3	×	×	×	×	×	×	×	×	×	×
Pattern 4	O	O	O	O	O	O	O	O	O	O
	4	3	4	9	4	9	4	4	7	4
	3			7	3	3	3	3	3	
Pattern 5	Δ	Δ	Δ	Δ	Δ	Δ	Δ	O	Δ	Δ
								25		
	3	3	3	3	3	3	3	3	4	3
Pattern 6	O	O	O	O	O	O	O	O	O	O
	9	4	7	8	6	14	10	4	8	5
	4		4	4	4	5	5		5	4

Experimental results of sponge manipulations are shown in Table . In the first row of each pattern, ○ denotes convergence with $\epsilon = 1[\text{mm}]$, Δ denotes convergence with $\epsilon = 2$, and × for no convergence. Second and third rows denote the numbers of iterations that are needed for convergence within $\epsilon = 1$ and 2, respectively. Fig. (a) and (b) illustrate the experimental results of pattern 2 and 4, respectively.

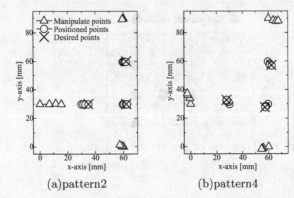

(a)pattern2   (b)pattern4

Fig. 12. Motion of positioned and manipulated points

According to the results, we can find that the error norm is converged within $\epsilon = 1$ in pattern 1, 4, and 6, manipulations without deformation. In pattern 2, 5 with deformation, the errors are converged in 2. One of the reasons is on accuracy of the vision sensor. In the experiments, the accuracy is $0.72[\text{mm}]$. In addition, inappropriateness of the locations of manipulated points on the objects is also one of the reasons. Pattern 3 denotes the stretching operations. Thus, the manipulation is failed since the robots do not pinch the object.

6   Conclusions

In this paper, indirect simultaneous positioning of deformable objects were discussed as an example of manipulation of deformable objects. First, we have proposed a coarse model of deformable objects for their positioning operations. Second, indirect simultaneous positioning of deformable objects have been formulated. Based on the formulations, we analyzed the indirect positioning. As the result, we derived the conditions that the given positioning can be achieved. Then, we have proposed a novel iterative control method to realize indirect simultaneous positioning based on the coarse object model. The validity of the method has been shown through experimental results using the textile fabrics, and effects of the model errors on the convergence were investigated. Then, we conclude that very coarse identifications can be utilized for the proposed method. In addition, we apply the proposed control method to compressing operations by grasping. In compressing operations, the error can be converged in a desired region.

In this article, initial locations of operation points on a deformable object were given before executing the manipulation. However, the task may be failed in or excessive forces may be exerted on the object in the case that the configuration of the positioned points is not appropriate. Then, task planning including configuration of operation points is important. Therefore, we need a method to plan configurations of robot fingers on a deformable object [ ]. In compressing operation, it is impossible to prove that stable grasp is maintaining during manipulations in all cases since we do not take states of grasping into consideration. Therefore, we have to add information of grasping states to control law. Use of force sensor for this purpose is one of the important future works.

References

1. Wada, T., Hirai, S., Hirano, T., Kawamura, S., "Modeling of Plain Knitted Fabrics for Their Deformation Control", Proc. of IEEE Int. Conf. on Robotics and Automation, pp.1960–1965, 1997
2. Wada, T., Hirai, S., Kawamura, S., "Planning and Control of Indirect Simultaneous Positioning Operation for Deformable Objects", Proc. of IEEE Int. Conf. on Robotics and Automation, pp.2572–2577, 1999   ,
3. Taylor, P. M. et al.(Ed.), "Sensory Robotics for the Handling of Limp Materials", Springer-Verlag, 1990
4. Ono, E., Kita, N., Sakane, S., "Strategy for Unfolding a Fabric Piece by Coorperative Sensing of Touch and Vision", Proc. of Int. Conf. on Intelligent Robots and Systems, pp.441–445, 1995
5. Hirai, S., Wakamatsu, H., and Iwata, K., "Modeling of Deformable Thin Parts for Their Manipulation", Proc. IEEE Int. Conf. on Robotics and Automation, pp.2955–2960, 1994
6. Wakamtatsu, H., Hirai, S., Iwata, K., "Static Analysis of Deformable Object Grasping Based on Bounded Force Closure", Proc. IEEE Int. Conf. on Robotics and Automation, pp.3324-3329, 1996
7. Howard, A. M. and Bekey, G. A., "Recursive Learning for Deformable Object Manipulation", Proc. of Int. Conf. on Advanced Robotics, pp.939–944, 1997.
8. Sun, D., Liu, Y., Mills, J. K., "Cooperative Control of a Two-Manipulator System Handling a General Flexible Object", Proc. of Int. Conf. on Intelligent Robots and Systems, pp.5–10, 1997
9. Terzopoulos, D., Platt, J., Barr, A., Fleischer, K., "Elastically Deformable Models", Proc. of Siggraph 87, Computer Graphics, 1987, Vol.21, No.4, pp.205–214
10. Louchet, J., Provot, X., Crochemore, D., "Evoluntionary Identification of Cloth Animation Models", Computer Animation and Simulation'95: Proc. of the Eurograpics Workshopin Maastricht, pp.44–54, 1995
11. Nastar, C. and Ayache, N., "Frequency-Based Nonrigid Motion Analysis: Application to Four Dimensional Medical Images", IEEE Trans. on Pattern Analysis and Machine Intelligence", Vol.18, No.11, pp.1067–1079, 1996
12. Wada, T., Hirai, S., Kawamura, S., "Indirect Simultaneous Positioning Operations of Extensionally Deformable Objects", Proc. of Int. Conf. on Intelligent Robots and Systems, pp.1333–1338, 1998   ,
13. Wada, T., Hirai, S., Kawamura, S., "Analysis and Planning of Indirect Simultaneous Positioning Operation for Deformable Objects", Proc. of Int. Conf. on Advanced Robotics, pp.141–146 1999

Shape Recognition Algorithm Robust under Partial Occlusions and Affine Deformations

J. L. Lisani[1], L. Moisan[1], P. Monasse[1], and J.M. Morel[2]

[1] Universitat de les Illes Balears, Cra. de Valldemossa, km. 7.5
07071 Palma de Mallorca, Spain
`joseluis@ipc4.uib.es`
[2] CMLA ENS-Cachan, 61 av du Pdt Wilson, 94235 Cachan Cedex, France
`moisan, monasse, morel@cmla.ens-cachan.fr`

Abstract. We design a generic contrast and affine invariant planar shape recognition algorithm. By generic, we mean an algorithm which delivers a list of all shapes two digital images have in common, up to any affine transform or contrast change. Affine invariance must not be considered as a weak requirement in shape recognition since it is well known that if 3D objects with smooth boundaries are being observed, then the deformation of the objects' images, far enough from the occlusion boundaries, is locally an affine transform. We define as "shape elements" all pieces of level lines of the image. We then discuss an efficient local encoding of the shape elements. We finally show experiments. Applications aimed at include image registration, image indexing, optical flow.

1 Introduction

The shape recognition problem has many different and very specific meanings, because each author somehow builds his own definition. In many cases, shape recognition is built for a specific application, like e.g. automatic character recognition, or fingerprint recognition. Another approach, related to psychophysics, tries to define what we really mean when stating that two shapes look alike. Recently, various strategies to rigorously define distances between shapes have been proposed [ ]. This distance method allows large nonparametric deformations. In this communication, we shall restrict ourselves to the case where perturbations boil down to contrast changes, planar affine transforms and occlusions. This restrictive framework is just sufficient to recognize an image which has undergone a xerocopy or a photograph (if it is a painting) and is thereafter subject to contrast changes and an arbitrary framing (occlusion on the boundary). The affine invariant framework is a well acknowledged topic [, , ,].

The restrictions we are taking are not arbitrary, but result from a hopefully rigorous invariance analysis. We first argue that the local contrast invariant information of an image is completely contained in its level lines ([,]), which turn out to be Jordan curves. In order to overcome the occlusion phenomena, we wish to have an encoding as local as possible. The locality is obtained by segmenting each level line into its smallest meaningful parts which must finally

H. H. Nagel and F. J. Perales (Eds.): AMDO 2000, LNCS 1899, pp. 15– , 2000.
© Springer-Verlag Berlin Heidelberg 2000

be described by small codes. The curve segmentation-encoding process must therefore be itself invariant.

Moreover, the description of the curves must involve some smoothing since level lines are influenced by the quantization process. Thus, smoothing must be performed in order to get rid of this influence. Another reason to smooth shapes, is given by the "scale space ideology" [ ]. Indeed, many of the fine scale oscillations of the shapes may be parts of the shape; the analysis of the shape would be lost in those details.

Following [ ], the only contrast invariant, local, smoothing and affine invariant scale space leads to a single PDE,

$$\frac{\partial u}{\partial t} = |Du|\text{curv}(u)^{\frac{1}{3}}, \tag{1}$$

where Du is the gradient of the image, $\text{curv}(u)$ the curvature of the level line and t the scale parameter. This equation is equivalent to the "affine curve shortening" ([ ])

$$\frac{\partial x}{\partial t} = |\text{Curv}(x)|^{\frac{1}{3}}\boldsymbol{n}, \tag{2}$$

where x denotes a point of a level line, $\text{Curv}(x)$ its curvature and $\boldsymbol{n}$ the signed normal to the curve, always pointing towards the concavity.

This equation is the only possible smoothing under the invariance requirements mentionned above. This gives a helpless bottleneck to the local shape recognition problem, since it is easily checked ([ ]) that no further invariance requirement is possible. Despite some interesting attempts [ ], there is no way to define a projective invariant local smoothing. The use of curvature-based smoothing for shape analysis is not new[, ,].

The contrast invariance requirement leads us to describe the shapes in terms of mathematical morphology [ ]. In [ ], connected components of level sets are proven to be invariant under contrast changes and [ ] proposed to take as basic elements of an image the boundaries of the level sets (the so called **level lines**), a complete representation of the image which they call **topographic map**. A fast algorithm for the decomposition of an image into connected components of level lines is described in [ ] and its application to a semi-local scale-space representation in [ ]. Each one of these connected components is a closed Jordan curve and in many cases, we shall identify the term "shape" with these Jordan curves.

In Section , a fast algorithm to perform equation ( ) is derived by going back to the mathematical morphology formalism ([,]) and defining first an affine distance and then affine erosions and dilations. This leads us to an axiomatic justification for a fast algorithm introduced by Moisan ([,]). This presentation follows the general line of a book in preparation [ ]. Section is devoted to a discussion of the basic requirements of computer based algorithms for shape recognition. In Section , we explain how to segment the smoothed curves into affine invariant parts and how these pieces of level lines can be encoded in an efficient way for matching. Section   gives a first account of what can be done with the generic algorithm.

2   Affine Invariant Mathematical Morphology and PDE's

We first define an "affine invariant distance" which will be a substitute to the classical euclidean one. We consider shapes X, subsets of $\mathbb{R}^2$. Let $x \in \mathbb{R}^2$ and Δ an arbitrary straight line passing by x. We consider all connected components of $\mathbb{R}^2 \setminus (X \cup \Delta)$. If $x \notin \bar{X}$, exactly two of them contain x in their boundary. We denote them by $\mathrm{CA}_1(x, \Delta, X)$, $\mathrm{CA}_2(x, \Delta, X)$ and call them the "chord-arc sets" defined by x, Δ and X, and we order them so that area($\mathrm{CA}_1(x, \Delta, X)$) $\leq$ area($\mathrm{CA}_2(x, \Delta, X)$).

Definition 1. *Let X be a "shape" and $x \in \mathbb{R}^2, x \notin \bar{X}$. We call affine distance of x to X the (maybe infinite) number $\delta(x, X) = \inf_\Delta \mathrm{area}(\mathrm{CA}_1(x, \Delta, X))^{1/2}$, $\delta(x, X) = 0$ if $x \in X$.*

Definition 2. *For $X \subset \mathbb{R}^2$. We call affine a-dilate of X the set $\tilde{D}_a X = \{x, \delta(x, X) \leq a^{1/2}\}$. We call affine a-eroded of X the set $\tilde{E}_a X = \{x, \delta(x, X^c) > a^{1/2}\} = (\tilde{D}_a X^c)^c$.*

Proposition 1. *$\tilde{E}_a$ and $\tilde{D}_a$ are special affine invariant (ie they commute with area preserving affine maps) and monotone operators.*

Proof. It is easily seen that if $X \subset Y$, then for every x, $\delta(x, X) \geq \delta(x, Y)$. From this, we deduce that $X \subset Y \Rightarrow \tilde{D}_a X \subset \tilde{D}_a Y$. The monotonicity of $\tilde{E}_a$ follows by the duality relation $\tilde{E}_a X = (\tilde{D}_a X^c)^c$. The special affine invariance of $\tilde{D}_a$ and $\tilde{E}_a$ follows from the fact that if $\det A = 1$, then area(X) = area(AX).

Remark : One can show that $\tilde{E}_a$ and $\tilde{D}_a$ are affine invariant in the sense of Definition 14.19, in [ ] that is, for every linear map A with $\det A > 0$, $A\tilde{E}_{(\det A)^{1/2}a} = \tilde{E}_a A$.

We shall now use the following theorem in order to give a standard form to $\tilde{E}_a$ and $\tilde{D}_a$:

Theorem 1. *(Matheron Theorem). Let T be a translation invariant monotone operator acting on a set of subsets of $\mathbb{R}^n$. Then there exists a family of sets $\mathbb{B} \subset \mathcal{P}(\mathbb{R}^n)$ which can be defined as $\mathbb{B} = \{X, 0 \in T(X)\}$, such that*

$$T(X) = \bigcup_{B \in \mathbb{B}} \bigcap_{y \in B} X - y = \{x, \exists B \in \mathbb{B}, x + B \subset X\} \qquad (3)$$

Conversely,   defines a monotone, translation invariant operator on $\mathcal{P}(\mathbb{R}^n)$

Definition 3. *We say that B is an affine structuring element if 0 is in interior of B, and if there is some b > 1 such that for every line Δ passing by 0, both connected components of $B \setminus \Delta$ containing 0 in their boundary have an area larger or equal to b. We denote the set of affine structuring elements by $\mathbb{B}_{\text{aff}}$.*

Proposition 2. *For every set X,*

$$\tilde{E}_a X = \bigcup_{B \in \mathbb{B}_{\text{aff}}} \bigcap_{y \in a^{1/2}B} X - y = \{x, \exists B \in \mathbb{B}_{\text{aff}}, x + a^{1/2}B \subset X\}$$

Proof. We simply apply Matheron theorem. The set of structuring elements associated with $\tilde{E}_a$ is $\mathbb{B} = \{X, \tilde{E}_a X \ni 0\}$. Now,

$$\tilde{E}_a X \ni 0 \Leftrightarrow \delta(0, X^c) > a^{1/2} \Leftrightarrow \inf_{\Delta} \text{area}(CA_1(0, \Delta, X))^{1/2} > a^{1/2}$$

This means that for every Δ, both connected components of $X \setminus \Delta$ containing 0 have area larger than some number $b > a$. Thus, X belongs to $a^{1/2}\mathbb{B}_{\text{aff}}$ by definition of $\mathbb{B}_{\text{aff}}$.

By Proposition , x belongs to $\tilde{E}_a X$ if and only if for every straight line Δ, chord-arc sets containing x have an area strictly larger than a. Conversely we can state :

Corollary 1. *$\tilde{E}_a X$ is obtained from X by removing, for every straight line Δ, all chord-arc sets contained in X which have an area smaller or equal than a.*

2.1 Application to Curve Affine Erosion/Dilation Schemes

Let c_0 be a Jordan curve, boundary of a simply connected set X. Iterating affine erosions and dilations on X gives a numerical scheme that computes the affine shortening c_T of c_0 at a given scale T. In general, the affine erosion of X is not simple to compute, because it can be strongly non local. However, if X is convex, then it has been shown in [ ] that it can be exactly computed in linear time. In practice, c will be a polygon and the exact affine erosion of X –whose boundary is made of straight segments and pieces of hyperbolae– is not really needed; numerically, a good approximation of it by a new polygon is enough. Now the point is that we can approximate the combination of an affine erosion plus an affine dilation of X by computing the affine erosion of each *convex component* of c, provided that the erosion/dilation area is small enough. The algorithm consists in the iteration of a four-steps process:

1. **Break the curve into convex components.**
2. **Sample each component.**
3. **Apply discrete affine erosion to each component.**
4. **Concatenate the pieces of curves obtained at step 3.**

• **Discrete affine erosion.** This is the main step of the algorithm: compute quickly an approximation of the affine erosion of scale σ of the whole curve. The first step consists in the calculus of the "area" A_j of each convex component $C^j = P_0^j P_1^j ... P_{n-1}^j$, given by $A_j = \sum_{i=1}^{n-2} \left[P_0^j P_i^j, P_0^j P_{i+1}^j \right] / 2$. Then, the effective area used to compute the affine erosion is $\sigma_e = \max \left\{ \sigma/8, \min_j A_j \right\}$. We restrain the erosion area to σ_e because the simplified algorithm for affine erosion may give a bad estimate of the continuous affine erosion+dilation when the area of one component is less than the erosion parameter. The term $\sigma/8$ is rather arbitrary and guarantees an upper bound to the number of iterations required to achieve the final scale. The discrete erosion of each component is defined as the succession of each middle point of each segment $[AB]$ such that

1. A and B lie on the polygonal curve
2. A or B is a vertex of the polygonal curve
3. the area enclosed by $[AB]$ and the polygonal curve is equal to σ_e

• **Iteration of the process**. To iterate the process, we use the fact that if E_σ denotes the affine erosion plus dilation operator of area σ, and $h = (h_i)$ is a subdivision of the interval $[0, H]$ with $H = T/\omega$ and $\omega = \frac{1}{2} \left(\frac{3}{2} \right)^{2/3}$, then

$$E_{(h_1 - h_0)^{3/2}} \circ E_{(h_2 - h_1)^{3/2}} \circ ... \circ E_{(h_n - h_{n-1})^{3/2}} \left(c_0 \right) \longrightarrow c_T$$

as $|h| = \max_i h_{i+1} - h_i \to 0$, where c_T is the affine shortening of c_0 described above by ( ).

The algorithm has linear complexity in time and memory, and its stability is ensured by the fact that each new curve is obtained as the set of the middle points of some chords of the initial curve, defined themselves by an integration process (an area computation). Hence, no derivation or curvature computation appears in the algorithm.

3   Requirements for the Local Encoding of Curves

Humans have little problems in recognizing familiar objects in a 2D image even when lighting conditions vary or objects have been partially occluded, independently of perspective effects.

Therefore, any reliable computer based vision algorithm for shape recognition, should satisfy these three previous requirements, namely :

1. Invariance under changes in lighting conditions. Specifically, we should ask our algorithms to be invariant under contrast changes.
2. Invariance under perspective transformations. This is in general a too strong requirement. Indeed, as shown in [ ], a previous local smoothing of an image, made necessary in order to reduce quantization effects and image complexity, can commute only with planar affine transforms. Thus, we shall only ask in practice this weaker invariance. Notice, however, that if 3D objects with smooth boundaries are being observed, then the deformation of the objects' images, far enough from the occlusion boundaries, is locally an affine transform. Indeed, as remarked in [ ] every C^1 map is locally an affine transform.

A weaker requirement, which we will also investigate, is similarity invariance (invariance under translations, rotations and uniform scaling).

3. Recognition of partially occluded objects. Therefore, shapes must be described as locally as possible in order to prevent side effects of the loss of some part of a shape in the description of its other parts.

Three more requirements may be introduced in order to improve the reliability and feasibility of the algorithms :

4 A scale-space representation [ ] : such a representation, provided it is invariant enough, provides us with more and more sketchy versions of the shapes to be recognized. This is required, as mentionned in the introduction, in order to reduce the complexity of the shape descriptors and to eliminate various noises in the fine levels shape description, particularly the quantization effects. Therefore, recognition algorithms should be integrated in a scale-space framework, which, as we have seen, can be, at most, affine invariant.

5 Uniqueness [ ], different shapes must have different descriptors. This requirement is never completely achieved, and must be replaced by a somewhat vague requirement, according to which shapes which do not look alike should not be matched. Here, visual inspection remains a valid criterion to decide of the validity of an algorithm. We shall therefore try to show many examples.

6 Incremental description : The fact of adding new features to the description of the shape must not disturb the previous description, but simply add a new information to it.

7 Completeness of the image description : We want ALL shapes present in the image to undergo the shape comparison algorithm. By "all", we mean that the list of the shapes of the image must enable us to fully reconstruct the image. If (e.g.) we match Image 1 with itself, the list of matching shapes will be of course equal to the list of all shapes present in Image 1. Now, this list being complete, we will be able to reconstruct fully the image 1 from this list. In the general case, we want to be able to show an image containing all shapes of Image 1 which match Image 2 and only them. This image will therefore be the "intersection of Images 1 and 2" (see [ ] for the definition of image intersection algorithms in Mathematical Morphology.)

The first requirement leads us to describe the shapes in terms of mathematical morphology, as explained in section . The second requirement (affine invariance) constrains us in two ways : clearly, descriptors of the shape must be (at least) affine invariant and we have mentionned the impossibility of requiring more invariance in the context of local smoothing. In the next section, we shall discuss which kind of features we can use. The second constraint is less obvious and related to the fourh requirement : the scale-space representation of the shape shall also be affine invariant. Typical scale-space representations, based on a gaussian-type filtering, do not satisfy this requirement. An affine invariant scale space based on partial differential equations (PDE) have been proposed in [ ] and is equivalent to the "affine curve shortening" proposed simultaneously by [ ]. Recently, a fast scheme for the computation of the affine shortening, applied directely to the level lines of an image, has been proposed in [ ] and [ ] (see Section   for a detailed description of the algorithm).

The third and fifth requirements are somehow contradictory. We must be able to find a description of the shapes local enough to allow local matching but global enough to prevent that several parts of different shapes have the same description. This trade-off can only be dealt with in an experimental context first, and then with statistical arguments which we shall not develop here.

The sixth requirement is very important in terms of robustness and reliability of the shape descriptions. It means that any new feature introduced in the description of a shape will either be redundant or improve the description, but never disturb the previous information that we had. In fact, the seven given design criteria define a generic, algorithm to shape recognition.

Following these seven design criteria, we have developped two algorithms for shape recognition, one of them more restrictive, only dealing with the problem of recognizing shapes under similarity transform, and a more general one, providing registration under affine transforms.

4   Algorithms for the Description of the Shapes in an Image

4.1   Similarity Invariant Description of Curves

In the search for an invariant description of a curve, the starting point for the sampling must be invariant, and so must be the sampling mesh. Typically, inflexion points have been chosen because they are affine invariant. Now, since the curve is almost straight at inflexion points, their position is not robust, but the direction of the tangent to the curve passing through them is. Another affine invariant robust semilocal descriptor is given by the lines which are bitangent to the curve (see Fig.).

Fig. 1. Inflexion points (marked with small triangles) and bitangents of a closed curve. The area defined by each bitangent and the original curve is marked ($A1$)

Our reference system is formed by such a line, and the next and previous tangents to the curve which are orthogonal to it (see Fig.). The intersections

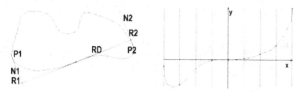

Fig. 2. Left: Local reference system for similarity invariant normalization: reference direction (RD), normal directions (N1, N2) and reference points (R1, R2). The portion of the curve normalized with this reference system starts at P1 and ends at P2, passing through the inflexion point. Right: Similarity invariant normalization. The y-ordinate of the marked points is used to encode the piece of curve

of each one of these lines with the reference line provide two reliable points independent of the discretization of the curve. The portion of the curve to be normalized is limited by these points. Normalization consists in a similarity transform that maps the reference line to the x-axis and that sets the distance between the two reference points to 1. We discretize each one of the normalized portions of the curve with a fixed number n of points, and we store, for each discretized point, its y coordinate (see Fig.). This set of n values is used to compare portions of curves.

4.2   Affine Invariant Description of Curves

If we look at Fig. , we can observe that the portion of the curve between the points defining the bitangent, together with the bitangent itself, define an area $(A1)$, from which further invariant features can be computed. In particular, we can compute the barycenter of this area, an affine invariant reference point. We compute then the line $B1$ parallel to the bitangent and passing through the barycenter. $B1$ divides the initial area into two parts and we compute the barycenter of the part which does not contain the bitangent (see Fig.). This second barycenter is a second reference point. Finally a point in line $B1$ such that the area of the triangle formed by this point and the two preceding barycenters is a fixed fraction of the initial area $A1$ is a third reference point (see Fig.). We therefore obtain three nonaligned points, that is an affine reference system. This strategy is related to [ ]. The discretization points are taken at uniform intervals of length on the normalized curve. The total length of the normalized curve is also used in the code. This set of $2n+1$ values is what we use to compare portions of curves.

5   Experimental Results

Figure   displays a picture of a man and the same picture after the man has moved and their level lines after smoothing with the iterative scheme described

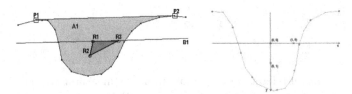

Fig. 3. Left: Local reference system for affine invariant normalization: reference points (R1, R2, R3). The portion of the curve to be encoded has endpoints P1 and P2. Right: Affine invariant normalization. The length of the normalized piece of curve together with the x and y coordinates of the marked points are used to locally encode the curve

in section . Clearly some level lines have suffered a significant deformation and some others are affected by the disocclusion of the left arm of the man. Even if some parts of the level line remain unchanged, registration methods based on global matching would fail in detecting those lines. In Figure , we show the result of the matching of several pieces of a level line in the first image with other pieces of level lines in the second image.

Figure   displays two frames of the 'walking man' sequence. Observe that occlusion and deformation are both present in the images (occlusion of the arm and deformation in the position of the legs). Figure   shows the result of the matching of a level line describing the man in the first image (in this case it is easy to find an unique level line, since there is a big contrast between the man and the background), and the level lines in the second image. Observe that, despite the occlusion and the deformation, the registration method (affine invariant) is able to retrieve the correct level line in the second image.

Acknowledgements

The first author gratefully acknowledges partial support by CICYT project, reference TIC99-0266.

References

1. L. Alvarez, F. Guichard, P. L. Lions, J. M. Morel, *Axioms and Fundamental Equations on Image Processing*, Technical Report 9231, CEREMADE, 1992 and Arch. for Rat. Mech. Anal. 16(9), 200-257, 1993.   ,   ,
2. H. Asada and M. Brady. *The curvature primal sketch.* IEEE Trans. Pattern Analysis and Machine Intelligence, 8(1), 2-14, 1986.
3. K. Astrom. *Affine and projective normalization of planar curves and regions,* ECCV 94, pp. B :439-448, 1994.

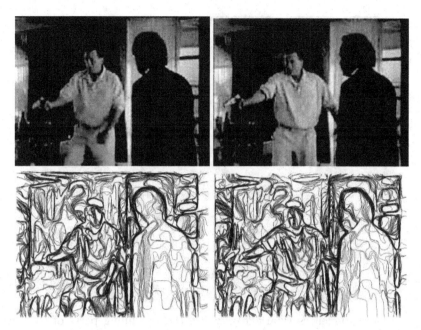

Fig. 4. Up: Original images (from the film 'Analyze This' (Warner Bros)). Down: their smooth level lines (smoothing method of section)

4. C. Ballester, E. Cubero-Castan, M. Gonzalez, J. M. Morel. *Image intersection and application to satellite imaging.* Preprint.
5. S. K. Bose, K. K. Biswas and S. K. Gupta. Model-based object recognition : the role of affine invariants. AIEng, 10(3) : 227-234, 1996.
6. V. Caselles, B. Coll, and J. M. Morel. *A Kanisza programme.* Progress in Nonlinear Differential Equations and their Applications, 25, 1996.
7. V. Caselles and B. Coll and J. M. Morel, *Topographic maps*, preprint CEREMADE, 1997. To appear in I. J. C. V.   ,
8. V. Caselles and J. L. Lisani and G. Sapiro and J. M. Morel, *Shape preserving histogram modification*, IEEE Trans. on Image Processing, February 1999.
9. Y. Cheng. *Analysis of affine invariants as approximate perspective invariants*, CVIU, 63 (2).
10. Cohignac, T. and Lopez, C. and Morel, J. M., *Integral and Local Affine Invariant Parameter and Application to Shape Recognition*, ICPR pp. A:164-168, 1994.
11. G. Dudek and J. K. Tsotsos. *Shape representation and recognition from multiscale curvature*, CVIU, 68(2), pp. 170-189, 1997.
12. O. Faugeras and R. Keriven, *Some recent results on the projective evolution of 2D curves.* In Proc. IEEE International Conference on Image Processing, vol. 3, pp. 13-16, Washington, October 1995.
13. F. Guichard and J. M. Morel, *Image iterative filtering and PDE's*, Preprint, 1999. Book in preparation.   ,
14. R. A. Hummel, H. J. Wolfson. *Affine invariant matching.* DARPA88, pp. 351-364, 1988.

Fig. 5. Correspondences (marked in white, the remaining parts of the curves in black) between some pieces of a level line in the first image (left) and some pieces of other level lines in the second image (right). Up: By using the similarity invariant registration method based on inflexion points. Down: By using the affine invariant registration method based on bitangents

15. P. Kempenaers, L. Van Gool, and A. Oosterlinck. *Shape recognition under affine distortions.* VF91, pp. 323-332, 1991.
16. A. Mackworth and F. Mokhtarian, *A theory of multiscale, curvature-based shape representation for planar curves*, IEEE Trans. Pattern Analysis and Machine Intelligence, 14 : 789-805, 1992.   ,
17. G. Koepfler, L. Moisan, *Geometric Multiscale Representation of Numerical Images*, Proc. of the Second Int. Conf. on Scale-Space Theories in Computer Vision, in Springer Lecture Notes in Computer Science, vol. 1682, pp. 339-350, 1999.
18. G. Matheron, *Random Sets and Integral Geometry*, John Wiley, N. Y., 1975.
19. L. Moisan, *Traitement numérique d'images et de films: équations aux dérivées partielles préservant forme et relief*, PhD dissertation, Université Paris-Dauphine, France, 1997.   ,
20. L.Moisan, *Affine Plane Curve Evolution : a Fully Consistent Scheme*, IEEE Transactions On Image Processing, vol. 7:3, pp. 411-420, 1998.   ,   ,
21. P. Monasse, *Contrast Invariant Image Registration*, Proc. of I. V. Conf. on Accoustics, Speech and Signal Processing, Phoenix, Arizona, vol 6, 1999, pp. 3221-3224.
22. P. Monasse and F. Guichard, *Fast Computation of a Contrast-Invariant Image Representation*, IEEE Transactions on Image Processing, Vol. 9, Number 5, pp. 860-872, May 2000. Preprint CMLA 9815, available at *http://www.cmla.ens-cachan.fr*

Fig. 6. Original images (from the 'walking man' sequence, kindly provided by the Computer Graphics and Vision Group from the UIB Dept. of Mathematics, CYCIT project TIC98-C302)

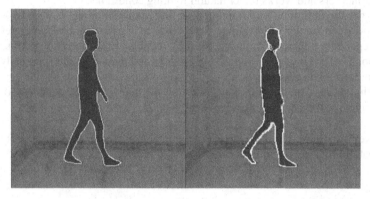

Fig. 7. Corresponding level lines (white) between the images in figure

23. P. Monasse and F. Guichard, *Scale-Space from a Level Lines Tree*, Proc. of 2nd Int. Conf. on Scale-Space Theories in Computer Vision, Corfu, Greece, 1999, pp. 175-186.
24. G. Sapiro and A. Tannenbaum, *Affine Invariant Scale Space*, International Journal of Computer Vision, 11 (1), 25-44, 1993.   ,
25. J.Serra, *Image Analysis and Mathematical Morphology*, Academic Press, 1982.
26. A. P. Witkin, *Scale space filtering*, Proc. IJCAI, 1019-1023, 1983.   ,
27. L. Younes *Computable elastic distances between shapes*, SIAM J. of Applied Mathematics, Vol. 58, Number 2, pp. 565-586, April 1998.

Adaptation of ASM to Lips Edge Detection

Laboratoire des Images et des Signaux, Institut National Polytechnique de Grenoble
LIS, INPG, 46 avenue Félix-Viallet, 38031 Grenoble Cedex, France
Tel: +33 (0)4 76 57 43 63   Fax: +33 (0)4 76 57 47 90
alice.caplier@inpg.fr

Abstract: Seeing the talker's lips in addition to audition can improve speech understanding which is rather based on lips shape temporal evolution than on absolute mouth shape. In this article, we propose an adaptation of *Active Shape Model* (ASM) to the extraction of lips shape over an image sequence. The algorithm does not require any make-up or markers and works under natural lighting conditions.

After the definition of a training base, initial mouth model is iteratively deformed under constraints according to spatiotemporal energies depending either on luminance or hue. A robust prior detection of four points of the model is proposed in order to automatically and accurately initialize the egde detection.

The success of our approach is tested on many image sequences of multi-speakers with multi-speaking.

Keywords: Active Shape Model, automatic lips edge detection, ACP, natural lighting conditions.

1   Introduction

Our research is a part of an advanced audio-visual communication tool which integrates both audio and visual features. It aims at improving speech understanding in the presence of acoustic noise by extracting lips shape. It is well known that seeing the talker's lips in addition to audition can improve speech intelligibility (cf. labial reading for deafs).

Extracting lips boundaries is a difficult task because lips shape is highly variable. Variability comes from individual appearence (spatial variability), locutions (temporal variability) and lighting (spatiotemporal variability). In order to detect deformable templates, many approaches have been developped [5]. In this paper, we focuse on the *Active Shape Model* (ASM) proposed in [4]. The efficiency of ASM has been widely proved in the litterature for detecting pedestrians in [1], for localizing moving hands in [6] and for face modelisation in [7]. We explain how the method has been adapted to the difficult problem of lips edge detection.

H. H. Nagel and F. J. Perales (Eds.): AMDO 2000, LNCS 1899, pp. 27-37, 2000.
© Springer-Verlag Berlin Heidelberg 2000

In a training step, a model point for open mouth and a model point for closed mouth are defined. The deformations of such models are learned on a training base with multi-speakers of multi-speakings and are then limited to the principal ones after a Principal Components Analysis (see section 2).

With ASM, there is a crucial problem with initialisation. Either initialisation is hand-made so that the processing is no more autonomous. Either initialisation involves algorithms which have a too high computational cost for real-time implementations [4]. In this paper, the initial shape is the average shape which comes from the training step and which has been automatically put and resized in the frame to be processed after the detection of four points of the model in a preprocessing step (see section 3).

As written in [2] : " the real information in lipreading lies in the temporal changes of lip positions rather than in the absolute lip shape". Temporal information must be taken into account to improve lips boundaries detection. In section 4, *spatiotemporal* energy functions are proposed to deform the initial shape.

2   Training Step

In this section, two mouth models are defined and we learn how each mouth shape is allowed to be modified. This yields to an *allowable deformation domain* [4].

2.1   Models of Open and Closed Mouth

A mouth is described with a set of discrete points called *landmarks*. We put the main landmarks as the corners of the mouth (or comissures), the arch of Cupidon... Main landmarks are in black on figure 1. Others points are equi-distributed between the main points. This yields to a 23 points model for a closed mouth and to a 30 points model for an open mouth (cf. figure 1). It should be noted that these models do not contain any curve description (no parabol, no quartic), they belong to the class of free form deformable templates.

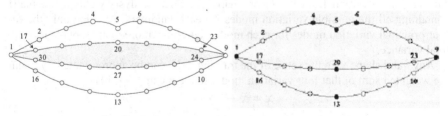

Fig. 1. Landmarks distribution : open mouth and closed mouth models

2.2   Training Step

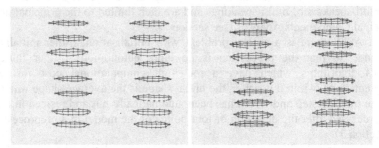

Fig. 2. Training bases : left, 16 handly-labelled closed mouths ; right, 20 handly-labelled closed mouths

For each model, a training base is handly built. Such a base contains 16 images for closed mouths and 20 images for open mouths (cf. Figure 2). These frames come from different speakers with different locutions. With these bases, we learn the average shape for an open mouth (resp. for a closed mouth) and how an open mouth (resp. a closed mouth) is deformed according to the speaker and what he is saying. Figure 3 shows on the top the 16 closed mouths superimposed on each other. Each mouth is aligned on the first mouth of the base, the average mouth is computed and the position of each landmark in comparaison with the same average landmark is studied.

2.3   Principle Component Analysis (PCA)

PCA has been shown to be very useful because of its capability to reduce the dimensionality and to extract the important features in terms of amount of variance retained.

A mouth shape is described by the coordinates of all the landmarks. Let vector x represents the set of these coordinates. For each shape in the training base, we calculate its deviation from the mean shape $\bar{x}$. Such analysis yields a big matrix containing all the possible variation modes for each landmark. Keeping only the first four principal variation modes for each model represents more than *80* percents of the total variance.

Any valid shape x, in the sense of the training data, can be approximated by adding the weighted sum of that four variation modes to the mean shape [4]:

$$x = \bar{x} + Pb \tag{1}$$

where P is a matrix containing the first four eigenvectors and $b = (b_1, b_2, b_3, b_4)$ is a vector of four weights characteristic of shape x.

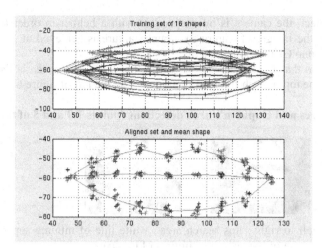

Fig. 3. Mouths aligning and average shape

3   Preprocessing Step

3.1   Initial Shape: Average Shape

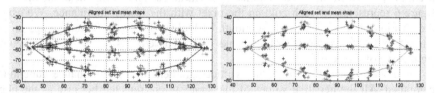

Fig. 4. Average shapes : left, average open mouth ; right, average closed mouth

Initial shape is the average mouth shape coming from the training step (cf. Figure 4).

3.2   Placing the Initial Shape

Images acquisition

Fig. 5. micro-camera

In our project, the camera is interdependant with a helmet in order to center the mouth within the image (cf. figure 5). Frame capture is achieved at 25 images per second by a mono CCD colour camera.

According to that frame acquisition system, the *lips search area* is limited to 1/4 and 2/3 from the top of each frame as mentionned on the left of figure 6.

Commissures and Cupidon's arch detections (points 1,9 and 5 of the model)

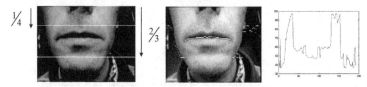

Fig. 6. From left to right : lips search area ; white line of minima superimposed on mouth frame ; curve of Y-axis of the minima of luminance

In order to automatically put the initial mouth shape, we are loocking for three particular points i.e. both corners and the Cupidon's arch (points *1*, *5* and *9* of the model). This is an improved version of the robust initialisation proposed in [3].

By noting that at the frontier between both lips, there is a very dark line of luminance, commissures are detected as follows: on each column of the *lips search area*, the pixel with the lowest luminance is extracted. The white line at the middle of figure 6 represents on each column the pixel with the lowest luminance. We extract the position of both corners of the mouth by looking for the important jumps on that white line, that is by detecting both peaks on the curve of Y-axis of such minima (cf. right curve of figure 6).

In order to detect point *5*, the vertical gradient of the luminance function is computed. All the negative values of that gradient are rejected because as the upper lip contours are concerned, vertical gradient values are positive: the skin is clearer than the lip. Point *5* is detected as the pixel of the frame which has the maximum vertical gradient and which is located on the upper vertical line going through the middle point between both commissures.

Fig. 7. Automatic detection of points 1, 5 and 9

Figure 7 shows the results of automatic detection of points *1*, *9* and *5* on different frames. Results are quite good even in case of bearded men.

Detection of a 4th point

In order to completly define the translation and the resizing to be applied to the average initial mouth, we propose to detect another point which is the point with the maximum of hue gradient located on the vertical line going through the middle point between both comissures and below the comissures. Hue is computed as

$$hue(x,y,t) = \frac{256 * \operatorname{Im}G(x,y,t)}{\operatorname{Im}R(x,y,t)}$$ as defined in [8] where ImG is the green

component of colour frame and ImR is the red one. Figure 8 shows the result of detection of this point on different frames. The lower cross indicates the position of detected point (others points are the detected Cupidon's Arch and commisures).

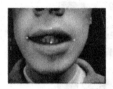  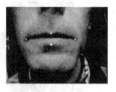

Fig. 8. automatic detection of the 4th point (cross on each frame)

This point may then correspond either to point *27* or to point *13* of the model in case of an open mouth (respectively either to point *13* or to point *20* of the model for a closed mouth). In order to correctly identify the detected point, the distance d between the detected Cupidon's arch and the detected point is computed and this distance is compared with $d_{27} = dist(pt_5, pt_{27})$ and $d_{13} = dist(pt_5, pt_{13})$ computed on the average open mouth model (respectively with $d_{13} = dist(pt_5, pt_{13})$ and $d_{20} = dist(pt_5, pt_{20})$ computed on the average closed mouth model). Following rules are then applied :

- for an open mouth

$$if \ |d - d_{27}| \prec |d - d_{13}| \ \Rightarrow \ det\,ected \ po\,int = pt_{27}$$
$$else \ det\,ected \ po\,int = pt_{13}$$

- for a closed mouth

$$if \ |d - d_{20}| \prec |d - d_{13}| \ \Rightarrow \ det\,ected \ po\,int = pt_{20}$$
$$else \ det\,ected \ po\,int = pt_{13}$$

As a result of such processing, on frames of figure 8, from left to right, the detected point is identified as pt_{27}, pt_{13} and pt_{13} respectively.

Putting and resizing the average shape

Initial shape is the average shape which must be adjusted to the frame to be processed. Points *1,9,5* and *20* (or *27* or *13*) of the average shape are aligned with the position automatically detected and identified in the frame to be processed. Translations and rotations are necessary to make coincide points *1* and *9* of the average model with those detected on the frame. Points *5* and *20* (or *27* or *13*) controll the increasing or decreasing of the average shape size. Figure 9 shows the initial shape before (average shape) and after (final initial shape) automatic positioning. On the right frame, the average shape has been enlarged because of the detection of both commissures. On this exemple, it should be noticed that the right position of commissures is not easy to detect even visually.

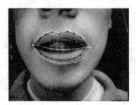

Fig. 9. On each frame, the black mouth corresponds to the average mouth and the white mouth is the initial shape for lips detection after automatic translation and resizing

4   Lips Detection Algorithm

4.1   Energy Functions

Starting with the initial shape, each point is moved perpendicularly of the contours in order to fit with a pixel of "maximum" information.

Spatiotemporal gradient of luminance for upper lip

Each point of the upper lip are moved according to the spatiotemporal gradient of the luminance function: the lip is darker than the face skin (spatial gradient) and with the hypothesis that the lighting of the scene is uniform, any motion induces a temporal variation of the luminance function (temporal gradient). Gradients $U(x,y,t)$ and $D(x,y,t)$ associated to up and down motions respectively are defined as following [9]:

$$U(x,y,t) = (\frac{\partial}{\partial t} - \frac{\partial}{\partial y}) * I(x,y,t)$$

$$D(x,y,t) = (\frac{\partial}{\partial t} + \frac{\partial}{\partial y}) * I(x,y,t)$$

where G is a Gaussian filter

and I is the luminance function:

$$I(x,y,t) = \frac{1}{3}\big(\text{Im }R(x,y,t) + \text{Im }G(x,y,t) + \text{Im }B(x,y,t)\big).$$

In order to be insensitive to the sign of U and D, they are converted into energy functions [9]:

$$E_u(x,y,t) = G * U^2(x,y,t)$$
$$E_d(x,y,t) = G * D^2(x,y,t)$$

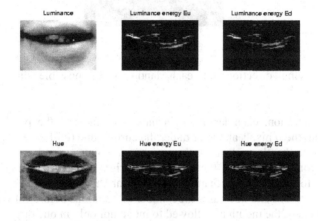

Fig. 10. Comparisons between « luminance » energies and « hue » energies

Top line of figure 10 shows E_u and E_d for a frame. High values of energy are represented in white and low values are represented in black. High values are located near lips edges especially for the upper lip.

Spatiotemporal gradient of hue for lower lip

Same spatiotemporal energy functions are computed for the lower lip but in this case, spatiotemporal gradient of hue is considered. Because of shadow between the lower lip and the chin, the spatiotemporal gradient of luminance is not enough discriminant ; there is very little contrast between the frontier of the lower lip and the skin as you can see on the exemple on the left frame of first line of figure 10. On this frame, it is very easy to see the edge of the upper lip but it is much more difficult to see the edge of the lower lip. In such case, hue is much more discriminant (see first frame of second line of figure 10). Figure 10 shows the " hue " energy and the " luminance " energy for a same frame. For lower lip, " hue " energy is more discrimant than " luminance " energy. Indeed, the maxima of « hue » energy function are located at the edge of that lip (see the white edge at the bottom of lower lip on « hue » energy frames of figure 10). In case of « luminance » energy, no such clear minima appear for the lower lip so that the detection algorithm should fail in finding right positions of the lower lip edge points.

4.2   Iterative Constrained Deformation

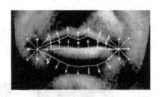

Fig. 11. Moving direction for each landmark (4 possible directions for the commissures)

At each iteration, each landmark is moved to fit with the pixel of maximum energy among the n pixels above or under the current one (cf. figure 11). The value of n is chosen to be dependant of the processed point. Indeed, the value of n is decreasing from the center of the model to the right and left corners. Middle points are allowed to moved faster than the points near the corners. Such evolution of n induces good results and decreases the number of iterations before convergence.

The corners of the mouth are allowed to move not only in one direction but in four directions (cf. figure 11) because it is not easy to determine the direction which is rightly perpendicular to the countour at these points.

Once all the landmarks have been moved according to the maximum energy information, we obtain what we call *the maximum energy shape*. We search in the *allowable deformation domain* the shape which fits at best with *the maximum energy shape*. This process is repeated until the contour does no more change. Figure 12 shows the result of lips detection for open mouths. Each mouth is very different from one person to another. But those differences have been taken into account in the training step because the training base is made of frames from different locutors. Results are thus good in all cases. Figure 13 shows results for lips detection of closed mouths.

5   Conclusion

We presented an adaptation of ASM for lips detection in a spatiotemporal framework. This yields to an automatic detection algorithm. A real time implementation of that algorithm is under study. Having a helmet on the head for that application should be a drawback. We are also developping an algorithm which localise the mouth in a frame whatever the camera centring is. The presented algorithm will be suited to others acquisition systems.

 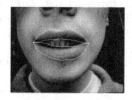 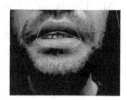

Fig. 12. Lips detection results in case of open mouths

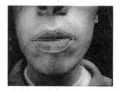  

Fig. 13. Lips detection results in case of closed mouths

Acknowledgements

The author would like to thank N. Mottin and C. Rigaud for the implementation of some parts of the Matlab code and M. Liévin for the scheme of figure 5.

6   References

[1]   A. Baumberg, D. Hogg. *Learning Flexible Models from Image Sequences.* ECCV94, Stockolhm, Sweden, 299-308, 1994.

[2]   C. Bregler, Y. Konig. *Eigenlips for Robust Speech Recognition.* IEEE ICASSP, Adelaide, Australia, 669-672, 1991.

[3]   A. Caplier, P. Delmas, D. Lam. *Robust Initialisation for Lips Edges Detection.* 11th SCIA, Kangerlussuaq, Greeland, June 7-11, 523-528, 1999.

[4]   T. Cootes, C. Taylor, D. Cooper, J. Graham. *Active Shape Models : Their Training and Application.* Computer Vision and Image Understanding, 61(1): 38-59, 1995.

[5]   A. Jain, Y. Zhong, M. Dubuisson-Jolly. *Deformable Template Models: a review.* Signal Processing, 71, 109-129, 1998.

[6]   C. Kervran. *Learning Probabilistic Deformation models from Image Sequences.* Signal Processing 71, 155-171, 1998.

[7]   A. Lanitis, C. J. Taylor, T.F. Cootes. *Automoatic Interpretation and Coding of Face Images Using Flexible Models.* IEEE Trans. on PAMI, vol.19, N. 7, 743-755, July 1997.

[8] M. Liévin, F. Luthon. *Unsupervised Lip Segmentation under Natural Conditions*. Proc. of IEEE Int. Conf. On Acoustic, Speech and Signal Processing (ICASSP99), Phoenix, Arizona, 1999.

[9] R. P. Wildes. *A Measure of Motion Salience for Surveillance Applications*. Proc. of ICIP, Chicago, Illinois, USA, October 1998.

Elastic Deformations Using Finite Element Methods in Computer Graphic Applications*

M. Mascaró, A. Mir, and F. Perales

Dep. Matemàtiques i Informàtica. (U. Gràfics i Visió),
Universitat de les Illes Balears (UIB), Ctra. de Valldemossa km. 7,5. CP: 07071
{mascport,paco}@anim.uib.es
dmiamt0@ps.uib.es

Abstract. Deformation tools constitute an important topic in computer animation. This paper shows how we can give an exact value to the basic parameters in a dynamical elastic deformation system based on finite elements for 2D objects. We look for an optimal value for the time step (Δt) in the dynamical system, and an optimal area for the basic square finite element of the object. Fine time step adjustment is important to reduce the computational cost of the system, and guarantee the realistic look of the result (final deformation of the object). Then several results from different physical conditions are compared, in order to find a good system of measuring the difference between them. Finally, using this measurement parameter we can relate the size of the finite elements with the error between several deformations of the same object. The deformations are rendered using the Open Inventor application (VRML).

Keywords: elasticity, render, VRML, Open Inventor, elastic deformation, finite element, mesh generator.

1 Introduction

In this article we analyze an elastic deformation model based on finite elements [,] (see [ ] and [ ] for more examples of similar models). We present a deformation model in the "physical model" category. A more detailed study of the deformation model classification can be found in [ ], and in [, , , ,], we can see several examples of physical models. The aim of this work is to obtain the solution of the movement equation taking into account the elasticity parameters [ ] in order to obtain the best results with the lowest computational cost. In this way we can optimize on the one hand the spatial discretization of the object, and on the other the time step of the differential equation model. Thus we reduce the number of iterations in the dynamic system and the size of the matrix related to our deformation model.

Section 2 presents a brief description of the deformation model, establishing its bases and obtaining the ordinary differential equation that will manage our numeric algorithm. Section 3 explains how to obtain the optimal mesh size to make

---

* Suported by the project TIC98-0302 of CICYT.

H. H. Nagel and F. J. Perales (Eds.): AMDO 2000, LNCS 1899, pp. 38–   , 2000.

the finite element structure. In Section 4 we refine the time step parameter in order to reduce the computational cost of the dynamic algorithm. An optimal value for the time step provides the numerical solution with the quantity of iterations necessary to reach the final position of the object. Thus the system does not make superfluous iterations, and guarantes the right strain wave transmission and system stability of the numerical algorithm. Section 5 defines the level of detail of the deformation process. In this section we define an error measurement that lets us compare several deformations with identical physical conditions on the same object with different finite elements sizes. We also present examples of this measurement process. The last section makes a short survey of the principal concepts laid out in this paper, and draws some conclusions about this work.

The model discussed in this article is a physical model that tries to simulate deformation very realistically, by using algorithms based only on physical parameters. Elastic deformation tools are useful in many commercial sectors and industries and can be found in generating deformable object animations, generating computer animation, fixing strength conditions of certain materials, in architecture design, clothing factories, medical research, etc.

The deformation model analyzed in this work is based on the elasticity theory (strain tensor and deformation tensor), and on the variational formulation presented in [ ].

2   A Dynamic Model to Simulate Elastic Deformations Based on Square Finite Elements

For the computational process, the object to be deformed is represented as a quadrangular mesh and the physical conditions corresponding to the deformation (the object's physical properties, and external forces) are taken into account. The physical deformation can be calculated without user interaction, and represented dynamically with computer animation tools - VRML and Open Inventor.

Let Ω be the 2D object that we are going to deform. Using the deformation tensor ( ) and the strain tensor ( ) definitions, and relating them using Hookes law

$$\varepsilon_{ij} = \frac{\partial u_i}{\partial x_j} + \frac{\partial u_j}{\partial x_i} \,, \tag{1}$$

$$\sigma_{ij} = \lambda \left(\sum_{k=1}^{2} \varepsilon_{kk} \right) \delta_{ij} + 2\mu\varepsilon_{ij} \,, \; i,j = 1,2 \,, \tag{2}$$

we can obtain the deformation process equation expressed in partial derivatives:

$$\begin{cases} \rho\frac{\partial^2 u}{\partial t^2} - \sum_{j=1}^{n} \frac{\partial}{\partial x_j}\sigma_{ij} = f_i, \ i = 1,\ldots,n \ \text{en} \ Q_T, \\ u_i = 0, \ i = 1,\ldots,n \ \text{en} \ \Gamma_0 \times (0,T), \\ \sum_{j=1}^{n} \sigma_{ij}n_j = 0, \ i = 1,\ldots,n \ \text{en} \ \Gamma_1 \times (0,T), \\ u_i\left(\cdot,0\right) = u_{0,i}, \ i = 1,\ldots,n \ \text{en} \ \Omega, \\ \frac{\partial u_i}{\partial t}\left(\cdot,0\right) = u_{1,i}, \ i = 1,\ldots,n \ \text{en} \ \Omega. \end{cases} \qquad (3)$$

where $Q_T = \Omega\left(0,T\right)$, $\Gamma = \partial\Omega = \Gamma_0 \bigcup \Gamma_1$, and Γ_1 is the part of the $\partial\Omega$ to wich we apply external forces, ρ represents the density of the object, f_i are the external forces applied to the Ω and u is the vector deformation of the object.

Using the technique described in [ ] we can obtain the following equation

$$\rho B\xi'' + \gamma B\xi' + A\xi = L \Rightarrow \rho B\xi'' + \gamma B\xi' + \underbrace{B^{-1}A}_{B}\xi = \underbrace{B^{-1}L}_{L}. \qquad (4)$$

In above equation:

- γ is the damping factor of the deformation, generated by the finite element analysis.
- Matrix B represents the strain relations between the verteices of the object.
- Matrix A represents the physical conditions of the object (internal forces).
- Vector L represents external forces which cause the deformation of the object.
- Vector ξ represents the position of each vertex on the meshed object at some step of the deformation simulation.

Performing a discretization process by time on ( ) we can generate the next expression:

$$\rho B \left(\frac{\xi\left(t + \Delta t\right) - 2\xi\left(t\right) + \xi\left(t - \Delta t\right)}{\Delta t^2}\right)$$

$$+\gamma B\left(\frac{\xi\left(t + \Delta t\right) - \xi\left(t - \Delta t\right)}{2\Delta t}\right) + A\xi\left(t\right) = L \qquad (5)$$

The γ factor is very important for simulating realistic deformation results. Null values generate deformation simulations without energy loss, which consequently present results with expanding and contracting movements for a long time. Thus using the equation defined in ( ) we can reach the final equation of the dynamic process:

$$B\left(\frac{\rho}{\Delta t^2} + \frac{\gamma}{2\Delta t}\right)\xi\left(t + \Delta t\right) = L + \frac{\rho B}{\Delta t^2}\left(2\xi\left(t\right) - \xi\left(t - \Delta t\right)\right)$$

$$+\frac{\gamma B}{2\Delta t}\xi\left(t - \Delta t\right) - A\xi\left(t\right) \qquad (6)$$

A simulation of the deformation is simply a question of solving the linear equation ( ) where the unknown values are the positions of the vertices of the object at the instant $t + \Delta t$, represented in ( ) by the $\xi_{t+\Delta t}$ vector.

3   Fixing an Optimal Size for the Mesh Finite Elements. Level of Detail in Deformation

In this section we fix the optimal size of the object's finite elements, in order to find the minimal vertex quantity in the object that produces a stable deformation process, (the right strain waves caused by external forces applied to the object).

First, we represent external forces f using the spatial and time components: $f(x, y, t) = f_e(x, y) \cdot f_t(t)$, where f_e is the spatial component and f_t is the time component. Once that is done, we calculate the Fourier transformation of the component expressions $f_t(t)$, $F(w)$. We then define a spatial interval $[w_m, w_M]$ where $F(w)$ function is greater than a certain upper boundary. In association with the lower and upper frequencies w_m and w_M we can define the minor and major periods as $T_m = \frac{2\pi}{w_M}$ and $T_M = \frac{2\pi}{w_m}$. Then, transverse and longitudinal wave transmission velocities through a material with Lame λ and μ coefficients are $v_t = \sqrt{\frac{\mu}{\rho}}$, $v_l = \sqrt{\frac{\lambda + 2\mu}{\rho}}$, where ρ is the material's density. Thus, the transverse and longitudinal wave of the strains caused by the forces f in the maximal and minimal period are:

$$\lambda_{m.t} = v_t \cdot T_m, \ \lambda_{M,t} = v_t \cdot T_M, \ \lambda_{m,l} = v_l \cdot T_m, \ \lambda_{M,l} = v_l \cdot T_M.$$

Now we must take mesh h for the finite elements to verify

$$h \leq \frac{\min\{\lambda_{m,t}, \lambda_{m,l}\}}{10} = \frac{T_m \cdot \sqrt{\frac{\mu}{\rho}}}{10} = \frac{2\pi}{w_M} \cdot \sqrt{\frac{\mu}{100 \cdot \rho}} = \frac{\pi}{5 w_M} \cdot \sqrt{\frac{\mu}{\rho}}.$$

By way of example of all the concepts laid out in the text above, we can apply a 1 N force on the examined object for 1 second. From a mathematical point of view, the time component of the force can be expressed as

$$f_t(t) = \begin{cases} 1, & \text{si } t \in (0, 1), \\ 0, & \text{otherwise.} \end{cases}$$

The value of the Fourier transformation is $F(w) = \frac{1}{2}\pi \left(\frac{i}{w} - \frac{ie^{iw}}{w} \right)$. The picture of $|F(w)|$ can be examined in Figure . We can take $w_m = 0$ and $w_M = 20$ using the symmetric aspect of $|F(w)|$, ($|F(20)| \approx 0.0854$).Thus the mesh size h must obey the following expression:

$$h \leq \frac{\pi}{5 w_M} \cdot \sqrt{\frac{\mu}{\rho}} = \frac{\pi}{100} \cdot \sqrt{\frac{\mu}{\rho}}.$$

4   Time Step Adjustment for Optimal Processing

To obtain the maximum speed of calculation we look for a Δt value which enables us to make the necessary number of iterations whilst maintaining system stability.

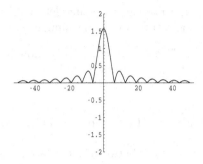

Fig. 1. $f_t(t)$ Fourier transform plot

The value chosen for Δt must be less than the smallest transmission wave period of the system, to guarantee correct propagation of the strains inside the deformed object. This kind of analysis normally generates very small time step values. In order to estimate our Δt value we suppose that the smallest wave period is T_n, where $T_n = \frac{2\pi}{\omega_n}$ and ω_n is the absolute value of the largest eigenvalue associated with the generalized and nonlinear eigenvalue problem of the final differential system

$$A\phi = \omega^2 \rho B\phi ,$$

where A is the strain matrix, B is the mass matrix of the deformation model, and ω^2 is the biggest eigenvalue of the system. Thus, for fine odjustment, the recommended value of Δt would be approximately $\frac{T_n}{10}$.

Now we have all the necessary items to calculate T_n, and the problem associated with calculating Δt in our system is reduced to a generalized, nonlinear eigenvalue problem. We can see a detailed method for efficient computation of the generalized and nonlinear eigenvalue problem in appendix A.

5   Level of Detail in Computing Deformation Simulations

The importance of the definition of the level of detail concept in elastic deformation models is rather similar to that of the level of detail concept used in 3D scene visualization. That is, depending on the precision with which we wish to simulate the deformation of the object, we must apply one size or another for the finite elements of the object in the mesh generation process. A greater value for the level of detail parameter produces a smaller matrix for the dynamic deformation process.

To determine the meshing level needed to compute the results with a predefined precision, we need a measurement tool that lets us know the error generated in the simplification of the problem. In our model we define the deformation error as the difference between the deformations calculated starting from certain physical parameters. Which are selected according to the future use of the deformation results. Thus, it is possible to render the same deformation with different levels of detail, depending on the future use of the simulation results.

Hence, a deformation simulation - which is good enough for some specific purposes - can be obtained at a low computational cost.

5.1   Computing Differences between Several Deformations

In order to detect the differences between deformation results, we measure the deformation of the boundary of the object under the same physical conditions, but with disctint levels of detail; applying the following function:

$$\widetilde{E}(\Gamma_0, \Gamma_1) =$$
$$\int_{s_0}^{s_1} \sqrt{(S_0(s) - S_1(s))^2 + (K_0(s) - K_1(s))^2} \cdot \sqrt{(x_1'(s))^2 + (y_1'(s))^2} \, ds, \quad (7)$$

where Γ_0 and Γ_1 are the curves associated with the boundary of two deformed objects represented with different levels of detail but the same physical features. $S_0(s)$ and $S_1(s)$ are the associated arc length for the parameterization of the curves with $s \in (s_0, s_1)$:

$$S_i(s) = \int_{s_0}^{s} \sqrt{x_i'(s)^2 + y_i'(s)^2} \, ds,$$

where $\Gamma_i(s) = (x_i(s), y_i(s))$, $i = 0, 1$. To fix the concepts, we suppose that the finest mesh is associated with curve Γ_1.

The reason for the $S_1'(s)$ factor's presence in the defined function ( ) is because if $S(x)$ is defined as the arc length of the parameterization on any curve, we see that normally the expression $\int_{x_0}^{x_1} \varphi(S(x)) \cdot S'(x) \, dx$ does not depend on the parameterization involved in the process:

$$\begin{cases} \int_{x_0}^{x_1} \varphi(S(x)) \cdot S\prime(x) \, dx = \int_{t_0}^{t_1} \varphi(t) \cdot S'(x) \, \frac{dt}{S'(x)} = \int_{t_0}^{t_1} \varphi(t) \, dt, \\ t = S(x), \\ dt = S'(x) \, dx, \\ dx = \frac{dt}{S'(x)}. \end{cases}$$

Therefore, with the definitions of the paragraph above, we can say that results generated by the use of the function $\widetilde{E}$ in the curves to compare is not affected by the parameterization used. For this reason we define the function $\widetilde{E}$ as the measurement of the existing differences between two examined deformations.

44   M. Mascaró et al.

5.2   Fixing the Error between Our Optimal Deformation and others Deformations

The algorithm to compute the differences between two deformations is:

1. We apply the same deformation conditions to two objects with different level sof detail in their finite element mesh, in order to compare the results of each deformation. One of the finite element mesh size corresponds to a level of detail to produce good deformation results. The second mesh size will be a simplification of this precise mesh (finite elements greater than the precise one, Figure   ).
2. In order to apply function $\widetilde{E}$ on each spline as shown above . We define this computed value as the error present in the simplified deformation.

5.3   Example of the Error Computation Generated by a Simplified Deformation

We take the same object meshed at two different finite elements sizes (fine level of detail and relaxed level of detail), and we deform them with those physical parameters: (Figure   ):

 - Vertices in P are the fixed vertices of the object during the deformation process.
 - On the vertices in set F we apply the following force: ($Fx = -5N$, $Fy = -5N$) for 0 to 1 seconds.
 - The rest of the object's vertices are free vertices without any external force on them.
 - The material properties of the deformed object are: density ($1.8\,g/cm^3$), Poisson's ratio (0.22), softening coefficient (3), and Young's module ($1000GPa$).
 - We compute the deformation over 2 seconds.

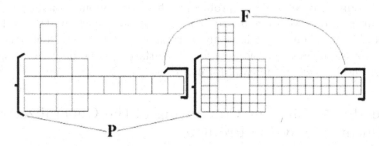

Fig. 2. Simulating a deformation in an object meshed at different levels of detail

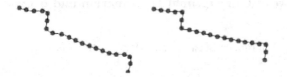

Fig. 3. On the left we have the spline obtained from the simplified deformation. On the right we have the spline from the precise deformation

In order to simplify the presentation of the results we compute the error in only part of the boundary. The differences can be seen in Figure   .

Two cubic splines obtained from respectively deformed boundaries can be observed in Figure   ; the value of the differences generated by the simplification process is 1.924.

6   Conclusions

In this paper we have presented several benefits to applying a finite element deformation model :

- We have calculated the optimal Δt to apply in the dynamic process. We then obtain the consequent reduction of the number of iterations while maintaining the stability of the deformation model.
- We define a precise finite element size to mesh the object in a way that generates a finite element mesh that guarantees a good transmission of the strain waves caused inside the object by the external forces. At the same time we get the precise number of vertices that must be in the object to reach a good solution without using superfluous information. We this reduce the size of the matrix in the dynamic problem.
- If we are using elastic deformation tools in animation work, precision is not the main goal, so we have defined a system to compute the error produced by a simplified deformation problem with a low computational cost.
- In future work, we are going to generalize all the topics to 3D. The level of detail is more important if we are working with 3D objects. The generalization of the defined function ( ) for the surfaces can be done by using their first and second fundamental forms.

Appendix A: Efficient Computing of the Generalized and Nonlinear Eigenvalue Problem

The basic generalized and nonlinear eigenvalue problem is:

$$A\phi = \omega^2 \rho B\phi ,$$

where A and B are symmetric and B is positive definite. We can convert it into a equivalent system:

$$\left(B^{-1}A\right)\phi = \omega^2\phi .$$

Now we must calculate the inverse matrix of B and this process is computationally inefficient. In addition the matrix $\left(B^{-1}A\right)$ is not symmetric. Thus the efficient way to solve this problem is to solve an equivalent system in which the eigenvalues are the same as those of the original problem.

We can recover a symmetric eigenvalue problem using the *Cholesky* decomposition in the mass matrix

$$B = L \cdot L^T .$$

Multiplying the equation above by L^{-1}, we get

$$C\left(L^T\phi\right) = \omega^2\rho\left(L^T\phi\right) \quad where \quad C = L^{-1}A\left(L^{-1}\right)^T .$$

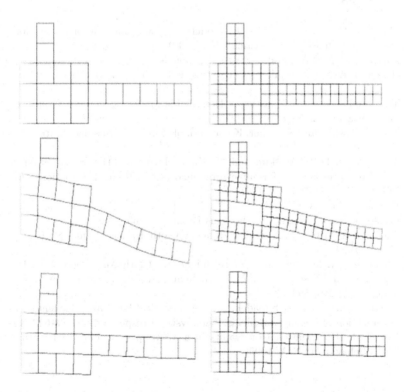

Fig. 4. On the left we have the results from the simplified deformation. In the right we have the results from the precise deformation. Rendered time steps correspond to 0, 0.33, and 1.5 seconds

Matrix C is symmetric and its eigenvalues are the same as those of the original problem, so we need only calculate the matrix C. To do this we need to compute L^{-1} and we must also make an inverse computation. The efficient way to form C is first to solve the equation

$$Y \cdot L^T = A ,$$

for the lower triangle of the matrix Y, and then solve

$$L \cdot C = Y ,$$

and obtain the lower triangle of the symmetric matrix C.

Once we get matrix C, to obtain its major eigenvalue we can apply the method to it. Now we can obtain the period T_n.

In our case the computational cost of the *Cholesky* decomposition is on the order of $O(n^2)$, because the mass matrix B in our model is maximum with nine values different than null for each row.

References

1. Mascaró, M. Mir, A. Perales, F. Modelado y animación de objetos deformables basado en la teoría de la elasticidad. CEIG 97, pp. 95-110, 1997.
2. Mascaró, M. Mir, A. Perales, F.Visualización de deformaciones dinámicas mediante elementos finitos triangulares y cuadrangulares. CEIG 99, pp. 47-61, 1999.   ,   ,
3. Terzopoulos, D. et. al. Elastically Deformable Models. Computer Graphics (Proc. Siggraph), 21, 4:205-214, 1987.
4. Terzopoulos, D. and Fleischer, K. Deformable Models. Visual Computer, 21, 4:306-331, 1988.
5. Terzopoulos, D. A. Witkin, and M. Kass. "Dynamic 3D models with local and global deformations: Deformable superquadratics". IEEE Transactions on PAMI, Vol. 13, n. 7, pp. 703-714, 1991.
6. Palmer, P. Mir, A. González, M. Simulació Dinàmica i Deformacions. Memoria de investigación. Universidad de las Islas Baleares. Junio, 1998.
7. Aono, M. A Wrinkle Propagation Model for Cloth. Proc. CG. Int'l, Springer-Verlag, 95-115, 1990.
8. Thalmann, N. M. and Yang, Y. Techniques for Cloth Animation. New Trends in Animation and Visualization, N. M-Thalmann and D. Thalmann, eds., John Wiley & Sons, 243-256, 1991.
9. Serón, F. J., Badal, J., Sabadell, F. J. A numerical laboratory for simulation and visualization of seismic wavefields. Geophysical Prospecting, 44,603-642, 1996.
10. Provot, X. Deformation Constraints in a Mass-Spring Model to Describe Rigid Cloth Behavior. INRIA. 1995.

Analysis of Human Motion Using Snakes and Neural Networks

K. Tabb, N. Davey, R. Adams and S. George

e-mail {K.J.Tabb, N.Davey, R.G.Adams, S.J.George}@herts.ac.uk
http://www.health.herts.ac.uk/ken/vision/
Tel: (+ 0044 / 0) 1707 286171
Fax: (+ 0044 / 0) 1707 284954

Department of Computer Science, University of Hertfordshire,
College Lane, Hatfield, Hertfordshire, UK. AL10 9AB

Abstract. A novel technique is described for analysing human movement in outdoor scenes. Following initial detection of the humans using active contour models, the contours are then re-represented as normalised axis crossover vectors. These vectors are then fed into a neural network which determines the typicality of a given human shape, allowing for a given human's motion deformation to be analysed. Experiments are described which investigate the success of the technique being presented.

Keywords: Human, Motion Analysis, Shape, Snake, Active Contour, Neural Network, Axis Crossover Vector

1 Introduction

This paper outlines a mechanism for analysing the motion and deformation of walking humans. A method based upon active contour models, snakes [1], and a neural network for categorisation is used [2, 3]. In previous papers we have discussed the classification of human shape in isolated static images taken from a motion sequence; in this study we discuss an individual's shape deformation during motion. The method discussed is part of a larger system designed to track moving pedestrians, a problem that has been the subject of much research [4, 5, 6]. We show that the periodic nature of human walking is clearly discernible from the deformation pattern, and that individual humans have a specific temporal pattern.

The paper is divided into 6 sections. Section 2 discusses the use of active contour models for detecting walking humans. Section 3 discusses the issues faced when using active contour data to train neural networks, and presents a solution in the form of the axis crossover vector. Section 4 summarises previous experimental findings using neural networks to identify human shapes, which leads into current work on human motion analysis using neural networks (section 5), along with experimental methods and results. Finally section 6 discusses the findings of this paper and details future work in this area.

H. H. Nagel and F. J. Perales (Eds.): AMDO 2000, LNCS 1899, pp. 48-57, 2000.

2   Identifying and Tracking Moving Humans Using Snakes

2.1   Snakes

In order to identify and track human outlines, the basic human shape must first be identified, and we use active contour models, 'snakes'. A snake is an energy minimising spline which can detect objects in an image and track non-occluded objects in a sequence of images. Snakes can be optimised for detecting and tracking particular classes of objects by customising their energy function so that detection of the desired characteristics, for example the curvature of an object's outline, or the presence of a particular colour, results in a reduction of the snake's overall energy. This reduction in energy has the effect of attracting the snake towards these desired features. Examples of a snake tracking a human can be seen in Figure 1. The active contour model used in these experiments was based on the Fast Snake model [7] as it allows for more autonomous object detection and tracking than the original model [1], although the techniques discussed in this paper are independent of the particular active contour model being used.

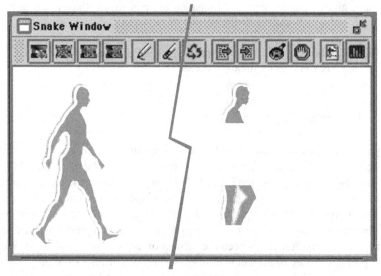

Figure 1: A target human detected and tracked in a sequence of frames, depicted here by the results of two discontiguous frames, using an active contour model. The target human has been dimmed in this figure to increase the snake's visibility

Once the snake's energy function has been defined, the user clicks an initial polygonal contour around the target object in the first frame of a movie. The snake then minimises its contour's energy according to its energy function, causing it to lock onto features in the image which are defined as salient by the energy function. Once the snake has stopped moving it is copied, in its relaxed position, into the next frame of the movie, where it again minimises its energy in an attempt to lock onto the target object in its new location in the image. This process continues until the end of the movie is reached. The success of the snake in detecting and tracking the target object is largely dependent on the relevance of the snake's energy function to the target class of object; the image quality following image preprocessing; the frame rate and speed of movement of the target object; the distance the contour's control points are from each other; and the level of occlusion of the target object. Once a snake loses focus from the target object, it rarely regains the successful detection and tracking of that target object.

A more detailed discussion of active contour models and their energy functions can be found in [8] and [9].

2.2   Tracking Walking Humans

In order to produce a clean and reasonably varied set of data, the 3D modelling and animation package 'Poser' [10] was used to simulate human movement. Snakes were relaxed around simulated humans in 30 different movies, all of which contained a single human walking from left to right. Each movie contained a different walk style and/or human build, providing a range of simulated human shapes and motions. All movies were 120 frames in duration, which allowed for at least 2 paces per person, despite individual differences in the length of stride and speed of movement from one human to another.

As described earlier, a snake is initialised around the human in the first frame of the movie. In subsequent frames, the snake is allowed to autonomously relax around the walking human, using its position in the previous frame as an initialisation in the next frame. In such a fashion the human is identified and tracked.

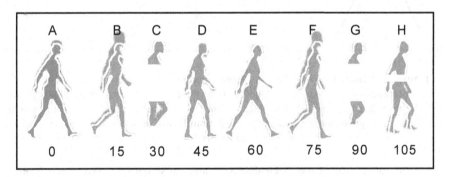

Figure 2: A target human detected and tracked through a sequence of 120 frames using an active contour. The frame numbers are shown below each frame; intermediate frames have been omitted. Above each frame is the pose identifier, referred to in the results sections of this paper. The target human has been dimmed in this figure to increase the snake's visibility

Figure 2 shows the results of a snake tracking a sample human over 120 frames of video footage. No objective measure exists of an active contour's success at tracking objects [8], but here the model was clearly successful as the humans were tracked in all of the 30 different instances. Speed is not a primary concern in this work, but it is worth noting that the relaxation times for the snakes in moving from one frame to another was often very fast.

As can be seen from Figure 2, the snake only obtains the outer edge of an object; 'holes' in between the human's legs do not form part of the contour. Despite the variation that humans adopt as they walk, their outer contour is identified in all cases.

3   Axis Crossover Vectors for Representing Human Shapes

3.1   Representation

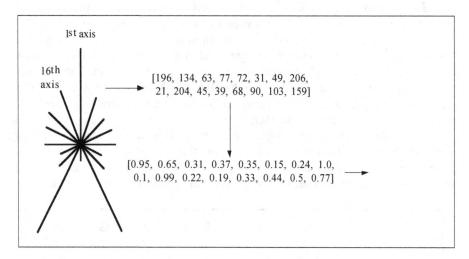

Figure 3: A human contour being re-represented as a 16-axis crossover vector. The snake's contour (left) has 16 axes projected from the contour's centre to its edges, giving 16 measurements (top vector). This vector is then normalised (bottom vector), to make it scale invariant, providing a compact representation for use in neural networks (visualised on right)

Once the target object has been detected and tracked in a movie, each frame's resultant contour can be stored as a vector of that contour's control points ((x,y) coordinates in the image), with vector length n where n is the number of control points along the snake's spline. However, this vector is not ideal for the purposes of shape analysis. By storing the absolute (x,y) locations of the control points, the active contour is location dependent; identically shaped contours in different parts of the image will have different vectors. The contour's vector is scale dependent too; differently sized contours which share the same shape will consist of different vectors. The contour is also rotation dependent; two identically shaped and sized contours will appear to have different vectors if they both consider different control points to be the 'first', as it is this control point which appears first in the vector. Finally, the length of the vector is determined by the number of control points along the contour, therefore identically shaped and sized contours which contain different numbers of control points will result in vectors of different lengths.

All of these factors make the comparison and analysis of active contours difficult. For the purposes of being used in neural networks, the native active contour vector is additionally unsuitable because it contains pairs of data, the x and y coordinates of the control point, requiring the network to associate an x coordinate with the correct y coordinate before analysis can take place.

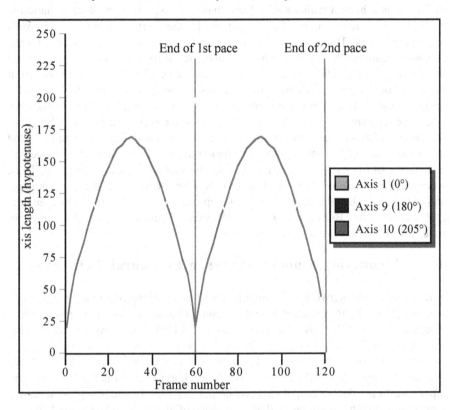

Figure 4: Axis length deformations over time, taken from a single walking human. The graph shows the differences in lengths of 3 of the 16 axes, at 0°, 180° and 205° from vertical, during two paces

One possible solution to the problem of analysing active contours is the axis crossover representation, presented in [2] and shown in Figure 3. A number of axes are projected outwards from the contour's centre, with the distance along those axes from the centre to the furthest edge the axis meets being stored in a vector. This vector is then normalised by its largest element, making the vector scale, location and rotation invariant. Furthermore such axis crossover vectors are independent of the number of control points on the contour, as the crossover vector's length is equal to the number of axes being projected, not to the number of control points on the snake. For more complicated situations the axis crossover representation offers more flexibility than discussed here; a more detailed description of its features can be found in [2].

3.2   Analysing Deformation

Having tracked the object with a snake, the relaxed contours are then converted into axis crossover vectors as described in Section 3.1. Figure 4 shows the deformation of 3 axes as a human walks along. Note that each axis' pattern of deformation is cyclical, closely repeating itself once per pace. Furthermore some axes are deformed more than others. The axis at 0°, which typically measures the distance from the contour's centre to the top of the head, shows little difference in movement during the walking motion. This reflects the fairly constant height that the head keeps from the centre of the body while walking. Conversely the axis at 180°, which typically measures the distance from the contour's centre to the crotch or feet (in the case where the legs are upright and the feet lie below the crotch), varies radically within each pace, reflecting the opening and closing of the human's legs. The length of the axis situated at 205° is has negative correlation to the 180° axis, where the opening and closing of the leg is again responsible for the axis growing and shrinking. Thus, when the leg is outstretched, the 180° axis is short whereas the 205° axis is long, and conversely when the human is standing up straight, the 180° axis is long and the 205° axis is short. Both the 180° and 205° axes extend and shrink only once per pace, coinciding with the stride being taken.

4   Identifying Human Shapes with Neural Networks

A range of neural network experiments have been performed to validate the axis crossover's ability to represent human contours in a scale-, location- and rotation-invariant manner [3]. Axis crossover vectors of different sizes were used, ranging from 4 axes to 24 axes, to identify the most appropriate axis crossover description for human shapes. The number of axes used has a direct relationship with the number of input units in the neural network: each axis' length is the input for one input unit. In the double output case one output unit was trained to represent human shapes, and the other non-human shapes. A range of hidden layers between 2 and $n-1$ units, where n is the number of input units in the network, were tested in order to identify the best generalisation ability.

Training data contained 150 human shapes, and 150 non-human shapes which consisted of 'outdoor furniture' shapes such as cars and streetlights. Active contours were relaxed around these shapes, and were then re-represented as axis crossover vectors, which could then be fed into the neural network.

Test data contained 10 unseen human shapes, and 10 unseen non-human shapes, again of outdoor furniture.

As is summarised in Figure 5, the experiments found that 16 axes offered the most suitable level of detail for encoding human contours using axis crossover vectors. Consequently a 16 input unit network was chosen for all further experimentation. In addition, by using two units in the network's output layer, a confidence value can be obtained which allows a crude measure of how 'human' the network considers the given axis crossover vector to be. The confidence value is simply the difference of the two output units' values.

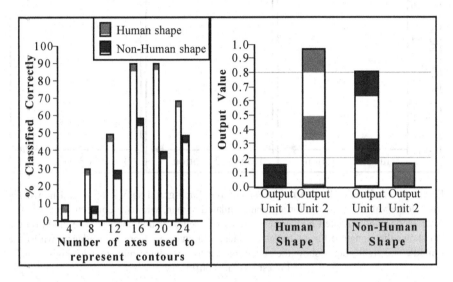

Figure 5: Results of neural networks classifying human and non-human axis crossover vectors. Left: Axis crossover vectors which used 16 axes were found to give the best results. Right: The mean confidence value when presented with human shapes (left pair of columns) and non-human shapes (right pair of columns)

5   Human Motion Analysis Using Neural Networks

As described in the previous section, a trained neural network, when presented with a human shape represented as an axis crossover vector, can produce a scalar value measuring the confidence of the network that the shape is human. The network used in section 4 was tested with 30 different simulated human motion sequences, each varying in weight and / or gait.

The motion patterns are periodic, repeating here after the 60th frame, or at the start of the second pace. This can be seen in Figure 6, where two consecutive paces are superimposed for each of the 3 humans. The frequency of a human's motion pattern is attuned to the frequency of their walking, so that the speed of walking can be identified from the confidence value/time graph.

A human's motion pattern forms a signature specific to that human. Whilst the motion pattern for a human is not identical from one pace to another, in the same way that poses A and E in Figure 2 are not identical, it can be seen from Figure 7 that motion patterns for a given human are more similar to each other than to other humans' motion patterns.

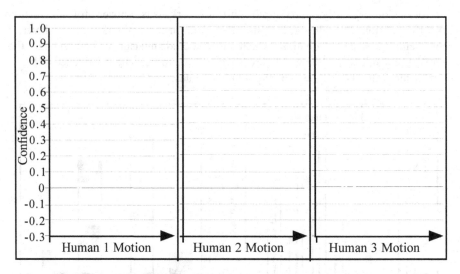

Figure 6: Analysis of human motion signatures. Each graph shows the neural network's confidence values over time for a given simulated human, with two consecutive paces for a corresponding simulated human being superimposed over one another. The graph on the left shows the signature for a simulated human with average overall confidence, whilst the middle and right graphs show the signatures for the simulated humans with highest and lowest overall confidence

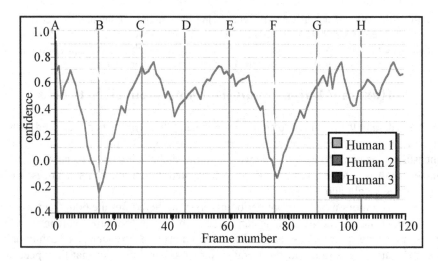

Figure 7: Neural network confidence value plotted against time for three simulated humans. 120 F rames corresponds to two paces. The pose identifiers labelled along the top of graph correspond to those in Figure 2

As the human walks, this confidence value will change, reflecting the fact that the typicality of the shape of a walking human varies over time. This can be clearly seen in Figure 7, where for some poses the network classes the humans as more non-human than human. See for example humans 2 and 3 in poses B and F. Moreover, there is considerable differences between humans so that, for example, human 1 is consistently classed as more human than humans 2 and 3 across all frames.

6   Discussion

In this paper we have shown how snakes can be used to identify human contours in an image, and then to track a moving simulated human. These contours can then be re-represented as fixed length, scale-, rotation- and location-invariant vectors. When the vector for a walking human is analysed over time, the deformation pattern of the human contour is observable , clearly showing a differential deformation pattern.

With a suitable set of images, a training set can be formed from the axis crossover vectors for a neural network classifier that identifies shapes as human or non-human, and it is the time dependent output of this network that can be used to analyse the motion pattern of a single walking human. As shown in Section 6, the output of the network is periodic, identifying single paces, so that speed of motion can be gauged. Moreover, individual differences between humans are apparent and these signatures could be used as identification tags. We are interested in extending this work to deal with the problems associated with occlusion. Our aim is to produce a model that will combine active contour models and neural networks and which will be able to track humans even during differing levels of occlusion, which will combine with previous studies on occluded human shapes [2]. This will involve prediction of the motion deformation pattern of a given human, which will in turn, involve the collection of a wider range of real human data, including footage of humans walking towards or away from the viewing point, and of real world noisy images.

References

1. Kass M., Witkin A. & Terzopoulos D. [1988]. *Snakes: active contour models*. In International Journal of Computer Vision (1988), pp. 321-331.

2. Tabb K., Davey N., George S. & Adams R. [1999]. *Detecting Partial Occlusion of Humans using Snakes and Neural Networks*. In Proceedings of the 5th International Conference on Engineering Applications of Neural Networks, 13-15 September 1999, Warsaw, pp. 34-39.

3. Tabb K., George S., Adams R. & Davey N. [1999]. *Human Shape Recognition from Snakes using Neural Networks*. In Proceedings of the 3rd International Conference on Computational Intelligence and Multimedia Applications, 23-26 September 1999, Delhi, pp. 292-296.

4. Sonka M., Hlavac V. & Boyle R. [1994]. Image processing, analysis and machine vision. Chapman & Hall.

5. Marr D. [1982]. Vision. W.H. Freeman & Company.

6. Baumberg A. M. & Hogg D. C. [1994]. An efficient method for contour tracking using active shape models. University of Leeds School of Computer Studies Research Report Series, Report 94.11.

7. Williams D.J. & Shah M. [1992]. *A fast algorithm for active contours and curvature estimation.* In CVGIP - Image Understanding 55, pp. 14-26.

8. Blake A. & Isard M. [1998]. Active Contours. Springer-Verlag.

9. Tabb K. & George S. [1998]. *Snakes and their influence on visual processing.* University of Hertfordshire Department of Computer Science Technical Report No. 309 Feb 1998.

10. MetaCreations [1999]. Poser 4 for Macintosh. www.metacreations.com

Stability and Complexity Study of Animated Elastically Deformable Objects*

P. Palmer, A. Mir, and M. González

Departament de Matemàtiques i Informàtica
Universitat de les Illes Balears
pere.palmer@uib.es
{dmiamt0,dmimgh0}@ps.uib.es

Abstract. The study of the motion of deformable models is one of the most important topics in computer animation. The model proposed by Terzopoulos et al. [ ] uses Lagrange's equation of motion and a variational principle to find the change of shape of deformable objects. We present in this work several methods for solving this equation numerically, and we study its complexity and stability, in order to find the best one. These methods have been classified in explicit and semi-implicit methods using central finite-difference methods and non-central finite-difference methods. We will see that the explicit methods are better than the semi-implicit ones because of lower computational cost in order to create the animation of non-highly deformable objects. Moreover, we will see that the behavior of non-central finite difference methods are better because they are stable. The study has been made for surfaces but can be easily generalizable to 3D curves and solids. To illustrate the applications we have displayed the animation of a held handkerchief and the free fall of a tablecloth over a table.

Keywords: Physically-based modelling, lagrangian dynamics, surface deformation, deformation energy, simulation, finite-difference methods, stability, animation.

1 Introduction

Deformations play an important role in Computer Graphics, allowing objects to assume interesting new shapes. Deformable objects are inherently more difficult to model than rigid objects. Since 1986 ([,]) , the Computer Graphics community has devoted much attention to the problem of modelling and animation of deformable objects, such as cloth and flesh, based not only on the Geometrical/Mathematical intrinsic characteristics of surfaces and solids, but also on their material properties in the context of continuum and discrete mechanics . Following [ ] the deformation-modelling techniques can be classified into three categories: geometrical, physical and hybrid. The "geometrical techniques" are

---

* Partially supported by CICYT contract TIC-98-0302

H. H. Nagel and F. J. Perales (Eds.): AMDO 2000, LNCS 1899, pp. 58–   , 2000.

the best in the computational cost sense, but they don't consider the physical properties of objects. The disadvantage is the poor realism of simulation deformation. See, by way of example, [,] and [ ]. Some of the main goals of this activity has been to produce animations of deformable objects with a high degree of realism. This approach has been included in a broader modelling framework, entitled "*physically modelling techniques*", where the objects are modeled and moved following the physical laws that govern their static and/or dynamic behavior. See [, , , ,] and [ ] for more details. The problem is that the complexity and computational cost, in almost all the cases, is very high. To avoid this drawback the so-called "*hybrid techniques*" have been developed. These techniques use concepts and methods from the two previous ones to view the deformable objects and their motion in as real a way as possible, thus reducing the computational cost and complexity using initial geometrical approximations. We can see in [, , , ,] some examples. An extended study of the previous classification can be found in [ ].

Coming back to the initial problem, the literature on modeling and animation of deformable objects shows that physically based techniques should be used to build and animate realistic deformable models. Another aspect in realistic animation is modeling the behavior of deformable objects. In order to do this we should approximate a continuous model by using discretization methods, such as finite-difference methods and finite-element methods (see [ ], and [ ] in the latter case). In the finite-difference discretization case, a deformable object is approximated by using a control points grid, where the points are allowed to move in relation to each other. The way that the points are allowed to move determines the properties of the deformable object. Included in these methods there are those that try to find the object motion by using Lagrange's motion model and by defining an object functional energy that measures the elastic deformation potential energy for the body. This functional can be based on the fundamental theorem of surfaces of Differential Geometry, as in [ ] and [ ] (see also [, ,]). Our way to solve the deformation problem belongs to this type of methods.

Compared to the former work by Terzopoulos et al. and Güdükbay and Özgüç ([ ]) our work can be viewed as a continuation and verification. Our model is similar but differs in the linear algebraic system associated to the numerical resolution of the differential equation related to the model, to obtain the animation of deformable objects. Using these ideas as a guide we present briefly in the next section the basic principles of the deformable model equation. In Section 3 we describe several finite-difference schemes to solve the deformation equation numerically and to obtain the linear algebraic system associated with it. To see which is the best way to solve the system we have carried out, in Section 4, a study of stability and complexity depending on the matrix which represents the deformation information. Section 5 is devoted to presenting some simulation results and finally we give some conclusions and suggestions for further research.

2   Equation of Elastically Deformable Model

Let Ω be our object. We suppose that Ω is a surface with local coordinates $p = (x_1, x_2)$ where $(x_1, x_2) \in [0, 1] \times [0, 1]$ (we suppose that the domain of parametrization of Ω is the unit square). The position of an object point at time t will be $\mathbf{r}(p; t) := \mathbf{r}(x_1, x_2; t) = (r_1(x_1, x_2; t), r_2(x_1, x_2; t), r_3(x_1, x_2; t))$. The initial position of the object is $\mathbf{r}^0(p) := \mathbf{r}^0(x_1, x_2) = (r_1^0(x_1, x_2), r_2^0(x_1, x_2), r_3^0(x_1, x_2))$.

The next step is to introduce the deformation energy. To do this, we are going to take into account the fundamental theorem of surfaces: two surfaces have the same shape if their metric tensor G and curvature tensor B are the same, where

$$G_{ij} = G_{ij}(\mathbf{r}(x_1, x_2; t)) = \frac{\partial \mathbf{r}}{\partial x_i} \cdot \frac{\partial \mathbf{r}}{\partial x_j}, \quad B_{ij} = B_{ij}(\mathbf{r}(x_1, x_2; t)) = n \cdot \frac{\partial^2 \mathbf{r}}{\partial x_i \partial x_j},$$

and n is the normal unit surface. See reference [ ] for a detailed discussion of these formulations. Using the above tensors we define the deformation energy for object Ω at time t as:

$$\varepsilon(\mathbf{r}) = \sum_{i,j=1}^{2} \int_{\Omega} \left[\eta_{ij} \left(G_{ij} - G_{ij}^0 \right)^2 + \xi_{ij} \left(B_{ij} - B_{ij}^0 \right)^2 \right] dx_1 dx_2,$$

where η_{ii} represents the object resistance to length deformation, $\eta_{12} = \eta_{21}$ represents the object resistance to shear deformation, ξ_{ii} represents the object resistance to bend deformation and $\xi_{12} = \xi_{21}$ represents the object resistance to twist deformation.

The motion equation for a deformable model can be written in Lagrangian form (see [ ]) using the previous functional as

$$\frac{\partial}{\partial t} \left(\mu \frac{\partial \mathbf{r}}{\partial t} \right) + \gamma \frac{\partial \mathbf{r}}{\partial t} + \frac{\delta \varepsilon(\mathbf{r})}{\delta \mathbf{r}} = f(\mathbf{r}, t), \tag{1}$$

where $\frac{\delta \varepsilon(\mathbf{r})}{\delta \mathbf{r}}$ is the first variational derivative for the deformation functional and $f(\mathbf{r}, t)$ is the net externally applied force. The first term is the inertial force due to the mass distributions. The second term is the damping force due to dissipation, and the third term is the elastic force due to deformation of the object away from its natural shape.

To create animations with this deformable model, the differential motion equation should be discretized by applying finite-difference approximation methods and solving the system of linked ordinary differential equations of motion obtained in this way. But, first of all, it is necessary to simplify the first variational derivative of functional $\varepsilon(\mathbf{r})$. Concerning the approximation of $\frac{\delta \varepsilon(\mathbf{r})}{\delta \mathbf{r}}$ it can be seen in [ ] that

$$\frac{\delta \varepsilon(\mathbf{r})}{\delta \mathbf{r}} \approx \sum_{i,j=1}^{2} -\frac{\partial}{\partial x_i} \left(\alpha_{ij} \frac{\partial \mathbf{r}}{\partial x_j} \right) + \frac{\partial^2}{\partial x_i \partial x_j} \left(\beta_{ij} \frac{\partial^2 \mathbf{r}}{\partial x_i \partial x_j} \right), \tag{2}$$

where $\alpha_{ij} = \eta_{ij}(p; t) \left(G_{ij} - G_{ij}^0 \right)$ and $\beta_{ij} = \xi_{ij}(p; t) \left(B_{ij} - B_{ij}^0 \right)$.

3   Numerical Resolution of Deformable Model

Equation ( ),which represents the surface movement and its deformation at the same time, can be solved using finite differences in both spatial and time coordinates. In order to do that we approximate spatial derivatives in order to transform the partial differential equation ( ) into an ordinary differential equation. So, using any of the finite-difference schemes described below, expressing the grid function $r(m,n)$ as the MN dimensional vector $\underline{r}$ in the grid vector notation, we transform the partial differential equation ( ) into the following differential equation:

$$\mathbf{M}\frac{d^2\underline{r}}{dt^2} + \mathbf{C}\frac{d\underline{r}}{dt} + \mathbf{K}(\underline{r})\underline{r} = \underline{f} \ , \tag{3}$$

where $\mathbf{M}$ is the $MN \times MN$ diagonal mass matrix, $\mathbf{C}$ is the $MN \times MN$ diagonal damping matrix and $\mathbf{K}(\underline{r})$ is the $MN \times MN$ stiffness matrix which contains all the information about the finite spatial discretization and the deformation properties of the object. Note that $\mathbf{M}$ is the mass matrix with $\mu(m,n)$ as diagonal elements, and $\mathbf{C}$ is also constructed similarly from $\gamma(m,n)$. As we can see below, the matrix $\mathbf{K}(\mathbf{r})$ is the most important in the numerical resolution of equation ( ).

To solve the differential equation, we use the following discrete time approximations:

$$\frac{d\underline{r}}{dt} \approx \frac{\underline{r}\,(t+\Delta t) - \underline{r}\,(t-\Delta t)}{2\Delta t}, \quad \frac{d^2\mathbf{r}}{dt^2} \approx \frac{\underline{r}\,(t+\Delta t) - 2\underline{r}\,(t) + \underline{r}\,(t-\Delta t)}{\Delta t^2}.$$

Independently of the of finite-difference scheme used to discretize the spatial coordinates, to solve equation ( ) we have to solve the following linear system of equations, associated to an explicit integration procedure for the ordinary differential equation:

$$\mathbf{A} \cdot \underline{r}\,(t+\Delta t) = \underline{b}\,(t), \tag{4}$$

where $\mathbf{A} = \frac{\mathbf{M}}{\Delta t^2} + \frac{\mathbf{C}}{2\Delta t}$ and $\underline{b}\,(t) = \underline{f}\,(t) - \left(\mathbf{K}(\underline{r}\,(t)) - \frac{2\mathbf{M}}{\Delta t^2}\right)\underline{r}\,(t) + \left(\frac{\mathbf{C}}{2\Delta t} - \frac{\mathbf{M}}{\Delta t^2}\right)\underline{r}\,(t-\Delta t)$. The previous system is easy to solve because matrix $\mathbf{A}$ is diagonal. We can write:

$$\underline{r}\,(t+\Delta t) = \mathbf{A}^{-1} \cdot \underline{b}\,(t) := \mathbf{S} \cdot \underline{b}\,(t),$$

where $S_{ij} = 0$, if $i \neq j$ and $S_{ii} = \left(\frac{m_{ii}}{\Delta t^2} + \frac{c_{ii}}{2\Delta t}\right)^{-1}$. Then, the original nonlinear partial differential equation ( ) has been reduced to a sequence of diagonal linear algebraic systems done by ( ).

This fact is different to the numerical integration through time carried out by Terzopoulos et al. As we can see in [,] (also in [ ]) they obtain a semi-implicit integration procedure

$$\mathbf{A}(t) \cdot \underline{r}\,(t+\Delta t) = \underline{g}_t, \tag{5}$$

where matrix $\mathbf{A}(t) = \mathbf{K}(\underline{\mathbf{r}}(t)) + \left(\frac{\mathbf{M}}{\Delta t^2} + \frac{\mathbf{C}}{2\Delta t} \right)$ and $\underline{\mathbf{g}}_t = \underline{\mathbf{f}}_t + \frac{2\mathbf{M}}{\Delta t^2} \cdot \underline{\mathbf{r}}(t) + \left(\frac{\mathbf{C}}{2\Delta t} - \frac{\mathbf{M}}{\Delta t^2} \right) \cdot$ $\underline{\mathbf{r}}(t - \Delta t)$.

To solve equation ( ) numerically we use the standard finite-difference approximation operators. In the first place we use a scheme based on *central finite-differences*, where the difference operators are done by

$$\frac{\partial \mathbf{h}}{\partial x_1} \approx \frac{\mathbf{h}(x_1 + \Delta x_1, x_2) - \mathbf{h}(x_1 - \Delta x_1, x_2)}{2\Delta x_1}, \text{ in a similar way for } \frac{\partial \mathbf{h}}{\partial x_2},$$

$$\frac{\partial^2 \mathbf{h}}{\partial x_1^2} \approx \frac{\mathbf{h}(x_1 + \Delta x_1, x_2) - 2\mathbf{h}(x_1, x_2) + \mathbf{h}(x_1 - \Delta x_1, x_2)}{\Delta x_1^2}, \text{ in a similar way for } \frac{\partial^2 \mathbf{h}}{\partial x_2^2},$$

$$\frac{\partial^2 \mathbf{h}}{\partial x_1 \partial x_2} \approx \frac{-\mathbf{h}(x_1 - \Delta x_1, x_2 + \Delta x_2) + \mathbf{h}(x_1 + \Delta x_1, x_2 + \Delta x_2) + \mathbf{h}(x_1 - \Delta x_1, x_2) - \mathbf{h}(x_1 + \Delta x_1 \Delta x_1, x_2)}{\Delta x_1 \Delta x_2}.$$

and so on up to fourth order derivatives. In this case the approximation error order is 2. Next, we use a *non central finite-difference* scheme where the approximation error order is 1. This method was used in [ ] and [ ] (see also [ ]). We define the following forward and backward first difference operators:

$$D_1^+ \mathbf{h}(x_1, x_2) = \frac{\mathbf{h}(x_1 + \Delta x_1, x_2) - \mathbf{h}(x_1, x_2)}{\Delta x_1}, \quad D_1^- \mathbf{h}(x_1, x_2) = \frac{\mathbf{h}(x_1, x_2) - \mathbf{h}(x_1 - \Delta x_1, x_2)}{\Delta x_1},$$

$$D_2^+ \mathbf{h}(x_1, x_2) = \frac{\mathbf{h}(x_1, x_2 + \Delta x_2) - \mathbf{h}(x_1, x_2)}{\Delta x_2}, \quad D_2^- \mathbf{h}(x_1, x_2) = \frac{\mathbf{h}(x_1, x_2) - \mathbf{h}(x_1, x_2 - \Delta x_2)}{\Delta x_2}.$$

Using the previous difference operators we define the second difference operator by

$$D_{12}^+ \mathbf{h}(x_1, x_2) = D_{21}^+ \mathbf{h}(x_1, x_2) = D_1^+ (D_2^+ \mathbf{h}(x_1, x_2)),$$
$$D_{11} \mathbf{h}(x_1, x_2) = D_1^- (D_1^+ \mathbf{h}(x_1, x_2)),$$
$$D_{12}^- \mathbf{h}(x_1, x_2) = D_{21}^- \mathbf{h}(x_1, x_2) = D_1^- (D_2^- \mathbf{h}(x_1, x_2)),$$
$$D_{22} \mathbf{h}(x_1, x_2) = D_2^- (D_2^+ \mathbf{h}(x_1, x_2)).$$

Now, using a grid of points to represent the continuous surface (where we apply the deformation) we can discretize the expressions involved in equation ( ) using the approximate variational derivate done by ( ).

Another aspect to take into account in the discretization process of equation ( ) is the surface boundary condition. We have considered two different boundary conditions. First of all we introduce a *free (natural) boundary condition* on the edges of a surface where the difference operator attempts to access nodal variables outside the discrete domain, setting the value of the difference operators to zero. This is equivalent to moving the boundary so as to amplify the square domain $[0, 1] \times [0, 1]$ and turn the values $\mathbf{r}(x_1, x_2)$ of the old boundary into the $\mathbf{r}(x_1, x_2)$ values of new boundary. After, we consider *regions of discretization in the boundary*. We make this clear with the first and second order finite-differences. In this case, we divide the square domain $[0, 1] \times [0, 1]$ into nine regions, as can be seen in Figure . In each of these regions we construct a new set of difference operators. For example, in zone VIII we have the following expressions for the approximations for the difference operators:

$$\frac{\partial h}{\partial x_1} \approx \frac{3\mathbf{h}(x_1, x_2) - 4\mathbf{h}(x_1 - \Delta x_1, x_2) + \mathbf{h}(x_1 - 2\Delta x_1, x_2)}{2\Delta x_1}$$

$$\frac{\partial h}{\partial x_2} \approx \frac{\mathbf{h}(x_1, x_2 + \Delta x_2) - \mathbf{h}(x_1, x_2 - \Delta x_2)}{2\Delta x_2}$$

$$\frac{\partial^2 h}{\partial x_1^2} \approx \frac{1}{\Delta x_1^2}(2\mathbf{h}(x_1, x_2) - 5\mathbf{h}(x_1 - \Delta x_1, x_2) + 4\mathbf{h}(x_1 - 2\Delta x_1, x_2)$$
$$- \mathbf{h}(x_1 - 3\Delta x_1, x_2))$$

$$\frac{\partial^2 h}{\partial x_2^2} \approx \frac{\mathbf{h}(x_1, x_2 + \Delta x_2) - 2\mathbf{h}(x_1, x_2) + \mathbf{h}(x_1, x_2 + \Delta x_2)}{\Delta x_2^2}$$

$$\frac{\partial^2 h}{\partial x_1 \partial x_2} \approx \frac{1}{4\Delta x_1 \Delta x_2}(\mathbf{h}(x_1, x_2) - 2\mathbf{h}(x_1 - \Delta x_1, x_2) + 3\mathbf{h}(x_1 - \Delta x_1, x_2 - \Delta x_2)$$
$$- \mathbf{h}(x_1 - \Delta x_1, x_2 + \Delta x_2) - 2\mathbf{h}(x_1, x_2 - \Delta x_2) + \mathbf{h}(x_1, x_2 + \Delta x_2)$$
$$+ \mathbf{h}(x_1 - 2\Delta x_1, x_2) - \mathbf{h}(x_1 - 2\Delta x_1, x_2 - \Delta x_2))$$

and so on with all the regions and each of the derivatives appearing in equation ( ). In the case of third and fourth order derivatives we have twenty-five different regions.

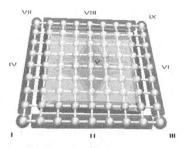

Fig. 1. Regions of discretization of boundary in order to compute the finite-difference operators

So, we have four ways of solving the partial differential equation ( ): (i) central finite-differences with free natural boundary, (ii) central finite-differences with a regions boundary, (iii) non central finite-differences with a free natural boundary and (iv) non central finite-differences with a regions boundary.

To find a numerical approximation of expression ( ), we can write this approximation as:

$$\mathbf{e}(x_1, x_2) = \sum_{i,j=1}^{2} -D_i(\mathbf{p}_{ij})(x_1, x_2) + D_{ij}(\mathbf{q}_{ij})(x_1, x_2), \tag{6}$$

where $\mathbf{p}_{ij}(x_1, x_2) = \alpha_{ij}(x_1, x_2) \cdot D_j \mathbf{r}(x_1, x_2)$ and $\mathbf{q}_{ij}(x_1, x_2) = \beta_{ij}(x_1, x_2) \cdot D_{ij}(\mathbf{r})(x_1, x_2)$ and D_i, D_j and D_{ij} are the finite-difference operators.

As we said above, using these four methods, we transform equation ( ) into the ordinary differential equation ( ), and using the discrete time derivative approximations we can integrate this equation through time using a step-by-step procedure, solving the diagonal linear algebraic system done by ( ). We can evolve the dynamic solution, which is a simulation of surface deformation, from given initial conditions at $t = 0$ by solving the linear algebraic system for the instantaneous configuration $r(t + \Delta t)$ using preceding solutions $r(t)$ and $r(t - \Delta t)$.

4   Study of Stability and Complexity

To see which is the best way of solving the system ( ) we need to study the system stability depending on the matrix $\mathbf{K}(\underline{\mathbf{r}}(t))$ we are using.

First of all, we introduce the following notation:

$$\mathbf{r}_n := \mathbf{r}(n\Delta t), \ \mathbf{f}_n := \mathbf{f}(n\Delta t), \ B(\underline{\mathbf{r}}(t)) := \mathbf{A}^{-1}\left(\frac{2\mathbf{M}}{\Delta t^2} - \mathbf{K}(\underline{\mathbf{r}}(t))\right),$$

and $\mathbf{D} := \mathbf{A}^{-1}\left(\dfrac{\mathbf{C}}{2\Delta t} - \dfrac{\mathbf{M}}{\Delta t^2}\right)$. In order to study the stability and taking into account that $r_0 = r_{-1}$, we have to find a matrix $\mathbf{G}_n$ and a vector $\mathbf{g}_n$ such that: $\mathbf{r}_n = \mathbf{G}_n r_0 + \mathbf{g}_n$. So, using equation ( ), we find the following recurrence relationships between matrices G_n and vectors g_n :

$$\mathbf{G}_n = \mathbf{B}(r_{n-1})\mathbf{G}_{n-1} + D\mathbf{G}_{n-2}, \quad \mathbf{g}_n = \mathbf{A}^{-1}\mathbf{f}_{n-1} + \mathbf{B}(r_{n-1})\mathbf{g}_{n-1} + D\mathbf{g}_{n-2}.$$

The system stability is given by the spectral radius $\rho(\mathbf{G}_n)$ of matrices $\mathbf{G}_n$. That is, the system is stable iff $\lim\limits_{n \to \infty} \rho(\mathbf{G}_n) = L \neq \infty$.

We have carried out two kinds of experiments and in the following two figures we show the spectral radius of matrix G_n in each iteration and experiment. In a first place we have deformed a plane with a fixed boundary, displayed in Figure , then we have deformed the same plane with only the four corners fixed, displayed in Figure . That is, in the first case we take the initial state $\mathbf{r}^0(x_1, x_2) = (x_1, x_2, 0)$, with $(x_1, x_2) \in [0, 1] \times [0, 1]$, and we deform the object $\mathbf{r}^0$ with $\mathbf{r}(x_1, 0; t) = (x_1, 0, 0)$, $\mathbf{r}(0, x_2; t) = (0, x_2, 0)$, $\mathbf{r}(x_1, 1; t) = (x_1, 1, 0)$ and $\mathbf{r}(1, x_2; t) = (1, x_2, 0)$ for all $t \in [0, T]$. In the second experiment we deform $\mathbf{r}^0$ with $\mathbf{r}(0, 0; t) = (0, 0, 0)$, $\mathbf{r}(0, 1; t) = (0, 1, 0)$, $\mathbf{r}(1, 0; t) = (1, 0, 0)$ and $\mathbf{r}(1, 1; t) = (1, 1, 0)$ for all $t \in [0, T]$. We have simulated an animation for a total time, T, of 2 seconds with 0.01 time increment. The plane is discretized into M rows by M columns (so, if the plane is a unit square and M is 11, the distance between points is 0.1), using a mass and damping density of 1 at each point. The horizontal, shear and vertical deformation resistance is fixed at 1 in the case of experiments displayed in Figure   and at 10 in the experiments of Figure . In this figure we show the evolution of the spectral radius in three different cases, varying

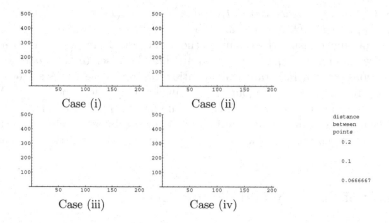

Fig. 2. Graphics of spectral radius in the experiments where we fix the boundary. In the horizontal axis, we represent the iteration n, and, in the vertical one, the spectral radius of matrix G_n. In each graph we have overlapped the results achieved in three different experiments, each one with different distance between points

the plane discretization ($M = \{6, 11, 16\}$) in order to study the evolution with different distances between points.

From Figures   and   we deduce that only with case (iii), that is, the explicit method using non-central-differences with a free natural boundary condition, we can guarantee the stability of the numerical resolution because $\lim_{n} \rho(G_n) = k$. The other cases aren't stable because (see Figures 2 and 3) $\lim_{n} \rho(G_n) = \infty$ and the convergence is very fast. The reason for this is the relevant importance played by point $(x_1, x_2; t)$ where we compute the derivative approximations to obtain matrix $\mathbf{K}$. Except in case (iv) of Figure   where after some oscillations we obtain a similar behavior to case (iii) of Figure .

4.1   Computational Cost of Model Behavior

We now consider the problem of obtaining the computational cost of our model behavior, done by equation ( ) in comparison with the development of Terzopoulos' system, which we can see in equation ( ). More precisely, we consider the study related to the simulation part in the case of a surface discretized in M rows and N columns, that is $M \times N$ points on the plane.

Previous to the simulation step it is necessary to construct the vectors and matrices which are necessary to solve the ordinary differential equation numerically. As the computational cost for each of the vectors and/or matrices is $O(M \times N)$, then the total computational cost in this part is also $O(M \times N)$.

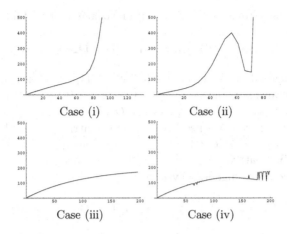

Case (i)   Case (ii)

Case (iii)   Case (iv)

Fig. 3. Graphics of spectral radius in the experiments where we only fix the four corners. In the horizontal axis, we represent the iteration n, and, in the vertical one, the spectral radius of matrix G_n

Recall that in each case the related equations are done by

$$\left(\frac{M}{2\Delta t^2} + \frac{C}{2\Delta t}\right) \underline{r}\,(t + \Delta t) = \underline{f}_r - \left(K(\underline{r}\,(t)) - \frac{M}{2\Delta t^2}\right) \underline{r}\,(t) + \left(\frac{C}{2\Delta t} - \frac{M}{\Delta t^2}\right) \underline{r}\,(t - \Delta t)$$

$$\left(\frac{M}{\Delta t^2} + \frac{C}{2\Delta t} + K(\underline{r}\,(t))\right) \underline{r}\,(t + \Delta t) = \underline{f}_r + \left(\frac{M}{2\Delta t^2}\right) \underline{r}\,(t) + \left(\frac{C}{2\Delta t} - \frac{M}{\Delta t^2}\right) \underline{r}\,(t - \Delta t)$$

that briefly we express as:

$$\mathbf{D_1} \cdot \underline{r}\,(t + \Delta t) = \underline{f}_r - \mathbf{A_1} \cdot r(t) + \mathbf{D_2} \cdot \underline{r}\,(t - \Delta t)$$

$$\mathbf{T_1} \cdot \underline{r}\,(t + \Delta t) = \underline{f}_r + \mathbf{A_2} \cdot \underline{r}\,(t) + \mathbf{D_2} \cdot \underline{r}\,(t - \Delta t)$$

Now we are going to analyze the computational cost, in time, of the simulation part in our linear algebraic system. To obtain matrix $K(\underline{r}\,(t))$ we first need to compute the expressions involved in equation ( ), which is of $O(M \times N)$ order, and after that, to build the precise matrix that is also of $O(M \times N)$ order, because we don't fill the whole matrix, but rather only the points that are involved in the deformation and movement of each point of the discrete surface. Finally, we obtain an $O(M \times N)$ order for this step.

As matrices $\mathbf{D_1}$ and $\mathbf{D_2}$ are diagonal we use an $O(M \times N)$ time order to compute them, which is, also the time necessary to compute the $\mathbf{A_1}$ matrix, because it is the difference between $K(\underline{r}\,(t))$ and $\frac{2M}{\Delta t^2}$ (a diagonal matrix).

On the other hand, the product of a vector by a matrix requires, in general, $O((M \times N)^2)$ time computing. So, this is the time necessary to compute $\mathbf{A_1} \cdot \underline{r}\,(t)$. But, to compute $\mathbf{D_2} \cdot \underline{r}\,(t - \Delta t)$ we need only $O(M \times N)$ time computing, because $\mathbf{D_2}$ is diagonal. Then, we have a $O((M \times N)^2)$ computational cost to obtain $\underline{f}_r - \mathbf{A_1} \cdot \underline{r}\,(t) + \mathbf{D_2} \cdot \underline{r}\,(t - \Delta t)$.

Finally we need to solve the diagonal linear algebraic system

$$\mathbf{D_1} \cdot \underline{\mathbf{r}}\,(t + \Delta t) = \underline{\mathbf{f}}_r - \mathbf{A_1} \cdot \underline{\mathbf{r}}\,(t) + \mathbf{D_2} \cdot \underline{\mathbf{r}}\,(t - \Delta t).$$

Since $\mathbf{D_1}$ is diagonal we can compute the inverse $\mathbf{D_1}^{-1}$ in linear time and at the same time we can make the product by $\underline{\mathbf{f}}_r - \mathbf{A_1} \cdot \underline{\mathbf{r}}\,(t) + \mathbf{D_2} \cdot \underline{\mathbf{r}}\,(t - \Delta t)$, so the computational cost of the whole process if $O((M \times N)^2)$.

In Terzopoulos' case we need to compute matrices $\mathbf{A_2}$ and $\mathbf{D_2}$, as in the previous case, with an order $O(M \times N)$, and we need the same time computing to obtain the $\mathbf{T_1}$ matrix.

To solve the linear algebraic system

$$\mathbf{T_1} \cdot \underline{\mathbf{r}}\,(t + \Delta t) = \underline{\mathbf{f}}_r + \mathbf{A_2} \cdot \underline{\mathbf{r}}\,(t) + \mathbf{D_2} \cdot \underline{\mathbf{r}}\,(t - \Delta t),$$

we need to compute the vector $\underline{\mathbf{f}}_r + \mathbf{A_2} \cdot \underline{\mathbf{r}}\,(t) + \mathbf{D_2} \cdot \underline{\mathbf{r}}\,(t - \Delta t)$ and in this case we use a time computing of order $O(M \times N)$ because $\mathbf{A_2}$ is diagonal. The matrix $\mathbf{T_1}$ isn't a diagonal matrix and depends on $\mathbf{K}(\underline{\mathbf{r}}(t))$. So, we must invert it in each step of integration. The time required to do it is very expensive. Thus, it is necessary to use a decomposition method to obtain $\mathbf{T_1}^{-1}$, so that the total computational cost order is $O((M \times N)^3)$.

Then, the explicit procedure to integrate through time the ordinary differential equation, represented by equation ( ), is more efficient, in the time computing sense, than the semi-implicit integration procedure, represented by equation ( ).

5 Simulation Examples

An implementation of those models has been made using the C++ language over several hardware platforms, also using OpenInventor®, a 3D modeling toolkit which simplifies visualization and scene composition tasks.

The following two figures show *artistic* animation sequences of deformable objects, the animations have been obtained with the explicit method using the central finite-difference scheme with a free natural boundary condition.

The first one, shown in Figure   represents a handkerchief held by its four corners in a gravity field. After two seconds, one of the corners is released, so this point is affected by the gravity field too. The Figure caption shows the experiment physical parameters. Note that the cloth discretization is a mesh of 21 rows by 21 columns.

The second one, Figure , represents a tablecloth falling over a table. The mesh discretization is the same as for the previous simulation. The collision between the tablecloth and the table hasn't been simulated, this is a goal of future work. The simulation parameters are shown in the Figure caption.

Notice the different evolution of the borders in the two experiments, the first one (Figure) is more elastic than the second (Figure).

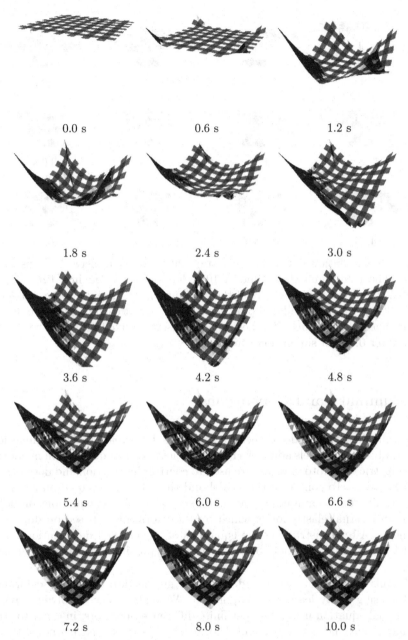

Fig. 4. A simulation example, the handkerchief held. A cloth held by its four corners, after 2 s. one corner is released. We can see the evolution over 10 s., the physical parameters of the cloth are $\eta_{11} = 1$, $\eta_{12} = \eta_{21} = 1$, $\eta_{22} = 1$, $\xi_{i,j} = 0 \forall i, j$, the mass and damping density equals 1 at each point of the discrete mesh, and the simulation time-step is 0.01 s

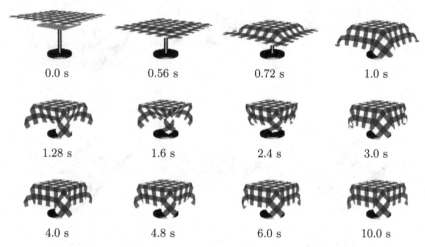

Fig. 5. A simulation example, the restaurant table. A tablecloth drops over a table. The total simulation time of 10 s. has been divided into time-steps of 0.01 s., the physical parameters of the cloth are $\eta_{11} = 4$, $\eta_{12} = \eta_{21} = 4$, $\eta_{22} = 4$, $\xi_{i,j} = 0 \forall i,j$, the mass and damping density equals 1 at each point of the discrete mesh. The collision effect has been made by setting fixed points at the middle mesh after 0.5 s. of simulation time

6   Summary and Conclusions

Physically based modeling is necessary if we want to create realistic animations. Physically based models add new characteristics to object description in addition to geometric descriptors, which are used to control the creation and development of the models. To construct the model and the differential equation associated with it, different techniques can be used, such as Lagrange equations of motion using an internal elastic force, which resists deformation, based on differential geometry. After constructing the equations of motion and deformation for the models, the equations should be solved as fast as possible using numerical methods.

In this paper we recover and explain a system for animating deformable models using a physically based approach. We analyze how to solve the partial differential equation using different finite-difference operators, in order to study the movement and deformation of deformable objects. We have studied the development of four (spatial) finite-difference resolution schemes depending on the error estimation and boundary treatment and, taking into account the advantages and disadvantages of each formulation. To make the integration through time we have used an explicit method that reduces the computational cost from $O((M \times N)^3)$ to $O((M \times N)^2)$ order, and to see which is possibly the best we have analyzed the stability for each one showing numerical examples. The system uses all the formulations for animating the models so that the user can decide which one to use in an animation and then compare the results. As can be seen from the section related to the stability we deduce that the explicit method with the differential scheme from Terzopoulos et al. is the bést one at this moment. Obviously, a finite-difference scheme with $O(h^2)$ approximation order is directly dependent on the point involved in it, and we haven't studied all of them, only the most appropriate. That is, the schemes using point neighboring to the point where we compute the derivative.

Another aspect that we have in mind is to generalize the study made in this paper for surfaces to curves and solids. Moreover, as physically deformable models are active, that is, they respond to external influences and interact with other objects, it is very interesting to study the response of the model in the presence of collisions, in order to incorporate deformable objects in a more complicated 3D scene. Moreover, we can improve the system if the collision of objects with themselves are considered, so that interpenetrating does not appear in the deformation simulation. Another extension may be the study of possible system parallelization in order to obtain shorter time responses.

At the present, we are working on the discretization of equation ( ) by using a different strategy from equation ( ); developing the expressions involved in equation ( ) in order to obtain a new expression for use in the numerical approach. So, if we suppose that η_{ij} is constant, in the case of the first term we take

$$\frac{\delta\varepsilon(\mathbf{r})}{\delta\mathbf{r}} \approx - \sum_{i,j=1}^{2} -\eta_{ij}\left(\left(\frac{\partial^2\mathbf{r}}{\partial x_i^2}\cdot\frac{\partial\mathbf{r}}{\partial x_j} + \frac{\partial\mathbf{r}}{\partial x_i}\cdot\frac{\partial^2\mathbf{r}}{\partial x_i\partial x_j}\right)\frac{\partial\mathbf{r}}{\partial x_j} + \left(\frac{\partial\mathbf{r}}{\partial x_i}\cdot\frac{\partial\mathbf{r}}{\partial x_j} - G_{ij}^0\right)\frac{\partial^2\mathbf{r}}{\partial x_i\partial x_j}\right),$$

and a similar expression for the second term. Next, we apply finite-differential operators in order to obtain the corresponding expression ( ) for the first term:

$$\mathbf{e}(x_1, x_2) = - \sum_{i,j=1}^{2} -\eta_{ij}\left((D_{ii}(\mathbf{r})\cdot D_j(\mathbf{r}) + D_i(\mathbf{r})\cdot D_{ij}(\mathbf{r}))D_j(\mathbf{r}) + \left(D_i(\mathbf{r})\cdot D_j(\mathbf{r}) - G_{ij}^0\right)D_{ij}(\mathbf{r})\right),$$

and an equivalent expression for the second term. The advantages of this new method are the following: we maintain the same order of approximation for methods (i) and (ii) but in this case we need fewer neighborhood points near the central point (x_1, x_2). So, we expect better results.

References

1. Agui, T., Nagao, Y. And Nakajma, M. An Expression Method of Cylindrical Cloth Objects-An Expression of Folds of a Sleeve using Computer Graphics. Trans. Soc. of Electronics, Information and Communications, J73-D-II, 7:1095-1097, 1990.
2. Aono, M. A Wrinkle Propagation Model for Cloth. Proc. CG. Int'l, Springer-Verlag, 95-115, 1990.

3. Decaudin, P. Geometric deformation by merging a 3d-object with a simple shape. In *Proc. of Graphics Interface*, pages 21–26, 1996.
4. do Carmo M. P. *Differential Geometry of Curves and Surfaces*. Prentice-Hall. USA 1976.
5. Dias,J. M. S., Galli, R., Palmer, P., and J. M. Rebordao, J. M. *Deformable objects with real-time realistic behavior for virtual scenarios (in The Internet en 3D)*. Academic Press, 1997.
6. Feynman, R. *Modeling the appearance of cloth*. PhD thesis, Departament of Electrical Engineering and Computer Science, MIT, Cambridge, 1986.
7. Greiner, G. Surface Construction on Variational Principles. *In: P. Laurent, A. Le Méhauté and L. Schumaker, eds., Wavelets, Images and Surface Fitting*, A. K. Peters, Wellesley, New York, pp. 277–286, 1994.
8. Güdükbay, U., and Özgüç, B. Animation of deformable models. *Computer-Aided Design*, 26(12):868–875, 1994.
9. Hing, N. Ng and Grimsdale, R. L. Computer Graphics Techniques for Modelling Cloth. IEEE Computer Graphics and Applications, 28-41, 1996.
10. Kimura, M., Saito, M. and Shinya, M. Surface deformation with differential geometric structures. *Computer-Aided Geometric Design*, 13:243–256, 1996.
11. Mascaró, M., Mir A., and Perales, F. Visualization of dynamic deformations through triangular and square finite elements. CEIG 99, pàg. 47-61. 1999. An references therein (in Spanish).
12. Metaxas, D. N. *Physics-Based Deformable Models*. Kluwer Academic Publishers, 1997.
13. Rudomin, I. J. Simulating Cloth using a Mixed Geometry-Phisycal Method. Doctoral Dissertation, Dept. of Computer and Information Science, Univ. Of Pennsylvania, 1990.
14. Serón, F. J., Badal, J., Sabadell, F. J. A numerical laboratory for simulation and visualization of seismic wavefields. Geophysical Prospecting, 44,603-642, 1996.
15. Shabana, A. A. *Dinamics of Multibody Systems*. John Wiley and Sons, 1988.
16. Terzopoulos, D. et. al. Elastically Deformable Models. Computer Graphics (Proc. Siggraph), 21, 4:205-214, 1987.
17. Terzopoulos, D. A. Witkin, and M. Kass. "Deformable Models: Physically Based Models with Rigid and Deformable Components". IEEE Computer Graphics and Applications, Vol. 13, n. 7, pp. 41-51, 1988.
18. Thalmann, N. M. and Yang, Y. Tecniques for Cloth Animation. New Trends in Animation and Visualization, N. M-Thalmann and D. Thalmann, eds., John Wiley & Sons, 243-256, 1991.
19. Tsopelas, N. Animation the Crumpling Behaviour of Garments. Proc. 2nd. Eurographics Workshop on Animation and Simulation, Blackwell, UK, 11-24, 1991.
20. Weil J. The Synthesis of Cloth Objects. Computer Graphics (Proc. Siggraph), 20:49-54, 1986.

Multi-part Non-rigid Object Tracking Based on Time Model-Space Gradients

T. Nunomaki[1], S. Yonemoto[1], D. Arita[1], R. Taniguchi[1], and N. Tsuruta[2]

[1] Laboratory for Image and Media Understanding, Department of Intelligent
Systems, Kyushu University
6-1, Kasuga-Koen Kasuga Fukuoka 816-8580 Japan
http://limu.is.kyushu-u.ac.jp/
[2] Department of Electronics Engineering and Computer Science, Fukuoka University
8-19-1, Nanakuma Jonan Fukuoka 814-0180 Japan

Abstract. This paper presents a shape and pose estimation method
for 3D multi-part objects, the purpose of which is to easily map objects
from the real world into virtual environments. In general, complex 3D
multi-part objects cause undesired self-occlusion and non-rigid motion.
To deal with the problem, we assume the following constraints:

- object model is represented in a tree structure consisting of deformable parts.
- connected parts are articulated at one point (called "articulation
  point").
- as a 3D parametric model of the parts, we employ *deformable superquadrics* (we call DSQ).

To estimate the parameters from the sensory data, we use time model-
space gradient method, which reduces the parameter estimation problem
into solving a simultaneous linear equation. We have demonstrated that
our system works well for multiple-part objects using real image data.

1 Introduction

Virtual environment applications such as augmented reality system, man-ma-
chine seamless interaction, video game console and tele-operation interface requires the system to estimate scene parameters for the natural objects such as
human bodies. To realize this requirement, we have been developing vision-based
3-D multi-part object tracking system which reconstructs the time-varying scene
parameters of objects including motion, shape deformation and dynamic surface
texture. In order to solve such a high DOF(Degrees of Freedom) estimation problem, we must consider how to reduce the computational cost, and how to increase
the estimation accuracy. Here, we assume that the objects can be represented
in a multi-part parameterized and constrained model which is articulated and
hierarchically structured. Based on this assumption we can reduce the parameter
search cost.

Our system acquires the scene parameters of the objects by two steps (Fig.).
First, with user's assist, an initial model is constructed from an initial frame

H. H. Nagel and F. J. Perales (Eds.): AMDO 2000, LNCS 1899, pp. 72–   , 2000.

data. To construct the initial model easily, we have developed a GUI based 3D modeler[ ] which can obtain shape and pose parameters of an object semi-automatically. And then, the model is tracked in the succeeding frames. This paper presents the tracking method, or, estimation of model parameters, in the succeeding frames.

Because the appearance of multi-part objects such as humans and animals changes considerably according to their shape deformation, their motion and viewing angle, it becomes very difficult to estimate their parameters with high DOF. We cannot assume 'rigid' shape model, and moreover, in practice, it is impossible to know the precise appearance-based object model, i.e., a set of "instance" object models, in advance. Rather we need a class object model (FISHER *et al.*,1997[ ]; BIEDERMAN,1987[ ]) which can be deformable, and the number of parameters required to represent the model should be as small as possible to make their estimation easier. Therefore, we have adopted *Deformable Superquadrics* model (METAXAS, *et al.*[ ]) as a primitive of geometric model description(see Sec. 3). In addition, we have employed a multiple camera system to relieve the difficulty caused by self-occlusion among the parts of the object.

In this paper, we briefly show our method for generic 3-D multi-part object tracking and demonstrate that the implementation system works well for multiple viewpoint image sequences in which a multi-part object causes self-occlusion.

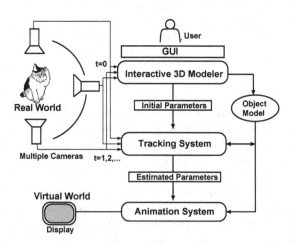

Fig. 1. System overview

2   Modeling of the Multi-part Object

In our system, we consider natural objects such as humans and animals. They are multi-part non-rigid objects which have strong constraints of joints between the parts. Here, we assume structural constraints as follows:

- an object model is represented in a tree structure consisting of deformable parts.
- connected parts are articulated at one point (called "articulation point").
- as a 3D parametric model of the parts, we consider *deformable superquadrics* [ ] (we call DSQ).

2.1   DSQ Geometry

When (η, ω) is a material coordinate, a point on SQ(*superellipsoids*) **e** is:

$$\mathbf{e}(\eta, \omega) = \begin{pmatrix} e_1(\eta, \omega) \\ e_2(\eta, \omega) \\ e_3(\eta, \omega) \end{pmatrix} = a \begin{pmatrix} a_1 \cdot C_\eta^{\epsilon_1} \cdot C_\omega^{\epsilon_2} \\ a_2 \cdot C_\eta^{\epsilon_1} \cdot S_\omega^{\epsilon_2} \\ a_3 \cdot S_\eta^{\epsilon_1} \end{pmatrix}, \tag{1}$$

where

$$C_w^\epsilon = \text{sign}(\cos w)|\cos w|^\epsilon, \quad S_w^\epsilon = \text{sign}(\sin w)|\sin w|^\epsilon,$$

and a, a_1, a_2, a_3 are scaling parameters, ϵ_1, ϵ_2 are squareness parameters.

Using SQ **e**, a point on DSQ **s** is expressed as follows:

$$\mathbf{s} = \begin{pmatrix} s_1 \\ s_2 \\ s_3 \end{pmatrix} = \begin{pmatrix} (\frac{t_1 e_3}{aa_3} + 1)e_1 + b_1 \cos(\frac{e_3 + b_2}{aa_3} \pi b_3) \\ (\frac{t_2 e_3}{aa_3} + 1)e_2 \\ e_3 \end{pmatrix}, \tag{2}$$

where t_1, t_2 are tapering parameters, and b_1, b_2, b_3 are bending parameters.

2.2   Multi-part Model Geometry

An object model is represented in a tree structure consisting of the 3D deformable parts. Fig. illustrates the multi-part model geometry. We use the word *level* to represent the depth of each part from the root node. Let $\mathbf{p}_{\phi_i}$ denote the position of a point with respect to the ϕ_i, the local coordinate system of a part n_i. When the level of a node should be represented, we use an additional suffix like ϕ_{i_k}, which means the coordinate system of a part n_i, whose level is k. Then, $\mathbf{p}_\Phi$, the position of a point with respect to the world coordinate system Φ can be expressed as follows:

- In the case of the root part, or $k = 0$

$$\mathbf{p}_\Phi = \mathbf{t}_{\phi_{i_0}}^\Phi + \mathbf{R}_{\phi_{i_0}}^\Phi \mathbf{p}_{\phi_{i_0}}, \tag{3}$$

where

- $\mathbf{t}^{\Phi}_{\phi_{i_0}} = (x_{i_0}, y_{i_0}, z_{i_0})^T$ is the position of the origin O_{i_0} of ϕ_{i_0} with respect to the world coordinate system Φ,
- $\mathbf{R}^{\Phi}_{\phi_{i_0}} = \mathbf{R}_z(w_{i_0})\mathbf{R}_y(v_{i_0})\mathbf{R}_x(u_{i_0})$ is the rotation matrix of ϕ_{i_0} with respect to Φ, where $\mathbf{R}_x(u), \mathbf{R}_y(v), \mathbf{R}_z(w)$ are the rotation matrix around X,Y and Z axes.

$$\mathbf{R}_x(u) = \begin{pmatrix} 1 & 0 & 0 \\ 0 & \cos u & -\sin u \\ 0 & \sin u & \cos u \end{pmatrix}, \mathbf{R}_y(v) = \begin{pmatrix} \cos v & 0 & \sin v \\ 0 & 1 & 0 \\ -\sin v & 0 & \cos v \end{pmatrix},$$

$$\mathbf{R}_z(w) = \begin{pmatrix} \cos w & -\sin w & 0 \\ \sin w & \cos w & 0 \\ 0 & 0 & 1 \end{pmatrix}.$$

- In the case of $k > 0$

$$\mathbf{p}_{\phi_{i_{k-1}}} = \mathbf{t}^{\phi_{i_{k-1}}}_{\phi_{i_k}} + \mathbf{R}^{\phi_{i_{k-1}}}_{\phi_{i_k}}(\mathbf{j}_{i_k} + \mathbf{p}_{\phi_{i_k}}), \qquad (4)$$

$$\mathbf{p}_{\Phi} = \mathbf{t}^{\Phi}_{\phi_{i_0}} + \mathbf{R}^{\Phi}_{\phi_{i_0}}(\mathbf{t}^{\phi_{i_0}}_{\phi_{i_1}} + \mathbf{R}^{\phi_{i_0}}_{\phi_{i_1}}(\mathbf{j}_{i_1} + \cdots (\mathbf{t}^{\phi_{i_{k-1}}}_{\phi_{i_k}} + \mathbf{R}^{\phi_{i_{k-1}}}_{\phi_{i_k}}(\mathbf{j}_{i_k} + \mathbf{p}_{\phi_{i_k}})) \cdots)), \quad (5)$$

where
- $\mathbf{t}^{\phi_{i_{j-1}}}_{\phi_{i_j}} = (x^{i_{j-1}}_{i_j}, y^{i_{j-1}}_{i_j}, z^{i_{j-1}}_{i_j})^T$ is the position of the origin O_{i_j} of ϕ_{i_j} with respect to the coordinate system of its parent part $\phi_{i_{j-1}}$,
- $\mathbf{R}^{\phi_{i_{j-1}}}_{\phi_{i_j}} = \mathbf{R}_z(w^{i_{j-1}}_{i_j})\mathbf{R}_y(v^{i_{j-1}}_{i_j})\mathbf{R}_x(u^{i_{j-1}}_{i_j})$ is the rotation matrix of ϕ_{i_j} with respect to $\phi_{i_{j-1}}$,
- s_{i_j} is the center position of DSQ n_{i_j} with respect to ϕ_{i_j},
- $\mathbf{j}_{i_k}$ is the position of the model center of part n_{i_k} with respect to ϕ_{i_j}.

Under the above geometry, establishing the world coordinate Φ, we translate it into the image coordinate $(U_m, V_m)^T$ by Tsai's camera model[ ].

For parameter estimation, we do not estimate translation parameters $\mathbf{t}$ or J because we assume constraints of joints between the parts. Translation parameters depend on only shape parameters and we calculate the translation parameters according to shape parameters.

2.3   Multi-part Object Model Description

From the definitions mentioned above,the model parameters of each part can be expressed as:

shape parameters: $(a, a_1, a_2, a_3, \epsilon_1, \epsilon_2, t_1, t_2, b_1, b_2, b_3)$
pose parameters: $(x, y, z, u, v, w, j_x, j_y, j_z)$

where shape parameters are DSQ parameters for each part in Eqs.( ),( ) and pose parameters are translation and rotation parameters in Eq.( )(in case it is the root part) , or Eq.( )(in case it is a non-root part).

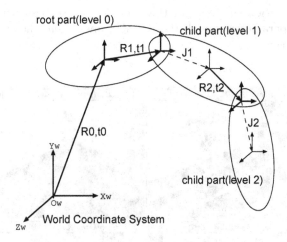

Fig. 2. Geometry of multi-part model

3   Multi-part Object Tracking

3.1   Tracking System

An outline of the 3D multi-part object tracking is as follows:

1. Acquire an initial model, referring to initial multi-viewpoint frames.
2. Acquire model sample points from the previous frame for every viewpoint.
3. Estimate model parameters for each part in accordance with the estimation strategy.
4. Refine the model parameters in accordance with the result of #3.
5. Repeat #2–#4 in the succeeding multiple-viewpoint frames.

3.2   Tool for Initial Modeling

The aims of our modeling tool is to construct a structure of an object model, and to estimate the initial model parameters, where the modeler fits the model view to initial multi-viewpoint image frames. In order to achieve them, our modeler have the following functions:

− multi-view overlay support of initial image frames
− virtual camera set up in the configuration in which real cameras are set
− interface of model parameter control

Fig.   shows typical display of the modeler. We can control scale, shape and pose parameters for each part model so as to fit the model views to all the overlaid multi-view frames. We can also fit the part models semi-automatically, using parameter estimation process. In this modeler, a user constructs the object model, whose parameters match the initial frames, from the root part in the structural order.

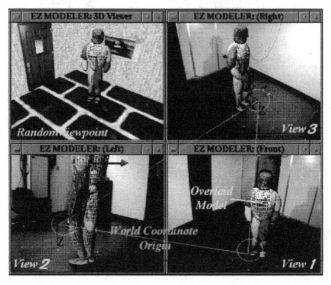

Fig. 3. GUI-based Initial Modeler

3.3   Acquiring Model Sample Points

In our methods, we use points with high textureness on model surfaces for tracking. Since we do not use the contours but points on the surfaces of the model for tracking, we can ignore the influence of complex background. It is difficult to extract its contour with high reliability, especially when the background of a part includes other parts. The procedure to acquire sample points on a model surface is as follows:

1. make projections of all model parts using a *Z-buffer* algorithm.
2. extract image features from the previous frame in accordance with eigenvalues [ ]
3. for each extracted feature point, obtain its corresponding material coordinates by finding the nearest vertex of a polyhedron approximating the model in DSQ. If a normal vector of the model surface on a sample point and the

---

[1] First, a user crops the image region of each part, and extracts the contour points. Then our modeler fits them to the part model using parameter estimation.

optical axis of the camera are nearly perpendicular to each other, the sample point will not be used for tracking because it is considered that the error of its calculated material coordinate is large. And, if a sample point is near to the boundary between the parts on image, the sample point will not be used for tracking because the point may be influenced by occlusion.

3.4   Estimation of Model Parameters

Estimation Strategy When we acquire sample points on the model surface, we can estimate the model parameters based on the *time model-space gradients*. In the proposed method, to reduce computation time we use a simple top-down strategy under the structural constraints, that is, estimation of the parameters of each part recursively according to the tree structure of the object.

estimation strategy:

1. Set $i = root$.
2. Estimate the parameters for the $part_i$(see 3.4.2).
3. **If** it has descendant parts, **then** estimate their parameters recursively (goto 2).
4. If not, stop the recursion.

Estimation of Model Parameters Our system adopts an estimation method based on *time model-space gradients* which can reduce computation time. For tracking, we assume that the brightness (an appearance in an image) of a point on a model surface does not change between adjacent frames. Let $I_j(\mathbf{p}, t)$ be the brightness of point j on the model surface whose model parameters are $\mathbf{p} = (p_1, p_2, ..., p_n)$ at time t. If model parameters are $\mathbf{p} = (p_1, p_2, ..., p_n)$ at time t and model parameters are $\mathbf{p} + \Delta\mathbf{p}$ at time $t + \Delta t$, we obtain the following equation.

$$I_j(\mathbf{p} + \Delta\mathbf{p}, t + \Delta t) = I_j(\mathbf{p}, t). \tag{6}$$

Here, let $\mathbf{v}_j(\mathbf{p})$ be the image coordinate (x_j, y_j) of the point j on the model surface whose model parameters are $\mathbf{p}$. We rewrite Eq.( ) in the form

$$I(\mathbf{v}_j(\mathbf{p} + \Delta\mathbf{p}), t + \Delta t) = I(\mathbf{v}_j(\mathbf{p}), t). \tag{7}$$

where the function $I(\mathbf{v}, t)$ is the brightness at the image point $\mathbf{v} = (x, y)$ at time t. If the brightness varies smoothly on the model surface, the brightness varies smoothly with x, y, and t. Then, by expanding the left-hand side of the Eq.( ) in a Taylor series and ignoring second- or higher-order terms, we obtain the following equation:

$$\Delta p_1 \left(\frac{\partial I}{\partial x} \frac{\partial x}{\partial p_1} + \frac{\partial I}{\partial y} \frac{\partial y}{\partial p_1} \right) + \cdots + \Delta p_n \left(\frac{\partial I}{\partial x} \frac{\partial x}{\partial p_n} + \frac{\partial I}{\partial y} \frac{\partial y}{\partial p_n} \right) + \frac{\partial I}{\partial t} = 0. \tag{8}$$

We obtain Eq.( ) by simplifying Eq.( ).

$$\Delta p_1 \frac{\partial I}{\partial p_1} + \cdots + \Delta p_n \frac{\partial I}{\partial p_n} + \frac{\partial I}{\partial t} = 0 \qquad (9)$$

Eq.( ) consists of model parameter changes and image gradients with respect to time and model space. We call Eq.( ) *time model-space gradient constraint equation.*

This single constraint is not sufficient to determine the parameters. It is clear that if sample points belong to the same model, their model parameters are common. Therefore, we collect Eq.( )s of sample points which are on the same model surface and obtain a simultaneous equation as follows:

$$\mathbf{A}_I \cdot \mathbf{x} = \mathbf{b}_I, \qquad (10)$$

where

$$\mathbf{A}_I = \begin{bmatrix} \dfrac{\partial I_1}{\partial p_1} & \cdots & \dfrac{\partial I_1}{\partial p_n} \\ \vdots & \ddots & \vdots \\ \dfrac{\partial I_k}{\partial p_1} & \cdots & \dfrac{\partial I_k}{\partial p_n} \end{bmatrix}, \mathbf{x} = \begin{bmatrix} \Delta p_1 \\ \vdots \\ \Delta p_n \end{bmatrix}, \mathbf{b}_I = \begin{bmatrix} -\dfrac{\partial I_1}{\partial t} \\ \vdots \\ \dfrac{\partial I_k}{\partial t} \end{bmatrix}, \qquad (11)$$

and k is the number of sample points. Ideally, it is sufficient to determine the model parameters when $k = n$. In fact, to reduce the influence of noise, we use more sample points and apply the least square method to the equation, that is, we estimate $\mathbf{x}$ which minimize

$$|\mathbf{A}_I \cdot \mathbf{x} - \mathbf{b}_I|^2. \qquad (12)$$

As mentioned above, our estimation method finally becomes a problem of liner system. Thus this method takes lower computation cost than our previous methods based on *analysis by image synthesis*[ ][ ] which have to be solved by a non-liner optimization method. However, since this method makes the assumption that the brightness on a model surface do not change, our method has a drawback that it is easily influenced by noise of observation. To overcome this problem we apply a smoothing filter to input images.

4   Experimental Result

4.1   Shape and Pose Estimation

For this experiment we prepared image sequences of moving upper half of the human body using six cameras. Multiple viewpoint image sequences are obtained by our capture system[ ] with PC-Cluster. Multiple cameras are calibrated by Tsai's method[ ]. First, we constructed the model which consists of four parts(body, right arm, left arm and head) and three joints. Then, we estimated pose and shape parameters over 120 frames. Fig. shows several input images and projected images of the estimated model. In this case, about 100~200 feature points are detected in each part and used to estimate the parameters. Although the object includes self-occlusion and texture of both arms are very similar to each other, these part models are tracked successfully on whole multiview sequences.

Computing time of the analysis using a 500MHz PentiumIII PC is about 1 sec for 1 frame of each view, and only 10 msec is required to minimize the formula   . Our proposed method can track the object 50-100 times faster than our previous method, which have employed a non-linear optimization technique.

4.2   Effect of the Number of Viewpoints

Next, to measure the effect of the number of viewpoints, we tracked a human in the samce scene as used in   with 2, 3 and 6 cameras and made a comparison among their estimation results. Fig. shows projected images of estimated model of each case at the last frame of image sequence. When we used 3 cameras, the estimation of body was more accurate than when used 2 cameras although the right hand was not correctly tracked. And when we used 6 cameras, the estimation of both arms was more accurate than when used 3 cameras. Up to 6 cameras, we have confirmed that estimation is more accurate as the number of viewpoints increases.

However, we have not yet investigated the effect of the increase of viewpoints in detail, especially how to arrange the viewpoints to get the accurate estimation. When a moving object is observed, optimal solution may not be acquired in advance. Rather it is necessary to control the viewpoints dynamically with active cameras or to select good positions to observe from a lot of cameras. We will start such directions.

5   Conclusion

To estimate shape and pose information for objects in time varying image sequences, we have adopted two kinds of information: one is a *a priori* object model, which consists of multiple-deformable parts; the other is an *a posteriori* observation, which means recovering 3D shape and pose parameters from multiple-viewpoint image sequences. The advantages of our approach is that non-rigid multi-part objects can be handled, and that, especially, self occlusion can be dealt with by multiple cameras. To estimate the model parameters we have used *time model-space gradient method*, which can drastically reduce the computational cost.

The future works are summarized as follows:

- Selection of adequate viewpoints when the number of viewpoints increases, which can reduce the computation time and can get more accurate parameter estimation.

---

[2] We can achieve faster calculation with an appropriate parallel processing scheme.

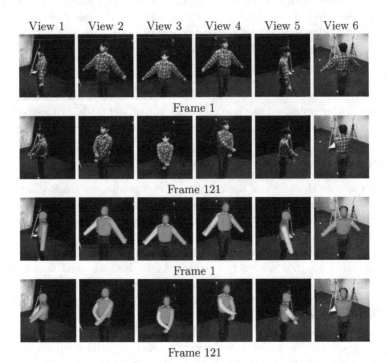

Fig. 4. Input sequence (top two rows) and estimated model views(bottom two rows)

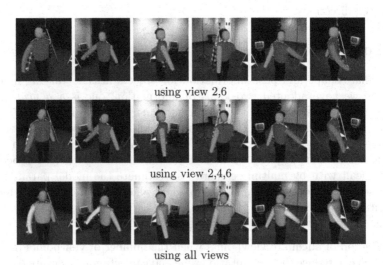

Fig. 5. Estimated model views when the number of cameras varies

- Development of a real-time system, using parallel processing techniques especially on our PC-cluster[ ].
- Introduction of more complex 3D model to represent natural objects with higher reality.

Then we will develop a system to map efficiently real world objects into a virtual environment for various applications.

References

1. Ichiki, A., Yonemoto S., Arita, D., Taniguchi, R.: A 3D Modeler with Parameter Estimation from Multiview Images. Tech. Rep. SIG-CVIM-115, IPSJ (1999) 49–56 (in Japanese)
2. Kakadiaris, I. A., Metaxas, D.: 3D Human Body Model Acquisition from Multiple Views. Proc. ICCV (1995) 618–623
3. Gavrila, D. M., Davis, L. S.: 3D Model-based Tracking of Humans in Action: a Multiview Approach. Proc. CVPR (1996) 73–80
4. Borges, D. L., Fisher, R. B.: Class-based recognition of 3D objects represented by volumetric primitives, Journal of Image and Vision Computing Vol.15, No.8 (1997) 665–664
5. Biederman, I.: Recognition-by-components: A theory of human image understanding, Psychological Review. Vol.94 (1987) 115–147
6. Metaxas, D., Terzopoulos, D.: Shape and Nonrigid Motion Estimation through Physics-Based Synthesis. IEEE Trans. PAMI, Vol.15, No.6 (1993) 580–591   ,
7. Shi, J., Tomasi, C.: Good Features to Track. Proc. CVPR (1994) 593–600
8. Nunomaki, T., Yonemoto, S., Tsuruta, N., Taniguchi, R.: Multi-Part Object Tracking Using Multiple Cameras. Proc. 4th Japan-France Congress on Mechatronics, Vol.2 (1998)) 540–545
9. Yonemoto, S., Tsuruta, N., Taniguchi, R.: Shape and Pose Parameter Estimation of 3D Multi-part Objects. Proc. ACCV (1998) 479–486
10. Ukita, N., Tokai, S., Matsuyama, T., Taniguchi, R.: Database Development of Multi-Viewpoint Image Sequences for Evaluation of Image Understanding Systems. Tech. Rep. of IEICE, PRMU99-58 (1999) 65–72 (in Japanese)
11. Tsai, R. Y.: A Versatile Camera Calibration Technique for High-Accuracy 3D Machine Vision Metrology Using Off-the-Shelf TV Cameras and Lenses. IEEE Trans. Robotics and Automation, Vol.3, No.4 (1987) 323–344   ,
12. Arita, D., Hamada, Y., Taniguchi, R.: A Real-time Distributed Video Image Processing System on PC-cluster. Proc. Int. Conf. Austrian Center for Parallel Computation(ACPC) (1999) 296–305

Spatio-Temporal Modeling in the Farmyard Domain

D. R. Magee and R. D. Boyle

School of Computer Studies, University of Leeds, UK
drm@scs.leeds.ac.uk

Abstract. A temporal modelling and prediction scheme based on modelling a 'history space' using Gaussian mixture models is presented. A
point in this space represents an abstraction of a complete object history as opposed to finite histories used in Markov methods. It is shown
how this 'History Space Classifier' may be incorporated into an existing
scheme for spatial object modelling and tracking to improve tracking
speed and robustness and to classify object 'behaviour' into normal and
abnormal. An application to the tracking and monitoring of livestock is
also presented in this paper.

Keywords: Behaviour Model, History Space Classifier, Livestock

1 Introduction

In recent years there has been much interest in object tracking [, , , , ,]
and temporal modelling [, , ,]. The combination of object tracking and temporal modelling gives rise to many exciting application possibilities. Isard and
Blake [ ] use a temporal model to improve the speed and robustness of their
object tracker. Wren and Pentland [ ] and Davis and Bobick [ ] use temporal models to classify observed human movements and in the case of the latter
use this information to trigger interactive responses in a virtual environment.
Johnson *et. al.* build a joint behaviour model in which a virtual human reacts
in a realistic manner to observed behaviour in a limited domain. Sumpter and
Bulpitt [ ] use object tracking and temporal modelling to predict the behaviour
of a flock of ducks or sheep for use in the control system of a robotic sheepdog.

These applications are merely the tip of the iceberg. As computer power
increases, costs come down and tracking algorithms become more robust the
number of applications for such techniques is endless. Today we see the prolifer-
ation of CCTV cameras throughout our environment, tomorrow a vision system
may be connected to these cameras analysing the movements of people, vehicles
and other moving objects in our environment if we decide that this is desirable.

We present here a temporal modelling scheme based on modelling an object
history which uses Gaussian mixture models to predict and classify future object
behaviour. The object history is based on modelling a complete object history
by a single point in an abstract 'history space'. We show how this 'History

H. H. Nagel and F. J. Perales (Eds.): AMDO 2000, LNCS 1899, pp. 83–   , 2000.

Space Classifier' can be incorporated into an existing object tracking scheme to improve speed and robustness and how the results of this may be used to classify object behaviour. We present an example application which is the monitoring of livestock to detect abnormalities.

2   Building Spatial Models of Livestock for Tracking

Previous work has described how multiple contour models of an object class may be built [ ] and how the variation within these models can be separated into independent components [ ]. These models are a variation on the Point Distribution Model [   ] in which a contour is modeled by a mean shape (described by a set of points) and a set of linear 'modes of variation'. We have applied this scheme to modelling livestock, building multiple models of cow outlines and separating the variation of each model into inter-animal, front legs and rear legs components as shown in figure   .

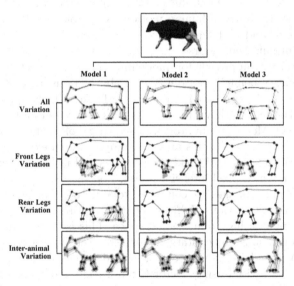

Fig. 1. Separating Object Variation Using a Hierarchical Scheme

These models are used in conjunction with a tracking algorithm to obtain the position and pose of individuals over time. The object tracker consists of three discrete components; i) A low level position estimator, ii) A stochastic stage using multiple discretised shape models and iii) A 'local search' algorithm using a single continuous model. The low level position estimator is used only for initialisation (and re-initialisation) and gives a rough estimate of position and scale. The stochastic stage uses discretised versions of the shape models described previously and iteratively samples possible solutions. Probabilities of particular solutions are updated after each iteration in a manner conceptually similar to the Markov Chain Monte Carlo algorithm [ ]. A predictor may be used to initialise these probabilities. The local search stage improves on the solution given by the stochastic stage by performing a local image search using the most appropriate continuous model. This scheme has been described in more detail previously [ ].

3   Building Temporal Models of Livestock Movements

There has been much related work in the field of temporal modelling and prediction. Initial efforts such as those by Terzopoulos and Szeliski [ ] used predictive filters such as the Kalman filter to make a prediction of future object behaviour. The application of these is limited as many objects of interest exhibit non-linear or multiple possible behaviours. These predictors may be combined with hand built [ ] or learned [ ] models of object (in particular human) kinematics. Recent work by Wren and Pentland [ ] uses multiple extended Kalman filters in modelling the dynamics of human motion. A complex model of human dynamics is built by hand and separate extended Kalman filters are used to model alternative 'atomic behaviours'.

An alternative approach for modelling complex object 'behaviours' is to 'learn' a model of behaviours from typical observations. If the state of an object can be represented by one of a finite number of tokens, techniques such as Markov chains and Hidden Markov Models may be used. Wren and Pentland [ ] use Hidden Markov Models to link together sequences of 'atomic behaviours'. These model a finite history of states and the computational expense of these models increases with the length of this history. Davis and Bobick [ ] use a 'motion history image' in which pixel intensity is based on time since motion last occurred at this pixel. These images are compared to a library of images of typical actions to classify unknown actions. Johnson *et. al.* [ ] represent a complete object history as a point in a high dimensional space. This is derived from the distances between a continuous object state vector and a set of prototypical state vectors. A maximum time decay limit operator is used to incorporate a history of states. This space is quantised using Vector Quantisation and a Markov Chain is used to make predictions about the likelihood of future histories. A CONDENSATION framework [ ] is required to make predictions about future object states as it is not possible to reconstruct a set of states from a point in the history space. Sumpter and Bulpitt [ ] also represent a history by a point in a high dimensional space, however this is works on a winner takes all approach using a spatial classifier based on a vector quantising (competitive learning) neural network. A set of leaky integrators are used to integrate pulses from the winning spatial classifier outputs. A second neural network is used to classify the 'history space' produced by the leaky integrators into possible next states and a feedback loop is used to allow the output to correct for erroneous spatial classification. This scheme relies on sets of histories resulting in particular next states being separable using a single vector quantisation prototype for each next state. This will not be the case for all data sets. This scheme is also not very computationally efficient for data sets with a large number of states as the computational expense of evaluating the neural networks is related to the number of states. Figures   and   illustrate the differences between the two 'history space' schemes of Johnson and Sumpter.

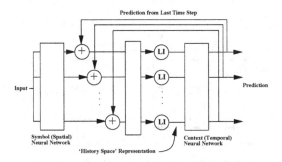

Fig. 2. The Sumpter and Bulpitt Prediction Scheme

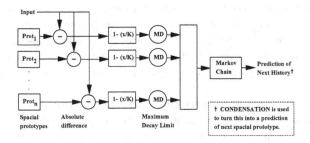

Fig. 3. The Johnson Prediction Scheme

In our spatial scheme we have multiple models and thus a measure of distance between an object state and a prototypical object state is only available when the same model is used for both. This precludes the formation of a history space such as that used in the Johnson scheme. A similar method to the Sumpter and Bulpitt scheme could be applied to our data however with the high dimensionality of our data this scheme would be slow. Also, as can be seen in figure   , the state transitions in our data are complex and a simple vector quantisation of a history space (as with the context networks) would not be appropriate[1]. We have developed an alternative 'History Space Classification' (HSC) scheme based on the Sumpter idea of 'winner takes all' however reducing the dimensionality of the history space using Principal Components Analysis (PCA) for improved prediction speed, and using Gaussian mixture models instead of neural networks to perform the temporal classification to deal with our complex history space. The scheme is detailed in figure[4].

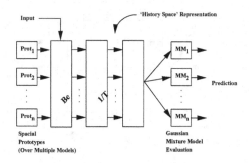

Fig. 4. Prediction scheme used in our system

It should be noted that there are two differences between our scheme and the Sumpter and Bulpitt scheme in addition to those mentioned previously. The first is the fact that there is no feedback loop in this scheme. In our scheme the low dimensionality mixture models have the power to generalise and thus give a sensible prediction for unseen histories (this is demonstrated in section 4). There is therefore no need to force the history into a previously observed state using feedback. In addition our spatial classification comes from an object tracker, rather than a neural network, and we must assume that this has some degree of correctness otherwise performing a prediction from this is not a sensible course of action. The second additional difference is the use of the reciprocal of the time since a state last occurred as the history space representation rather than a representation derived from a set of leaky integrators. This gives a precise, easily calculable (fast), approximately frame rate independent, two way mapping between a sequence of states and a point in the history space. No time constant needs to be determined for this scheme as in the Sumpter and Bulpitt method. No evaluation of different history schemes has been carried out as the scheme used is sufficient for the data sets we are working with. It is hypothesised that different representation schemes will work well for different data sets depending on the length and nature of the history required to make a prediction.

---

[1] Note: The Johnson scheme produces a much simpler space as there are no discontinuities caused by using the winner takes all approach. This space is suitable for vector quantisation.

3.1   Building Gaussian Mixture Models

There are two approaches that may be taken to build a Gaussian mixture model of a probability density function from a training set of multivariate data points (histories in our example). The first is the 'kernel method' or 'adaptive kernel method' in which each data point in the set of training examples is modeled by a single Gaussian. This is described well by Silverman [ ]. This results in a model with a large number of Gaussian mixtures which can take considerable computational expense to evaluate. An alternative approach is to build a mixture model with fewer Gaussian mixtures than training data points which may be done using the Expectation Maximisation (EM) algorithm [ ]. This is a two stage iterative scheme which computes the local maximum likelihood fit of an arbitrary number of Gaussians to a data set. This scheme is heavily dependent on how the Gaussians are initialised (this is not covered by the EM algorithm) and can lead to an over specific mixture model (see figure). Another drawback of this scheme is that, if the training data is locally sparse, mixtures may become singularities. Cootes and Taylor [ ] present a scheme which combines the kernel method with the EM algorithm by altering the M step as in the table in figure . In this scheme singularities never occur and the result is less dependent on the initialisation of the mixture model.

Standard EM Algorithm	Cootes and Taylor Modified EM Algorithm
E-step: Compute the contribution of the i_{th} sample to the j_{th} Gaussian $$p_{ij} = \frac{w_j G(\mathbf{x}_i : \mu_j, \mathbf{S}_j)}{\sum_{j=1}^{m} G(\mathbf{x}_i : \mu_j, \mathbf{S}_j)}$$	**E-step:** Compute the contribution of the i_{th} sample to the j_{th} Gaussian $$p_{ij} = \frac{w_j G(\mathbf{x}_i : \mu_j, \mathbf{S}_j)}{\sum_{j=1}^{m} G(\mathbf{x}_i : \mu_j, \mathbf{S}_j)}$$
M-step: Compute the parameters of the Gaussians $$w_j = \frac{1}{N}\sum_{i=1}^{N} p_{ij} \; , \; \mu_j = \frac{\sum_{i=1}^{N} p_{ij}\mathbf{x}_i}{\sum_{i=1}^{N} p_{ij}}$$ $$\mathbf{S}_j = \frac{\sum_{i=1}^{N} p_{ij}(\mathbf{x}_i - \mu_j)(\mathbf{x}_i - \mu_j)^T}{\sum_{i=1}^{N} p_{ij}}$$	**M-step:** Compute the parameters of the Gaussians $$w_j = \frac{1}{N}\sum_{i=1}^{N} p_{ij} \; , \; \mu_j = \frac{\sum_{i=1}^{N} p_{ij}\mathbf{x}_i}{\sum_{i=1}^{N} p_{ij}}$$ $$\mathbf{S}_j = \frac{\sum_{i=1}^{N} p_{ij}[(\mathbf{x}_i - \mu_j)(\mathbf{x}_i - \mu_j)^T + \mathbf{T}_i]}{\sum_{i=1}^{N} p_{ij}}$$

Fig. 5. EM Algorithms to fit a mixture of m Gaussians to N samples $\mathbf{x}_i$. $\mathbf{T}_i$ is the kernel covariance of a sample calculated using the adaptive kernel method

We use the Cootes and Taylor modification of the EM algorithm to build our mixture models. In our scheme we initialise the mixture means uniformly across the range of the data removing mixtures for which the mean is the nearest mixture mean to no data point in the training set. Initial mixture covariances are calculated from the covariance of the training set, the number of Gaussians

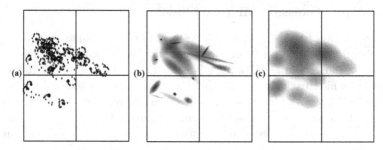

Fig. 6. Building Gaussian Mixture Models: (a) Raw Data (b) Standard EM Algorithm (c) Cootes and Taylor Modified EM Algorithm

and the dimensionality as in the kernel method [ ]. The initialisation is such that more mixtures than required are selected. This results in mixtures becoming co-incident (having equal mean and covariance) during the course of the EM iterations. Under such circumstances we modify the scheme to merge these mixtures after the M stage of the iteration. This results in a mixture model with an identical density description which is computationally more efficient to evaluate.

3.2 Comparing Mixture Model Densities

The scheme described previously produces a set of Gaussian mixture models which represent probability density functions (PDFs) within the history space. To make a prediction from this set of models that a newly observed history will result in a specific next state we must determine the relative probability that the history comes from each model distribution. Statistically the probability of a continuous distribution resulting in a particular sample value is zero. To obtain a non-zero probability (P) we must integrate the PDF (ϕ) over some area local to the sample. Over a suitably small local area this is approximately equal to the product of the PDF magnitude at the sample and this area (δA_l) as in equation .

$$P(\bar{x}) = \int_{\delta A_l} \phi(\bar{x})\delta a \approx \phi(\bar{x}) \times \delta A_l \qquad (1)$$

To the authors knowledge there is no statistically correct method to determine size of the local area (δA_l) over which to integrate as this will depend on the range of, and magnitude of variation within the PDF. It can be shown however that it is valid to use the same area if the probability that a sample comes from either of two distributions is equal when considering the complete range of the data (proof is omitted for brevity). In our example there is significant variation in the range of the model PDFs and as such it would be incorrect to use the same value of δA_l for all models. As no scheme is available for the selection of δA_l we take the approach of calculating uniform distributions with roughly similar ranges to the mixture model PDFs (ϕ_U). Examples of this can be seen in figure .

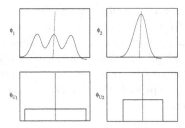

Fig. 7. Comparing PDFs with uniform PDFs with the same Range

It is hypothesised that these distributions are similar enough in range and variation to use the same value of A_l for each pair of distributions. We can thus calculate the relative probability ($P_{Rel(Uniform)}(\bar{x})$) that a sample results from a mixture model distribution or the corresponding uniform distribution as in equation .

$$P_{Rel(Uniform)}(\bar{x}) = \frac{\phi(\bar{x}) \times \delta A_l}{(\phi(\bar{x}) \times \delta A_l) + (\phi_U(\bar{x}) \times \delta A_l)} = \frac{\phi(\bar{x})}{\phi(\bar{x}) + \phi_U(\bar{x})} \qquad (2)$$

The relative probabilities obtained in equation   can be compared across mixture models and as such relative probabilities of a history resulting in a particular next state may be calculated as in equation .

$$P_{Rel}(\bar{x}_i) = \frac{P_{Rel(Uniform)}(\bar{x}_i)}{\sum\limits_{n=1}^{N} P_{Rel(Uniform)}(\bar{x}_n)} \qquad (3)$$

This method of comparison gives significantly more robust prediction for seen and unseen data than simple comparison of PDF heights (for our data sets).

4   Evaluation of Predictor Scheme

There are many metrics and tests that may be used to evaluate a predictor scheme, however these may be broadly divided into two types; success measures and failure measures. Success measures (such as average error) measure how well a predictor predicts future states for unseen data and failure measures (such as the proportion of erroneous predictions) measure the robustness of the prediction scheme. It is important to evaluate a predictor scheme using both success measures and failure measures to obtain an accurate description of its properties.

In our scheme there are multiple spatial models and thus a simple error measure is not always available, however we can look at the proportion of correct model predictions and the errors within the set of correct predictions. An alternative approach is to evaluate the scheme as a finite state predictor, looking at prediction probabilities for newly observed states. In our application multiple next states are possible from a given history and as such a unit (100% Probability) prediction for the next observed state is not what is desired. The predictor should assign a 'significant probability' to any next state that has a 'reasonable probability' of actually occurring. It is difficult to determine what a 'significant probability' or a 'reasonable probability' should be as this depends on the nature of that particular prediction.

In this evaluation we state that any new state observed has a 'reasonable probability' of being observed (as it has been observed) and any probability greater than the probability given by a uniform predictor is a 'significant probability'. From this we define a measure 'Probability Drop Out' which is the proportion of unseen future states that are assigned a probability of less than that given by a uniform predictor. As a measure of success we also examine the mean and standard deviation of predicted probabilities for each next state observed. These are broken down by the next state observed as these predictions should have similar context (average results are shown). All results shown are from leave 2 out tests from a set of 12 sequences of healthy walking cows (approx. 1000 frames). The results for first and second order Markov chains are also presented for comparison.

The results shown in figure   show that the HSC scheme assigns a reasonable probability to actual next states observed for unseen data on average, although this is lower than the average for the Markov chain results. Markov chains however have higher drop out rates and standard deviations. Examining the individual results we see that the high average prediction of Markov chains is due to unrealistically high probability predictions for certain frames averaged with very low probability predictions in others. This makes the Markov chain unsuitable for our application which requires a robust prediction mechanism. These results are discussed further in section 5.

To evaluate the predictor as a behaviour classifier we used sequences of limping and normally walking humans as insufficient data of lame cows was available. A single two space (inter and intra-person) spatial model was built of human outlines and the spaces quantised exactly as in the three space models of cows. Eight sequences were taken of five individuals (4 Normal and 4 Limping) and a set of leave one sequence (of each person) out and leave one person out tests were conducted. It was found that simply comparing the outputs of the two predictors biased the results towards the lame predictor as for approximately half the walking cycle limping is identical to normal walking motion and thus the lame predictors fit well to healthy data. The solution to this was to discard frames where both predictors assigned 'significant probability' to the observed next state and perform the classification on the remaining frames comparing the mixture model outputs as in section   .

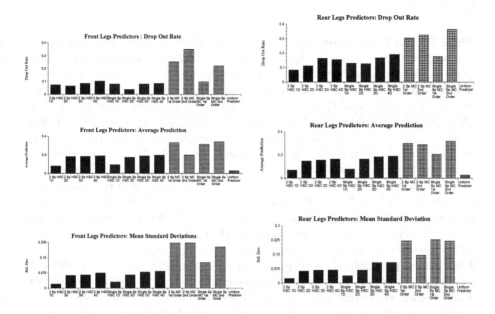

Fig. 8. Prediction Results for Cow Data

Data Sets	Lame Data		Healthy Data	
	Correct	Incorrect	Correct	Incorrect
Unseen Sequences of Seen People	81.25%	18.75%	100%	0%
Unseen Sequences of Unseen People	68.75%	31.25%	93.75%	6.25%

Fig. 9. Classification Results for Human Data (2D HSC Predictor)

In applications involving tracking it is important that a predictor can be evaluated faster than the desired frame rate for the tracking algorithm. Approximate average evaluation rates are given in figure   , using an entry level workstation (SGI R5000 180MHz 96MB). It should be noted that only one set of timing results is presented for our history space classifier scheme as the timings for the two space and single space versions are similar.

	HSCs				Markov Chains			
	1D	2D	3D	4D	SS 1st Odr	SS 2nd Odr	2S 1st Odr	2S 2nd Odr
Rate (f/sec)	900	350	135	91	2000	65	65	*

* 2 Space 2nd Order Markov Chain Evaluation takes several miniutes due to memory usage.

Fig. 10. Evaluation Rates for Predictor Schemes

5   Discussion

The Effect of Dimensionality Reduction: The Principal Components Analysis stage of the predictor (see figure) reduces the dimensionality of the history space in order to increase the speed of the predictor. The results in figure   show that history space classifier (HSC) predictors with a high dimensionality reduction (70 to 2,3 or 4 in the two space case) can give usable predictions. The effect of dimensionality reduction is twofold; decreased dimensionality gives a lower average prediction however at lower dimensionalities drop out rates are generally smaller (except for the single space 1D case). We can conclude that increasing the dimensionality makes the predictor more specific and less general. It does however appear there may be a limit to this and there is a dimensionality above which adding extra dimensions will have no effect. More results are required to verify this hypothesis. We must trade off generality, specificity and speed when choosing the dimensionality. In the example presented (cows) a 2 or 3 dimensional classifier would seem suitable.

Two Space predictors vs Single Space Predictors: It was hypothesised that making predictions about future front leg movements would be more robust if information about rear leg histories was used in addition to information about front leg histories (and vice versa). This was achieved by concatenating the front and rear legs history spaces before the Principal Components Analysis part of the predictor. No firm conclusions may be drawn on the relative merits of the single space and this two space scheme however the results suggest a single space predictor may be more suitable for the front legs predictors and a two space predictor may be more suitable for the rear legs predictor (this is based on drop out rates and standard deviations). This is a sensible result as the variation in position of the front legs is much larger (as they bend more) and thus there is more information about the position in the walking cycle in the front legs positions than the in the rear legs positions. We can conclude that the merits of the two schemes are application specific.

Use of Predictor as a Classifier: The results in figure   show that our History Space Classifier scheme has improved generality over Markov chain schemes which is seen in lower drop out rates and lower prediction standard deviations, however specificity is also required in order to make a behaviour classification. The results in figure   suggest that, even for the low dimensionality HSC used, enough specificity has been preserved in the predictor to make a reasonable classification even for unseen individuals in this relatively small test set.

6   Conclusions

We have presented a spatio-temporal modeling scheme using a hierarchical spatial model and a novel 'History Space Classifier' temporal prediction scheme. This scheme can be used to track objects and classify their movements into 'behaviours'. As an example the detection of lameness in cows is presented. The scheme has also been evaluated on sequences of limping humans. The prediction or classification can be performed faster than current video frame rates on a relatively inexpensive computer and has a relatively small memory requirement which means it may be incorporated into a 'real time' behaviour evaluation system.

Acknowledgments

This work was funded by the BBSRC. The authors would like to thank Prof. M. Forbes from the Leeds University dept. of Animal Physiology and Nutrition and the staff at ADAS Bridgets research institute for their help with data collection.

References

1. A. Baumberg and D. Hogg. An efficient method for tracking using active shape models. In *Proc. IEEE Workshop on Motion of Non-rigid Objects*, pages 194–199, 1994.   ,
2. T. F. Cootes and C. J. Taylor. A mixture model for representing shape variation. In *Proc. British Machine Vision Conference*, pages 110–119, 1997.
3. J. Davis and A. Bobick. The representation and recognition of action using temporal templates. In *Proc. IEEE Computer Society Conference on Computer Vision and Pattern Recognition*, pages 928–934, 1997.   ,
4. A. Dempster and D. Rubin N. Laird. Maximum likelihood from incomplete data via the em algorithm. *Journal of the Royal Statistical Society. Series B*, 39:1–38, 1977.
5. W. Gilks, S. Richardson, and D. Spiegelhalter. *Markov Chain Mote Carlo in Practice*. Chapman and Hall, 1996.
6. Michael Isard and Andrew Blake. Condensation – conditional density propagation for visual tracking. *International Journal of Computer Vision*, 29:5–28, 1998.   ,
7. N. Johnson, A. Galata, and D. Hogg. The acquisition and use of interaction behaviour models. In *Proc. IEEE Computer Society Conference on Computer Vision and Pattern Recognition*, pages 866–871, 1998.   ,
8. D. Magee and R. Boyle. Building shape models from image sequences using piecewise linear approximation. In *Proc. British Machine Vision Conference*, pages 398–408, 1998.
9. D. Magee and R. Boyle. Building class sensitive models for tracking application. In *Proc. British Machine Vision Conference*, pages 594–603, 1999.
10. D. Magee and R. Boyle. Feature tracking in real world scenes (or how to track a cow). In *Proc. IEE Colloquium on Motion Analysis and Tracking*, pages 2/1–2/7, 1999.   ,
11. A. Pentland and B. Horowitz. Recovery of nonrigid motion and structure. *IEEE Transactions on Pattern Analysis and Machine Intelligence*, 13:730–742, 1991.   ,
12. B. W. Silverman. *Density Estimation for Statistics and Data Analysis*. Chapman and Hall, 1986.   ,
13. N. Sumpter and A. Bulpitt. Learning spatio-temporal patterns for predicting object behaviour. In *Proc. British Machine Vision Conference*, pages 649–658, 1998.   ,

14. D. Terzopoulos and R. Szeliski. Tracking with Kalman snakes. *Active Vision*, pages 3–20, 1992.   ,
15. T. F.Cootes, C. J. Taylor, D. H. Cooper, and J.Graham. Training models of shape from sets of examples. In *Proc. British Machine Vision Conference*, pages 9–18, 1992.   ,
16. C. R. Wren and A. P. Pentland. Understanding purposeful human motion. In *Proc. IEEE International Workshop on Modelling People (MPEOPLE)*, pages 19–25, 1999.   ,

Recognition of Articulated Objects
in SAR Images

G. Jones III and B. Bhanu

Center for Research in Intelligent Systems
University of California, Riverside, California 92521 USA

Abstract. This paper presents an approach for recognizing articulated vehicles in Synthetic Aperture Radar (SAR) images based on invariant properties of the objects. Using SAR scattering center locations and magnitudes as features, the invariance of these features with articulation (e.g. turret rotation of a tank) is shown for SAR signatures of actual vehicles from the MSTAR (Public) data. Although related to geometric hashing, our recognition approach is specifically designed for SAR, taking into account the great azimuthal variation and moderate articulation invariance of SAR signatures. We present a recognition system, using scatterer locations and magnitudes, that achieves excellent results with the real SAR targets in the MSTAR data. The articulation invariant properties of the objects are used to characterize recognition system performance in terms of probability of correct identification as a function of percent invariance with articulation. Results are also presented for occluded articulated objects.

1 Introduction

In this paper we are concerned with recognizing articulated vehicles, starting with SAR image chips of various target vehicles from the MSTAR (Public) target data set [ ] and ending with identification of the specific vehicle type (e.g., a T72 tank). The major challenge is that the vehicles can be in articulated configurations such as a tank with its turret rotated. In addition, the articulated vehicles can be partially hidden (occluded). Previous work in recognizing articulated objects in optical images [ ] [ ], has used simple models (like scissors and pantograph lamps) and has used constraints around a joint to recognize these objects. Because of the unique characteristics of SAR image formation (specular reflection, multiple bounces, low resolution and non-literal nature of the sensor), it is difficult to extract linear features (commonly used in visible images), especially in SAR images at one foot resolution. Previous recognition methods for SAR imagery using templates [ ] [ ] are not well suited for the recognition of articulated objects, because each different articulation configuration requires a different template leading to a combinatorial explosion.

We approach the problem of recognizing articulated objects from the fundamentals of SAR images. We characterize the SAR image azimuthal variance to determine the number of models required. We demonstrate (and measure) the

H. H. Nagel and F. J. Perales (Eds.): AMDO 2000, LNCS 1899, pp. 96–   , 2000.
© Springer-Verlag Berlin Heidelberg 2000

SAR scattering center location and magnitude invariance with target articulation. Based on these invariants, we develop SAR specific recognition methods that use non-articulated models to successfully recognize articulated versions of the same objects. The key contributions of the paper are the development and evaluation of a method, based on location and magnitude invariant properties of scattering centers, to recognize articulated objects in one foot resolution SAR data.

2   SAR Target Image Characteristics

The typical detailed edge and straight line features of man-made objects in the visual world, do not have good counterparts in SAR images for sub-components of vehicle sized objects at one foot resolution. However, there are a wealth of peaks corresponding to scattering centers. The relative locations of SAR scattering centers, determined from local peaks in the radar return, are related to the aspect and physical geometry of the object, independent of translation and serve as distinguishing features. In addition to the scatterer locations, the magnitudes of the peaks are also features that we use in this paper.

Photo images of the MSTAR articulated objects, a T72 tank serial number (#) a64 and a ZSU 23/4 antiaircraft gun #d08 are shown in Fig. . Example SAR images and the regions of interest (ROI), with the locations of the scattering centers superimposed, are shown in Fig.   for baseline and articulated versions of the T72 and ZSU. The MSTAR articulated object data is all at one foot resolution and $30°$ depression angle. The ROIs are found in the MSTAR SAR object chips by reducing speckle noise using the Crimmins algorithm in Khoros [ ], thresholding at the mean plus two standard deviations, dilating to fill small gaps among regions, eroding to have one large ROI and little regions, discarding the small regions with a size filter and dilating to expand the extracted ROI. The parameters used in extracting ROIs are held constant for all the results reported. The scattering centers are extracted from the SAR magnitude data (within the boundary contour of the ROI) by finding local eight-neighbor maxima.

2.1   Azimuthal Variance

The typical rigid body rotational transformations for viewing objects in the visual world do not apply much for the specular radar reflections of SAR images. This is because a *significant* number of features *do not* typically persist over a few degrees of rotation. Since the radar depression angle is generally known, the significant unknown object rotation is ($360°$) in azimuth. Azimuth persistence or invariance can be expressed in terms of the average percentage of scattering center locations that are unchanged over a certain span of azimuth angles (when we compare scatterer locations in the ground plane of an image rotated by some azimuth increment with another image at the resulting azimuth angle). Since the objects in the MSTAR chips are not registered, we calculate the azimuth

(a) T72   (b) ZSU 23/4

Fig. 1. Articulated T72 tank and ZSU 23/4 antiaircraft gun photos

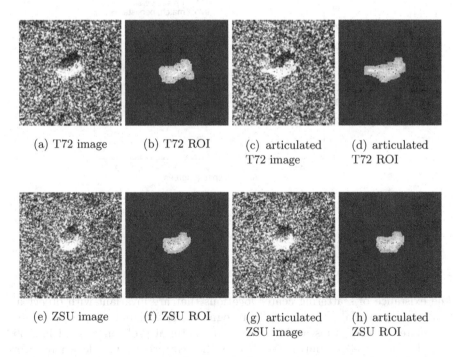

(a) T72 image   (b) T72 ROI   (c) articulated   (d) articulated
                                T72 image   T72 ROI

(e) ZSU image   (f) ZSU ROI   (g) articulated   (h) articulated
                                ZSU image   ZSU ROI

Fig. 2. SAR images and ROIs (with peaks) for T72 tank and ZSU 23/4 at 66° azimuth

invariance as the maximum number of corresponding scattering centers (whose locations match within a given tolerance) for the optimum integer pixel translation. This method of registration by finding the translation that yields the maximum number of corresondences has the limitation that for very small or no actual invariance it may find some false correspondences and report a slightly higher invariance than in fact exists. Figure   shows an example of the mean scatterer location invariance (for the 40 strongest scatterers) as a function of azimuth angle span using T72 tank #132, with various definitions of persistence. The cases labeled 'persists' in Figure   enforce the constraint that the scatterer exist for the entire span of angles and very few scatterers continuously persist for even 5°. Because of this azimuthal variation we model the objects at 1° increments. In the two cases not labeled 'persists' in Figure   , scintillation is allowed and the location invariance declines slowly with azimuth span. The 'within 1 pixel' results (that allow scintillation) are consistent with the one foot ISAR results of Dudgeon [ ], whose definition of persistence allowed scintillation.

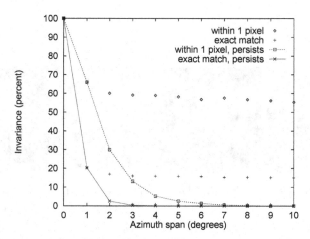

Fig. 3. Scatterer location persistence for T72 #132

2.2   Scatterer Location Invariance with Articulation

The existance of scattering center locations that are invariant with object articulation is crucial to successfully recognizing articulated objects with non-articulated models, thus avoiding the combinatorial problem of modeling 360 articulations x 360 azimuths. We express the scattering center location invariance with respect to articulation as the maximum number of corresponding scattering centers (whose locations match within a stated tolerance) for the optimum integer pixel translation. Given an original version of a SAR object image with n scattering centers, represented by points at pixel locations $P_i = (x_i, y_i)$

for $1 \leq i \leq n$ and a translated, distorted version $P_j' = (x_j', y_j')$ $(1 \leq j \leq n)$ at a translation $t = (t_x, t_y)$, we define a *match* between points P_j' and P_i as:

$$M_{ij}(t) = \begin{cases} 1 \text{ if } |x_j' - t_x - x_i| \leq l \text{ and} \\ \quad |y_j' - t_y - y_i| \leq l \\ 0 \text{ otherwise} \end{cases}$$

where $l = 0$ for an 'exact' match and $l = 1$ for a match 'within one pixel'. The scatterer location invariance, L_n, of n scatterers, expressed as a percentage of matching points, is given by:

$$L_n = \max_t \left\{ \frac{100}{n} \sum_{j=1}^{n} \min \left(\left(\sum_{i=1}^{n} M_{ij}(t) \right), 1 \right) \right\}$$

where each point P_j' is restricted to at most one match. Figure   shows the location invariance, L_{40}, of the strongest 40 scattering centers with articulation for the T72 tank and ZSU 23/4 antiaircraft gun as a function of the hull azimuth. The average articulation invariance is 16.5% for the exact match cases and 56.5% for the within one pixel cases.

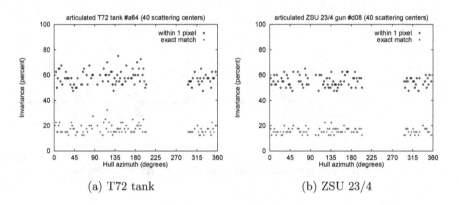

(a) T72 tank   (b) ZSU 23/4

Fig. 4. Scatterer location invariance with articulation

2.3   Scatterer Magnitude Invariance

Using a scaled scatterer amplitude (S), expressed as a radar cross section in square meters, given by $S = 100 + 10 \log_{10}(i^2 + q^2)$, where i and q are the components of the complex radar return, we define a percent amplitude change

(A_{jk}) as: $A_{jk} = 100(S_j - S_k)/S_j$. (This form allows a larger variation for the stronger signal returns.) A location and magnitude match $Q_{jk}(t)$ is given by:

$$Q_{jk}(t) = \begin{cases} 1 \text{ if } M_{jk}(t) = 1 \text{ and } |A_{jk}| \le l_A \\ 0 \text{ otherwise} \end{cases}$$

where l_A is the percent amplitude change tolerance. The scatterer magnitude and location invariance (I_n), expressed as a percentage of n scatterers, is given by:

$$I_n = \max_t \left\{ \frac{100}{n} \sum_{k=1}^{n} \min \left(\left(\sum_{j=1}^{n} Q_{jk}(t) \right), 1 \right) \right\}$$

Figure shows the probability mass functions (PMFs) for percent amplitude change for the strongest 40 articulated vs. non-articulated scattering centers of MSTAR T72 tank #a64 and ZSU #d08. Curves are shown both for the cases where the scattering center locations correspond within a one pixel tolerance and for all the combinations of scatterers whose locations do not match.

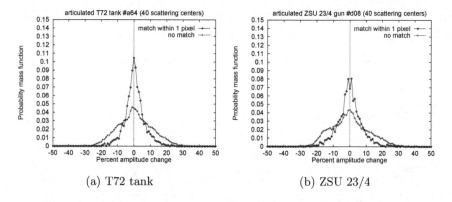

(a) T72 tank   (b) ZSU 23/4

Fig. 5. Scatterer magnitude invariance with articulation

3   SAR Recognition System

Establishing an appropriate local coordinate reference frame is critical to reliably identifying objects (based on locations of features) in SAR images of articulated objects. In the geometry of a SAR sensor the 'squint angle', the angle between the flight path (cross-range direction) and the radar beam (range direction), can be known and fixed at 90°. Given the SAR squint angle, the image range and cross-range directions are known and any local reference point chosen, such as a scattering center location, establishes a reference coordinate system. The relative distance and direction of the other scattering centers can be expressed in radar range and cross-range coordinates, and naturally tessellated into integer buckets that correspond to the radar range/cross-range bins. The recognition system takes advantage of this natural system for SAR, where a single basis point performs the translational transformation and fixes the coordinate system to a 'local' origin.

Our model-based recognition system uses standard non-articulated models of the objects (at 1° azimuth increments) to recognize the same objects in non-standard articulated configurations. Using a technique like geometric hashing [ ], the relative positions of the scattering centers in the range (R) and cross-range (C) directions are indices to a look-up table of labels that give the associated object type and pose. This is an efficient search for *positive* evidence that generates votes for the appropriate object (and azimuth). The models and recognition engine have evolved from the previous 2D version [ ] (which was applied to synthetic SAR data), which uses only the relative distances and the 'exact' scatterer locations, to a 6D version for the more challenging real MSTAR data, which uses more local features and accommodates a 'within 1 pixel' scatterer location uncertainty. In the 6D version the model look-up table labels contain four additional features: range and cross-range position of the 'origin' and the magnitudes (S) of the two scatterers. The model construction algorithm for the 6D recognition system is outlined in Fig. .

1. For each model Object do 2
2. For each model Azimuth do 3, 4, 5
3. Obtain the location (R, C) and magnitude (S) of the strongest n scatterers.
4. Order (R, C, S) triples by descending S.
5. For each origin O from 1 to n do 6
6. For each point P from O+1 to n do 7, 8
7. $dR = R_P - R_O$; $dC = C_P - C_O$.
8. At look-up table location dR, dC append to list entry with: Object, Azimuth, R_O, C_O, S_O, S_P.

Fig. 6. 6D model construction algorithm

For ideal data one could use the strongest scatterer as the origin, however any given scatterer could actually be spurious or missing due to the effects of noise, articulation, occlusion, or non-standard configurations. Thus, we model and use (for recognition) all the scattering center locations in turn as the origin, so the size of the look-up table models and the number of nominal relative distances considered in the recognition of a test image is $n(n-1)/2$, where n is the number of the strongest scattering centers used.

In contrast to many model-based approaches to recognition [ ], we are not 'searching' all the models; instead we are doing table look-ups based on relative distances between the strongest scatterers in the test image. Each query of the look-up table may generate votes for one or more potential candidate solutions. Comparison of each test data pair of scatterers with the model look-up table result(s) provides information on the range and cross-range translation and the percent magnitude changes for the two scatterers. Limits on allowable values for translations and magnitude changes are used as constraints to reduce the number of false matches. (The number of scattering centers used and the various constraint limits are design parameters that are optimized, based on experiments, to produce the best recognition results.) Here, votes are accumulated in a 4D space: object, azimuth, range and cross-range translation. Also a (city-block) weighted voting method is used to reduce the impact of the more common small relative distances. To accommodate some uncertainty in the scattering center locations, the eight-neighbors of the nominal range and cross-range relative location are also probed in the look-up table and the final translation results are summed over a 3x3 neighborhood in the translation subspace. This voting in translation space, in effect, converts the consideration of scatterer pairs back into a group of scatterers at a consistent translation. The process is repeated with different scattering centers as reference points, providing multiple 'looks' at the model database to handle spurious scatterers that arise due to articulation, noise or other factors. To handle identification with 'unknown' objects, we introduce a criteria for the quality of the recognition result (e.g., the votes for the potential winning object exceed some threshold v_{min}). The recognition algorithm is given in Fig. .

---

1. Obtain from test image the location (R, C) and magnitude (S) of n strongest scatterers.
2. Order (R, C, S) triples by descending S.
3. For each origin O from 1 to n do 4
4. For each point P from O+1 to n do 5, 6
5. $dR = R_P - R_O$; $dC = C_P - C_O$.
6. For DR from dR-1 to dR+1 do 7
7. For DC from dC-1 to dC+1 do 8, 9, 10
8. weighted_vote = |DR| + |DC|.
9. Look up list of model entries at DR, DC.
10. For each model entry E in the list do 11
11. IF $|tr = R_O - R_E|$ < translation_limit and $|tc = C_O - C_E|$ < translation_limit and $|1 - S_{EO}/S_O|$ < magnitude_limit and $|1 - S_{EP}/S_P|$ < magnitude_limit THEN increment accumulator array [Object, Azimuth, tr, tc] by weighted_vote.
12. Query accumulator array for each Object, Azimuth, tr and tc, summing the votes in a 3x3 neighborhood in translation subspace about tr, tc; record the maximum vote_sum and the corresponding Object.
13. IF maximum vote_sum > threshold THEN result is Object ELSE result is "unknown".

Fig. 7. 6D recognition algorithm

4   Recognition Results

In these experiments the models are non-articulated versions of T72 #a64 and ZSU23/4 #d08 and the test data are the articulated versions of these same serial number objects (with BRDM2 #e71 as an "unknown" confuser vehicle, when required). Recognition results are optimum using 38 scattering centers, a translation limit of ±5 pixels and a percent magnitude change of less than ±9%. Without the confuser, the overall forced recognition rate is 100% over a range from 14 to 40 scattering centers. In order to handle unknown objects we introduce a minimum vote threshold criteria for a target declaration; objects which fail to achieve the vote threshold are labeled as "unknown". This can be seen in Table , an example confusion matrix for a vote threshold of 2100 votes, where the T72s are all correctly classified and only 2 ZSUs are misclassified as unknown for a 0.990 probability of correct identification (PCI), while 32 BRDM2s are misidentified as targets for a 0.126 probability of false alarm (PFA).

A form of Receiver Operating Characteristic (ROC) curve, with PCI vs. PFA, can be generated by varying the vote threshold (e.g. from 1500 to 4000 in 50 vote increments). The ROC curve in Fig.   shows the excellent articulated object recognition results that are obtained with this system. Figure   shows how the PCI varies with the percent articulation invariance (for a within one pixel location match). The sets of curves are shown with different vote thresholds from 1700 to 2700 to generate failures that illustrate the effect of location invariance on recognition rate.

Table 1. Articulated object confusion matrix

MSTAR (Public) articulated test objects	Identification results		
	T72	ZSU	unknown
T72 315⁰ turret	98	0	0
ZSU 315° turret	0	92	2
BRDM2	32	0	222

There is no real SAR data with occluded objects available to the general public. In addition, there is no standard, accepted method for characterizing or simulating occluded targets. Typically occlusion occurs when a tank backs up into a tree line, for example, so that the back end is covered by trees and only the front portion of the tank is visible to the radar. Thus, the 'bright target' becomes a much smaller sized object. However, the tree tops can produce additional 'bright' peaks that can be of similar strength to target peaks at many azimuths. The occluded test data in this paper is simulated by starting with a given number of the strongest scattering centers and then removing the appropriate number of scattering centers encountered in order, starting in one of

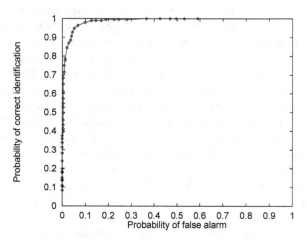

Fig. 8. Receiver Operating Characteristics

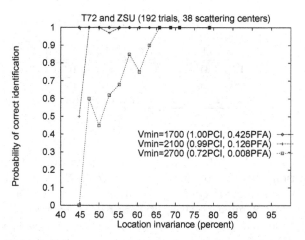

Fig. 9. Recognition rate and articulation invariance

four perpendicular directions d_i (where d_1 and d_3 are the cross range directions, along and opposite the flight path respectively, and d_2 and d_4 are the up range and down range directions). Then the same number of scattering centers (with random magnitudes) are added back at *random locations* within the original bounding box of the target. This keeps the number of scatterers constant and acts as a surrogate for some potential occluding object.

In the occluded articulated object experiments the models are non-articulated versions of T72 #a64 and ZSU23/4 #d08 and the test data are the articulated versions of these same serial number objects that are occluded in the manner described above. Figure   shows the effect of occlusion on recognition of these MSTAR articulated objects for various numbers of scattering centers used.

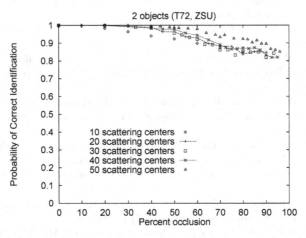

Fig. 10. Effect of occlusion on articulated object recognition

5   Conclusions

The large azimuthal variations in the SAR signatures of objects can be successfully captured by using models at $1°$ degree increments for a fixed depression angle. Useful articulation invariant features exist in SAR images of vehicles. In addition, where the scattering center locations are invariant with articulation, the corresponding magnitudes are also invariant within a small tolerance (typically less than a 10% change). The feasibility of a unique concept for a system to recognize articulated objects in SAR images based on non-articulated models is demonstrated. The great variability of the MSTAR SAR data can be successfully overcome by using the scatterer magnitude as well as location, by accommodating one pixel uncertainty in the scatterer location and by considering an object as a group of scatterers at a consistent translation.

Acknowledgements

This work was supported by DARPA/AFOSR grant F49620-97-1-0184. The contents and information do not necessarily reflect the position or policy of the U.S. Government.

References

1. Beinglass, A., Wolfson, H.: Articulated object recognition, or: How to generalize the generalized Hough transform. Proc. IEEE Conf. on Computer Vision and Pattern Recognition (June 1991) 461–466
2. Dudgeon, D., Lacoss, R., Lazott, C., Verly, J.: Use of persistent scatterers for model-based recognition. SPIE Proceedings: Algorithms for Synthetic Aperture Radar Imagery **2230** (April 1994) 356–368
3. Grimson, W. E. L.: Object Recognition by Computer: The Role of Geometric Constraints. MIT Press (1990)
4. Hel-Or, Y., Werman, M.: Recognition and localization of articulated objects. IEEE Workshop on Motion of Non-Rigid and Articulated Objects (November 1994) 116–123
5. Jones, G. III, Bhanu, B.: Recognition of Articulated and Occluded Objects. IEEE Trans. on Pattern Analysis and Machine Intelligence **21**(7) (July 1999) 603–613

6. Khoros Pro v2.2 User's Guide. Addison Wesley Longman Inc. (1998)
7. Lamden, Y., Wolfson, H.: Geometric hashing: A general and efficient model-based recognition scheme. Proc. Int. Conference on Computer Vision. (December 1988) 238–249
8. Novak, L., Owirka, G., Netishen, C.: Radar target identification using spatial matched filters. Pattern Recognition **27**(4) (1994) 607–617
9. Ross, T., Worrell, S., Velten, V., Mossing, J., Bryant, M.: Standard SAR ATR Evaluation Experiments using the MSTAR Public Release Data Set. SPIE Proceedings: Algorithms for Synthetic Aperture Radar Imagery V **3370** (April 1998) 566–573
10. Verly, J., Delanoy, R., Lazott, C.: Principles and evaluation of an automatic target recognition system for synthetic aperture radar imagery based on the use of functional templates. SPIE Proceedings: Automatic Target Recognition III **1960** (April 1993) 57–71

A Robust Method for Motion Estimation in Image Sequences

R. Mecke and B. Michaelis

Otto-von-Guericke-University of Magdeburg
Institute for Electronics, Signal Processing and Communications (IESK)
Postfach 4120, D-39016 Magdeburg, Germany
Phone: +49 391 67 114 83, Fax: +49 391 67 112 31
ruediger.mecke@e-technik.uni-magdeburg.de
http://iesk.et.uni-magdeburg.de/TI/

Abstract. In this paper a robust method for block-based motion analysis in monocular image sequences is considered. Due to the realized recognition of false measurements by a neural recognition system, gross errors in the motion trajectories are avoided. Assuming correspondences between regions in successive images, a model based recursive estimation technique is applied to estimate the motion of the observed image region. For this purpose a Kalman filter is used. The underlying kinematic model contains assumptions about the motion, especially constant velocity components are assumed. Particularly, the existence of problematic image situations (e.g. partial occlusion of objects) leads to gross errors in the measuring values and false motion parameters are estimated. In order to cope with this problem an extension of the filtering algorithm by a neural recognition system is proposed. This system recognizes typical problematic image situations and controls the adaptation of the filter. Selected results for real-world image sequences are described.

1   Introduction

Motion estimation techniques represent a focal point in the field of image sequence processing. These techniques try to interpret the changes in successive images as caused exclusively by motion of the objects contained in the scene. The analysis of image sequences is often done in a recursive manner. Recursive methods use the redundancy of motion information in temporal direction for a more robust and efficient motion analysis. The starting point is usually the measurement of displacement and rotation using correspondences in successive images. These correspondences can be generated using pixel-based matching algorithms [1]. In contrast to approaches determining correspondences of certain image features, such as line segments [2] or flexible contour models of objects [3], in this paper the gray-

H. H. Nagel and F. J. Perales (Eds.): AMDO 2000, LNCS 1899, pp. 108-119, 2000.
© Springer-Verlag Berlin Heidelberg

levels of image blocks are used immediately without any feature extraction. Therefore, our method is not restricted to certain specific object features. Using a set of image blocks it is possible to analyze articulated motion or deformable objects too.

2   Pixel-Based Matching Algorithm

For the measurement of image motion a pixel-based matching algorithm is used. In modification to the conventional block matching algorithm [1] the determination of displacement and *rotation* with *sub-pixel accuracy* is possible. The matching algorithm realizes a comparision of image regions in successive images by calculating a similarity criterion. In this approach quadratic image blocks are compared (see Fig. 1). At first the translational motion and afterwards the rotational motion is determined. In order to generate the compared image windows, the sequence images are interpolated at the position of the sample points $\mathbf{p}^i$. These points represent an equidistant quadratic grid, that can be located at any position and angle in the image.

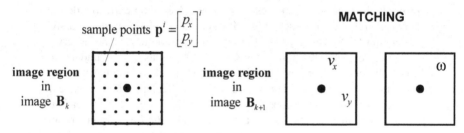

Fig. 1. Matching of image regions in successive images

The correspondences of image blocks in successive images are obtained using the following matching criterion:

$$\text{MAD}(a_k) = \frac{1}{255 \cdot A} \sum_{i=1}^{A} \left| \mathbf{B}_k(\mathbf{p}_k^i) - \mathbf{B}_{k+1}(\mathbf{p}_{k+1}^i) \right| \quad ; \quad \mathbf{p}_{k+1}^i = f(\mathbf{p}_k^i, m_k)$$

$$\text{translation:} \quad m_k = \mathbf{v}_k \quad ; \quad \mathbf{v}_{min} \leq \mathbf{v}_k \leq \mathbf{v}_{max}$$

$$\text{rotation:} \quad m_k = \omega_k \quad ; \quad \omega_{min} \leq \omega_k \leq \omega_{max}$$

$\mathbf{B}_k$...image k ; $\mathbf{p}_k^i$...i – th sample point in $\mathbf{B}_k$; f...motion function
A...number of sample points in the window

(1)

The function specified in Eq. 1 represents a simplified block-based correlation measure for the determination of translation (MAD_T) and rotation (MAD_R). These functions are generated by the comparison of a reference window in image $\mathbf{B}_k$ with all possible search windows located within a search area in the next image $\mathbf{B}_{k+1}$. Since they calculate the <u>M</u>ean <u>A</u>bsolute <u>D</u>ifference between two image windows, they are called MAD-functions. The coordinates of the minimum of the MAD_T-criterion represent the measured velocity $[v_x \ v_y]^\text{T}$ and the position of the MAD_R-minimum represents the measured angular velocity ω of the reference window. These values refer to the position respectively the angle at time k and make it possible, to measure the midpoint position $[p_x^M \; p_y^M]_{k+1}^T$ and the angle φ_{k+1}^M of the considered window in the next image. The index M indicates that these parameters represent measuring values.

In order to derive highly resolved measuring values from the discrete MAD-functions, an approximation of the similarity criteria around the minimum is realized. For this purpose the discrete minimum value of the MAD_R- and the MAD_T-criterion and their 2 respectively 4 neighboring values are approximated by the following model functions MAD^{mod}.

model function 1: $\quad MAD_T^{mod}(v_x, v_y) = c_T^{(5)} v_x^{\,2} + c_T^{(4)} v_y^{\,2} + c_T^{(3)} v_x + c_T^{(2)} v_y + c_T^{(1)}$ $\qquad$ (2)

model function 2: $\quad MAD_R^{mod}(\omega) = c_R^{(3)} \omega^2 + c_R^{(2)} \omega + c_R^{(1)}$

After determining the coefficients $c^{(i)}$ the minimum position of each of the model functions is calculated using the first derivations of the MAD^{mod}-functions.

Own experiments on real-world images have shown, that measuring values calculated by this procedure are corrupted by noise. Depending on the required accuracy the influence of noise can be more or less disturbing. Particularly, if there are applications with high requirements regarding the quality of motion parameters, it is necessary to minimize the influence of noise. In the next paragraph a recursive filtering algorithm is presented which is able to reduce the influence of noise.

3   Recursive Motion Estimation

The procedure which reduces the influence of noise from the measuring values is called *estimation*. Considering sequences of data the estimation is often realized in a recursive manner. In this paper such an estimation procedure is used to process the motion parameters (measuring values) calculated by the matching algorithm as described in the section before (see scheme shown in Fig. 2).

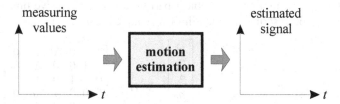

Fig. 2. Motion estimation for noise reduction

In the field of image sequence processing Kalman filtering techniques have been gained in their importance as a method for model-based state estimation problems during the past decades [4, 5]. These techniques are used ordinarily to estimate the motion parameters of scene objects.

Using the Kalman filter algorithm to estimate motion parameters, they are derived from two parts (see Fig. 3). The fist one is represented by the measuring values calculated by the pixel-based matching algorithm in this case. The second part is the underlying kinematic model that describes the assumptions about the motion in the image sequence. The filtering algorithm controls the influence of the two parts.

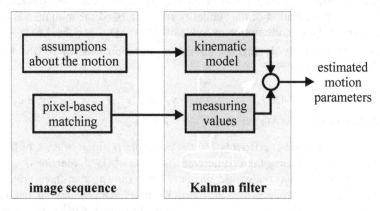

Fig. 3. Estimation of motion parameters

A set of motion parameters (for instance parameters for position and velocity) can be combined in the state vector **s**. The conventional Kalman filter, as described in [6], requires a linear model of the observed state vector **s** in the state space (*system model*). The definition of an appropriate system model requires assumptions about the observed motion. A simple kinematic model, applicable to monocular image sequences, assumes motion of rigid objects in a plain perpendicular to the cameras optical axis and is used in this paper. Furthermore, the motion in a short time interval is assumed to be constant and to be composed of a translational velocity $\begin{bmatrix} v_x & v_y \end{bmatrix}^{\mathrm{T}}$ and an angular velocity ω. The corresponding parameters for the position and the angle are $\begin{bmatrix} p_x & p_y \end{bmatrix}^{\mathrm{T}}$ and φ.

In many cases the motion of an object part between 2 successive time steps (time interval Δt) can be described by the following simple recursive kinematic model:

$$\mathbf{s}_{k+1} = \mathbf{H}_k\,\mathbf{s}_k + \mathbf{w}_k \quad ; \quad \mathbf{s} = \begin{bmatrix} \varphi \\ p_x \\ p_y \\ \omega \\ v_x \\ v_y \end{bmatrix} \quad ; \quad \mathbf{H}_k = \begin{bmatrix} 1 & 0 & 0 & \Delta t & 0 & 0 \\ 0 & 1 & 0 & 0 & \Delta t & 0 \\ 0 & 0 & 1 & 0 & 0 & \Delta t \\ 0 & 0 & 0 & 1 & 0 & 0 \\ 0 & 0 & 0 & 0 & 1 & 0 \\ 0 & 0 & 0 & 0 & 0 & 1 \end{bmatrix}^{\mathrm{T}} \qquad (3)$$

The uncertainty in the system model is considered by the separate stochastic noise vectors $\mathbf{w}_k$. Each element of $\mathbf{w}_k$ is assumed as caused by a zero-mean white Gaussian process. Using a set of state vectors **s** respectively system models it is possible to describe articulated motion or deformable objects too.

A measuring algorithm calculates the measurement vector **x** from correspondences of image regions in successive images (see section 2). The *measurement equation* represents the linear connection between the measurement vector $\mathbf{x}$ and the state vector $\mathbf{s}$ and can be written as follows:

$$\mathbf{x}_k = \mathbf{F}_k\,\mathbf{s}_k + \mathbf{n}_k \quad ; \quad \mathbf{x} = \begin{bmatrix} \varphi^M \\ p_x^M \\ p_y^M \end{bmatrix} \quad ; \quad \mathbf{F}_k = \begin{bmatrix} 1 & 0 & 0 & 0 & 0 & 0 \\ 0 & 1 & 0 & 0 & 0 & 0 \\ 0 & 0 & 1 & 0 & 0 & 0 \end{bmatrix} \tag{4}$$

The values of $\begin{bmatrix} p_x^M & p_y^M \end{bmatrix}^{\mathrm{T}}$ represent the measured midpoint position and φ^M is the measured angle of the considered image region. Since, as mentioned above, the measurement (matching) is always executed between two successive images, the current measurement vector $\mathbf{x}_k$ is derived from the sum of the vector $\mathbf{x}_{k-1}$ one time step before and the determined velocity components.

The noise in the measuring values is assumed by the stochastic noise vector $\mathbf{n}_k$. The elements of this vector are assumed to have a zero-mean Gaussian probability density function as the elements of the vector $\mathbf{w}_k$.

Fig. 4 shows the internal signal flow chart of the Kalman filter (see for instance [7]). The updated state vector $\hat{\mathbf{s}}_k^*$ is composed of two parts, whereof the first one is the vector $\hat{\mathbf{s}}_k$ and the second one represents the difference between $\mathbf{x}_k$ and the estimated measurement $\mathbf{F}_k\,\hat{\mathbf{s}}_k$. The Kalman gain $\mathbf{K}_k$ is calculated recursively and represents a variable amplification matrix for this difference. The predicted state vector at the next time step ($\hat{\mathbf{s}}_{k+1}$) is calculated using the system matrix $\mathbf{H}_k$ and the updated state vector at time k.

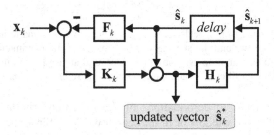

Fig. 4. Signal flow chart of the Kalman filter

The Kalman filter yields a recursive estimate $\hat{\mathbf{s}}$ of the state vector $\mathbf{s}$ which is optimal in the sense of a least square optimization criterion. This criterion minimizes the trace of the covariance matrix of the estimation error $\hat{\mathbf{s}} - \mathbf{s}$.

The stochastic properties of the noise vectors $\mathbf{w}_k$ and $\mathbf{n}_k$ are taken into consideration by the covariance matrices of both vectors. Conventionally the elements of the covariance matrices are assumed to be constant and are determined on the basis of knowledge about the noise characteristic. On the whole, they influence the smoothing capability of the filter.

For further details and the mathematical description of the well-known filter equations the reader is referred to the appropriate literature (for instance [7]).

Besides the capability of the filter, to reduce the influence of noise, there are some other important advantages. For instance the inclusion of an appropriate system model makes it possible, to predict the state vector one step into the future. Due to this capability, expectations about the motion parameters at the next time step are specified without calculating a measurement. They can be used effectively to reduce the search area in the matching algorithm.

In the field of image processing the measuring values have a specific characteristic, that depends on the type of the considered image data, the image contents and some other important conditions during the image acquisition. Particularly, the existence of *problematic image situations* leads to gross errors (outliers) in the measuring values. Such situations, for instance, arise from *overlapping motion* and *partial occlusion* of objects or *illumination changes* in the scene. Fig. 5 (on the left) shows the first image from a real-world image sequence that contains a moving object (bus). Parts of the object are partially occluded by other stationary objects in the foreground (specified in Fig. 5) during the motion.

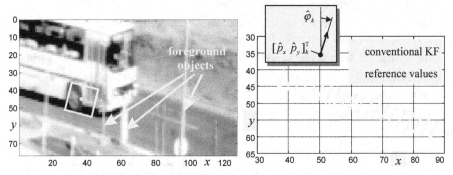

Fig. 5. *Left:* First image from a real-world image sequence. Problematic image situations are indicated by white arrows and the starting window for the motion estimation is depicted as a square; *Right:* Results of motion estimation (position and angle) for the image window using the conventional Kalman filter (KF) and the corresponding reference values at each time step

This occlusion leads to deformations of the matching criteria, if the occlusion appears in the reference window or in the search window. Since the measuring values for the position and the angle of the considered window (square in the image of Fig. 5, on the left) are derived from the minimum position of these matching criteria, the stream of measurements consequently contains outliers or useless values. An example for such distorted matching criteria is shown in Fig. 6 (column $k = 9$). There are no significant minima and the MAD-values are higher compared to the non-distorted matching criterion depicted in Fig. 6 (column $k = 5$).

Due to the existence of outliers in the measuring values, the above mentioned assumptions concerning the stochastic noise vector $\mathbf{n}_k$ are often incorrect. It can be noticed, that outliers are not taken into consideration in the conventional Kalman filter algorithm. As a result, the estimated state vector $\hat{\mathbf{s}}$ does not converge against the 'true' object motion or there is a considerable delay in the filter response.

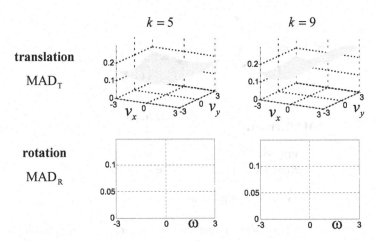

Fig. 6. Different MAD-criteria for selected time steps k

Consequently, the considered image region for the sequence in Fig. 5 (on the left) does not contain the same part of the moving object, as in the first image after the appearance of occlusion. In Fig. 5 (on the right) the estimated midpoint position $\begin{bmatrix} \hat{p}_x & \hat{p}_y \end{bmatrix}^T$ and angle $\hat{\varphi}$ of the image region are depicted in the coordinates of the image scene. Compared with the reference values it is visible, that there is a permanent divergence of the motion trajectory after the occlusion.

Obviously the conventional Kalman filter is not able to eliminate the influence of problematic image situations to the estimates, if there is no further adaptive component in the filter.

4   System for Robust Motion Estimation

In order to cope with the problems, arising from the problematic image situations described in the previous section, an extension of the conventional filtering structure is suggested. The idea is to evaluate the quality of the measuring values at each time step and to adapt certain parameters of the filter in dependence on the reliability of the measurement.

The proposed system for a robust motion estimation is shown in Fig. 7. A new approach is that both the MAD_R- and the MAD_T-criterion calculated by the pixel-based matching algorithm are used for the determination of the measurement vector $\mathbf{x}_k$ *and* as input for a recognition system. This system realizes an adaptation of the Kalman filter depending on several features of the MAD-criteria. For this purpose the elements of a later defined gating matrix $\mathbf{G}_k$ are adjusted. During the occurrence of problematic image situations it is later described, that these elements are small and the filter derives the motion parameters mainly from the underlying kinematic model.

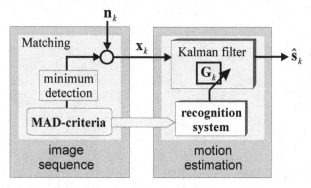

Fig. 7. Proposed system for robust motion estimation

Own investigations have shown that certain features of the matching criterion represent a measure for the reliability of the corresponding measuring value [8, 9]. In [9] a set of 6 simple features $f^{(i)}$ has been found empirically, that are suitable to describe the main properties of MAD-criteria. Furthermore it is necessary, that the used features are independent from the minimum position of the respective matching criterion. Essential features in this context are, for instance, the mean of the MAD-criterion and the value of the minimum. The features are elements of the feature vector $\mathbf{f}$. The feature extraction is realized separately for the MAD_R- and the MAD_T-criterion (see Fig. 8).

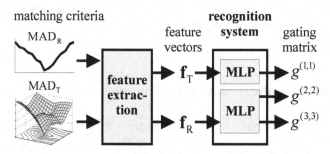

Fig. 8. Quality assessment of matching criteria

It is proposed to use a recognition system that assesses the quality of the respective MAD-function based on these features. The recognition system is realized by *artificial neural networks (ANN)*. In this case two simple Multi-Layer Perceptons (MLP) have been employed (see Fig. 8). Typically they consist of several layers of neurons. The output of each neuron is connected with the input of all neurons in the next layer. The first layer (input layer) stores the input vector $\mathbf{f}$. The outputs of the MLP's are equivalent to the diagonal elements of the above mentioned gating matrix $\mathbf{G}_k$.

Neural networks have the ability to learn their recognition task from examples. This feature is very useful, because the many different effects of problematic image situations on the matching criterion can be better described by typical examples (e.g. see Fig. 6) than by mathematical models. Another advantage of neural networks is their generalization ability, that means, they are able to produce an appropriate response also for those input data, which are similar to the training examples, but have never been trained before. Therefore, the variety of possible matching criteria can be considerably reduced and only typical candidates have to be contained in the training data set. Because of limitations in this paper a detailed description of the structure and training of the used feed-forward networks are left out here. For details the reader is referred to [9].

Fig. 9 shows the proposed filtering structure. Compared with the conventional Kalman filter (see Fig. 4) the difference between the measurement vector $\mathbf{x}_k$ and the estimated measurement $\mathbf{F}_k \hat{\mathbf{s}}_k$ is multiplied by the gating matrix $\mathbf{G}_k$, before the multiplication by the Kalman gain $\mathbf{K}_k$ is realized. So it is possible to weight each element of the difference vector corresponding to the output of the respective MLP.

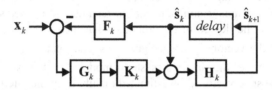

Fig. 9. Signal flow chart of the proposed filtering structure

The 3×3 gating matrix $\mathbf{G}_k$ is defined as follows:

$$\mathbf{G}_k = \begin{bmatrix} g_k^{(1,1)} & 0 & 0 \\ 0 & g_k^{(2,2)} & 0 \\ 0 & 0 & g_k^{(3,3)} \end{bmatrix} \ ; \ \ 0 \le g_k^{(i,j)} \le 1 \tag{5}$$

Due to the properties of the MLP's the diagonal elements $g_k^{(i,j)}$ represent floating point values. This is an essential advantage compared to those approaches (for instance [10]), using only two discrete values (1 or 0) for a „good/bad"-classification.

5   Selected Examples for the Representation of Results

The proposed system was tested for the analysis of several real-word image sequences. In this section selected examples are presented. Fig. 10 shows the first image from a sequence that contains problematic image situations. In this case parts of the moving object (toy) are partially occluded by stationary objects in the foreground. As a result, the state vector $\hat{\mathbf{s}}$ estimated by the conventional Kalman filter does not describe the 'true' motion of the considered image region. This error is visible in Fig. 10 (on the right), where the position and the angle of the respective image block is depicted at each time step. There is a permanent divergence of the estimated motion parameters after the first occlusion.

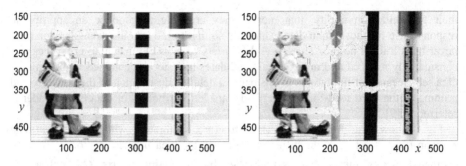

Fig. 10. Results of motion estimation using the proposed system (on the left) respectively the conventional Kalman filter (on the right)

Due to the recognition system (see section 4) the proposed system is able to recognize problematic image situations and to readjust the elements of gating matrix $\mathbf{G}_k$, depending on the degree of disturbance. That means that the incoming (false) measurements in the vector $\mathbf{x}_k$ are weighted less than before and the Kalman filter uses more and more the internal system model for the state vector update. Consequently, the state vector $\hat{\mathbf{s}}_k^*$ is estimated mainly from the internal system model. As a result in the example shown in Fig. 10 (on the left), the correct estimation of the image block position and angle is achieved even in case of partial occlusion.

The dark image blocks indicate, that the sum of the 3 diagonal elements $g_k^{(i,i)}$ of the gating matrix $\mathbf{G}_k$ is less than the threshold 1.5. This threshold is chosen only for the purpose of visualization. As mentioned above, the elements $g_k^{(i,i)}$ represent floating point values (see example in Fig. 11).

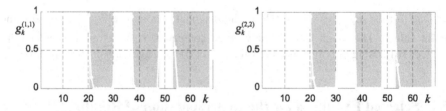

Fig. 11. Diagonal elements $g_k^{(1,1)}$ and $g_k^{(2,2)}$ determined by the recognition system for the upper image block of the sequence in Fig. 10 at each time step

The proposed system was tested for both indoor sequences acquired under definite lab conditions and real-word outdoor sequences. An example for the latter image sequences is shown in Fig. 12. There are various problematic image situations (e.g. overlapping motion, partial occlusion, shadows on moving objects and illumination changes) within the scene.

118   R. Mecke and B. Michaelis

Fig. 12. First image of the sequence TRAFFIC and position of selected image regions

In Fig. 13 the results of motion analysis for the TRAFFIC sequence are shown. The proposed system is able to cope with the occuring different problematic image situations. The reason for this capability is the above mentioned generalization property of the recognition system (see section 4).

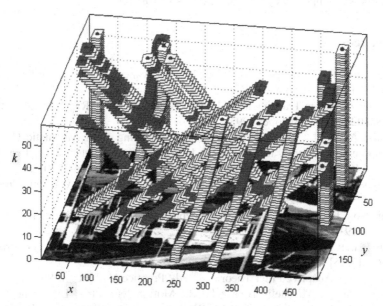

Fig. 13. Results of motion estimation for the TRAFFIC sequence (see Fig. 12) using the proposed system. For the purpose of a better visualization the estimated position and angle of the image blocks are plotted in the vertical direction. The dark blocks indicate, that the sum of the 3 diagonal elements $g_k^{(i,i)}$ of the gating matrix $\mathbf{G}_k$ is less than the threshold 1.5

6   Conclusions

The described results show, that the proposed system according to Fig. 7 makes it possible, to achieve a considerable improvement of the motion estimation in the case of problematic image situations. This system contains a neural recognition system, that realizes the adaptation of the motion estimation algorithm. The recognition system uses simple features of the matching criterion in order to assess the quality of the incoming measurements. A further improvement of the recognition capability can be expected when using more complex features of the matching criteria. Intended work in the future will investigate a motion estimation system for the analysis of color image sequences. Another goal is, to use object-specific shaped image regions instead of the presently used fixed quadratic blocks. The proposed system shall be used in future to analyze articulated motion and deformable objects.

Acknowledgements

This work was supported by the LSA grant 1441A/8386H .

References

1. Musmann, H. G.; Pirsch, P.; Grallert, H. J.: Advances in Picture Coding. Proc. of the IEEE, 1985, Volume 73, No. 4, 523-548.
2. Zhang, Z.: Token Tracking in a Cluttered Scene. Research Report N°2072, INRIA, ISSN 0249-6399, October 1993.
3. Blake, A.; et. al.: Affine-Invariant Contour Tracking With Automatic Control of Spatiotemporal Scale. In: Proc. of 4. Int. Conf. on ComputerVision, Berlin, May 11th-14th, 1993, IEEE Computer Society Press, ISBN 0-8186-3870-2.
4. Maybeck, P. S.: Stochastic Models, Estimation and Control. Academic Press Inc., Vol. 1-3, ISBN 0-12-48070(1or2or3)-X, 1982.
5. Sorenson, H. W.: Kalman Filtering: Theory and Application. IEEE Press, ISBN 0-87942-191-6, 1985.
6. Kalman, R. E.: A New Approach to Linear Filtering and Prediction Problems, 1960, In: [5] from this list, pp. 16-26.
7. Haykin, S.: Adaptive Filter Theorie. 3rd ed-, Prentice-Hall Inc., 1996.
8. Schnelting, O.; Michaelis, B.; Mecke, R.: Motion Estimation By Using Artificial Neural Networks, Proc. of IEEE-Workshop on Nonlinear Signal and Image Processing, Neos Marmaras, Greece, June 20th-22th, 1995, Vol. 2, pp. 714-717.
9. Mecke, R.: Grauwertbasierte Bewegungsschätzung in monokularen Bildsequenzen unter besonderer Berücksichtigung bildspezifischer Störungen, PhD Thesis, Otto-von-Guericke-University of Magdeburg, Department Electrical Engineering, 1999.
10. Rao, R. P. N.: Robust Kalman Filters for Prediction, Recognition, and Learning. Technical Report 645, University of Rochester, Computer Science Department, Rochester, New York, Dezember 1996.

Spectral Correspondence for Deformed Point-Set Matching

M. Carcassoni and E. R. Hancock

Department of Computer Science, Univerisity of York
York Y01 5DD, UK.

Abstract. This paper describes a modal method for point-set tracking in motion sequences. The framework for our study is the recently reported dual-step EM algorithm of Cross and Hancock [ ]. This provides a statistical framework in which the structural arrangement of the point-sets provides constraints on the pattern of correspondences used to estimate alignment parameters. In this paper our representation of point-set structure is based on the point-adjacency matrix. Using ideas from spectral graph-theory, we show how the eigen-vectors of the point-adjacency matrix can be used to compute point correspondence probabilities. We show that the resulting correspondence matching algorithm can be used to track deforming point-sets detected in motion sequences.

1 Introduction

Correspondence matching is key to the analysis of articulated and deformable objects in motion sequences. The reason for this is that correspondences between image features, such as points or lines, are required before the degree of articulation or deformation can be assessed via detailed alignment. If the arrangement of object features is represented using a relational structure such as an adjacency graph, then consistent correspondence patterns can be recovered using techniques such as inexact graph-matching [ ]. Moreover, using the structural arrangement of the features renders the estimation of correspondences quasi invariant to a variety of deformations. However, one of the shortcomings of existing inexact graph-matching methods is their computational overheads, which can render them unsuitable for motion sequence analysis.

An efficient alternative is to use a modal representation of the relational arrangement of features. Over the past decade, there has been considerable effort expended in developing modal models of point-set deformation, Although the literature on the topic is dense, there are two familiar examples which merit special mention. In the point distribution model of Cootes and Taylor [ ] the deformation of the point-set is modelled using the eigen-modes of the point-position covariance matrix for a set of training examples. By contrast, the finite element model of Sclaroff and Pentland [ ] uses the modes of vibration the points under elastic forces. Although this work has made considerable strides, it can be criticised on the grounds that it is based on a central clustering model. In other

H. H. Nagel and F. J. Perales (Eds.): AMDO 2000, LNCS 1899, pp. 120–   , 2000.

words, point-set deformation is measured relative to the centre-of-gravity. As a result a considerable body of information concerning the relational arrangement of the points is overlooked.

It is the modal analysis of relational structure which is central to the field of mathematics known as spectral graph theory. This is a term applied to a family of techniques that aim to characterise the global structural properties of relational graphs using the eigenvalues and eigenvectors of the adjacency matrix [ ]. Although the subject has found widespread use in a number of areas including structural chemistry and routeing theory, there have been relatively few applications in the computer vision literature. The reason for this is that although elegant, spectral graph representations are notoriously susceptible to the effect of structural error. In other words, spectral graph theory can furnish very efficient methods for characterising exact relational structures, but soon breaks down when there are spurious nodes and edges in the graphs under study.

Spectral methods for graph analysis invariably commence by computing the Laplacian matrix. This is closely related to the node adjacency matrix. The diagonal elements of the Laplacian matrix are equal to the degree of the nodes (vertices) and the off diagonal elements are unity if the corresponding nodes are connected by an edge, and are zero otherwise. However, it is also common to work with proximity or property matrices where the off diagonal elements reflect the difference in node attributes such as position [ ] or orientation [ ]. Once a matrix characterisation of the graph is to hand then the eigenvalues and eigenvectors are computed. The main idea behind spectral graph theory is to use the distribution of eigenvalues to provide a compact summary of graph-structure.

In the computer vision literature there have been a number of attempts to use spectral properties for graph-matching and object recognition. Umeyama has an eigen-decomposition method that matches graphs of the same size [ ]. Borrowing ideas from structural chemistry, Scott and Longuet-Higgins were among the first to use spectral methods for correspondence analysis [ ]. They showed how to recover correspondences via singular value decomposition on the point association matrix between different images. In keeping more closely with the spirit of spectral graph theory, yet seemingly unaware of the related literature, Shapiro and Brady [ ] developed an extension of the Scott and Longuet-Higgins method, in which point sets are matched by comparing the eigenvectors of the point proximity matrix. Here the proximity matrix is constructed by computing the Gaussian weighted distance between points. The eigen-vectors of the proximity matrices can be viewed as the basis vectors of an orthogonal transformation on the original point identities. In other words, the components of the eigenvectors represent mixing angles for the transformed points. Matching between different point-sets is effected by comparing the pattern of eigenvectors in different images. Shapiro and Brady's method can be viewed as operating in the attribute domain rather than the structural domain. Horaud and Sossa have adopted a purely structural approach to the recognition of line-drawings. Their representation is based on the immanantal polynomials for the Laplacian matrix of the line-connectivity graph. By comparing the coefficients of the polynomials, they are able to index into a large data-base of line-drawings. In another application involving indexing into large data-bases, Sengupta and Boyer have used property matrix spectra to characterise line-patterns. Various attribute representations are suggested and compared. Shokoufandeh, Dickinson and Siddiqi [ ] have shown how graphs can be encoded using local topological spectra for shape recognition from large data-bases.

The focus of this paper is to investigate the use of property matrix spectra for matching point-sets undergoing deformation in motion sequences. As mentioned above, spectral methods offer an attractive route to correspondence matching since they provide a representation that can be used to characterise graph structure at the global level. If used effectively, the spectral representation can be used for rapid matching by comparing patterns of eigenvalues or eigenvectors. Unfortunately, these advantages must be traded against their relative fragility to the addition of noise and clutter. For instance, although the methods of Horaud and Sossa [ ] and Shapiro and Brady [ ] work well for graphs that are free of structural contamination, they do not work well when the graphs are of different size.

To render the modal analysis more robust, we adopt a statistical framework. The framework for our study is provided by the recently reported dual-step EM algorithm of Cross and Hancock [ ]. This interleaves the processes of correspondence matching and point-set alignment in an iterative matching process. The idea underpinning the method is to use the consistency of the pattern of correspondences to constrain the estimation of alignment parameters. The method is proved effective in the matching of planar point-sets under affine and perspective geometries. Despite proving effective the method is computationally demanding. The reason for this is that the correspondence probabilities, which weight contributions to the expected log-likelihood function for alignment parameter estimation are computed using a time-consuming dictionary-based method. The aim in this paper is to address this deficiency by using a more efficient method for computing the correspondence probabilities using modal structure.

2   Dual-Step EM Algorithm

We are interested in the correspondence matching of deformed point-sets in motion sequences. The framework for our study is provided by the dual-step EM algorithm of Cross and Hancock [ ]. This statistical algorithm has been demonstrated to improve matching performance by interleaving the processes of alignment and correspondence. In this section we review this method before proceeding to show how modal structure can be used to constrain correspondence matching.

2.1   Prerequisites

The aim in this paper is to use the dual-step EM algorithm of Cross and Hancock [ ] to render the process of modal correspondence matching robust. Before we detail the algorithm, we provide some of the formal ingredients of the method.

Affine Geometry: Suppose that $\Phi^{(n)}$ is the geometric transformation that best aligns a set of image feature points $\mathbf{w}$ with their counterparts in a model $\mathbf{z}$ at iteration n of the algorithm. Each point in the image data set is represented by an augmented position vector $\boldsymbol{w}_i = (x_i, y_i, 1)^T$ where i is the point index. This augmented vector represents the two-dimensional point position in a homogeneous coordinate system. We will assume that all these points lie on a single plane in the image. In the interests of brevity we will denote the entire set of image points by $\mathbf{w} = \{\boldsymbol{w}_i, \forall i \in \mathcal{D}\}$ where $\mathcal{D}$ is the point set. The corresponding fiducial points constituting the model are similarly represented by $\mathbf{z} = \{\boldsymbol{z}_j, \forall j \in \mathcal{M}\}$ where $\mathcal{M}$ denotes the index-set for the model feature-points $\boldsymbol{z}_j$.

The Cross and Hancock alignment method [ ] is quite general and can be used with a variety of image deformation models. However, in this paper we confine our attention to affine deformations. The affine transformation has six free parameters. These model the two components of translation of the origin on the image plane, the overall rotation of the co-ordinate system, the overall scale together with the two parameters of shear. These parameters can be combined succinctly into an augmented matrix that takes the form

$$\Phi^{(n)} = \begin{pmatrix} \phi_{1,1}^{(n)} & \phi_{1,2}^{(n)} & \phi_{1,3}^{(n)} \\ \phi_{2,1}^{(n)} & \phi_{2,2}^{(n)} & \phi_{2,3}^{(n)} \\ 0 & 0 & 1 \end{pmatrix} \tag{1}$$

With this representation, the affine transformation of co-ordinates is computed using the following matrix multiplication $\boldsymbol{w}_i^{(n)} = \Phi^{(n)} \boldsymbol{w}_i$.

Correspondences: The recovery of the parameters of the transformation matrix Φ, requires correspondences between the point-sets. In other words, we need to know which point in the data aligns with which point in the model. This set of correspondences between the two point sets is denoted by the function $f^{(n)} : \mathcal{M} \rightarrow \mathcal{D}$ from the nodes of the data-graph to those of the model graph. According to this notation the statement $f^{(n)}(i) = j$ indicates that there is a match between the node $i \in \mathcal{D}$ of the model-graph to the node $j \in \mathcal{M}$ of the data-graph at iteration n of the algorithm.

2.2   The Dual-Step EM Algorithm

Cross and Hancock's contribution was to present an extension of the standard EM algorithm in which the structural consistency of correspondence matches can be used to gate contributions to the expected log-likelihood function [ ]. This idea is closely related to the hierarchical mixture of experts algorithm of Jordan and Jacobs [ ]. However, the method uses a dictionary method for computing the correspondence probabilities which is both localised and time consuming. The aim here is to replace the dictionary-based method used to compute the probabilities with a modal correspondence method.

Expected Log-likelihood: According to Cross and Hancock we seek both correspondence matches (i.e. the function f) and transformation parameters which maximise the expected log-likelihood

$$Q(\Phi^{(n+1)}|\Phi^{(n)}) = \sum_{i \in \mathcal{D}} \sum_{j \in \mathcal{M}} P(z_j|w_i, \Phi^{(n)}) \zeta_{i,j}^{(n)} \ln p(w_i|z_j, \Phi^{(n)}) \qquad (2)$$

The meaning of this expected log-likelihood function requires further comment. The measurement densities $p(w_i|z_j, \Phi^{(n+1)})$ model the distribution of alignment errors between the data-point position w_i and the the model point position z_j at iteration n of the algorithm. The log-likelihood contributions at iteration $n+1$ are weighted by the *a posteriori* measurement probabilities $P(z_j|w_i, \Phi^{(n)})$ computed at the previous iteration n of the algorithm. The individual contributions to the expected log-likelihood function are gated by the structural matching probabilities $\zeta_{i,j}^{(n)}$. These probabilities measure the consistency of the pattern of correspondences when the match $f^{(n)}(i) = j$ is made. Their modelling is the topic of Section 3.

Expectation: In the expectation step of the EM algorithm the *a posteriori* probabilities of the missing data (i.e. the model-graph measurement vectors, z_j) are updated by substituting the point position vector into the conditional measurement distribution. Using the Bayes rule, we can re-write the *a posteriori* measurement probabilities in terms of the components of the corresponding conditional measurement densities

$$P(z_j|w_i, \Phi^{(n)}) = \frac{\alpha_j^{(n)} p(w_i|z_j, \Phi^{(n)})}{\sum_{j' \in \mathcal{M}} \alpha_{j'}^{(n)} p(w_i|z_{j'}, \Phi^{(n)})} \qquad (3)$$

The mixing proportions are computed by averaging the *a posteriori* probabilities over the set of data-points, i.e. $\alpha_j^{(n+1)} = \frac{1}{|\mathcal{D}|} \sum_{i \in \mathcal{D}} P(z_j|w_i, \Phi^{(n)})$. In order to proceed with the development of a point registration process we require a model for the conditional measurement densities, i.e. $p(w_i|z_j, \Phi^{(n)})$. Here we assume that the required model can be specified in terms of a multivariate Gaussian distribution. The random variables appearing in these distributions are the alignment errors for the position predictions of the ith data point delivered by the current estimated data-point positions. Accordingly we write

$$p(w_i|z_j, \Phi^{(n)}) = \frac{1}{2\pi\sqrt{|\Sigma|}} \exp\left[-\frac{1}{2}(z_j - \Phi^{(n)} w_i)^T \Sigma^{-1} (z_j - \Phi^{(n)} w_i)\right] \qquad (4)$$

In the above expression Σ is the variance-covariance matrix for the position errors.

Maximisation: The dual step EM algorithm iterates between the two interleaved maximisation steps for alignment parameter estimation and estimating correspondence assignments.

- **Maximum *a posteriori* probability correspondence matches:** These are sought so as to maximise the *a posteriori* probability of structural match. The update formula is

$$f^{(n+1)}(i) = \arg\max_{j \in \mathcal{M}} P(\boldsymbol{z}_j | \boldsymbol{w}_i, \Phi^{(n)}) \zeta_{i,j}^{(n)} \qquad (5)$$

- **Maximum likelihood alignment:** In the case of affine geometry, the transformation is linear in the parameters. This allows us to locate the maximum-likelihood parameters directly by solving the following system of saddle-point equations for the independent affine parameters $\phi_{k,l}^{(n+1)}$ running over the indices $k = 1, 2$ and $l = 1, 2, 3$

$$\frac{\partial Q(\Phi^{(n+1)} | \Phi^{(n)})}{\partial \phi_{k,l}^{(n+1)}} = 0 \qquad (6)$$

For the affine transformation the set of saddle-point equations is linear, and are hence easily solved by using matrix inversion. The updated solution matrix is given by

$$\Phi^{(n+1)} = \left[\sum_{(i,j) \in f^{(n)}} P(\boldsymbol{z}_j | \boldsymbol{w}_i, \Phi^{(n)}) \zeta_{i,j}^{(n)} \boldsymbol{w}_i \, U^T \, \boldsymbol{w}_i^T \, \Sigma^{-1} \right]^{-1}$$
$$\times \left[\sum_{(i,j) \in f^{(n)}} P(\boldsymbol{z}_j | \boldsymbol{w}_i, \Phi^{(n)}) \zeta_{i,j}^{(n)} \boldsymbol{z}_j \, U^T \, \boldsymbol{w}_i^T \, \Sigma^{-1} \right] \qquad (7)$$

where the elements of the matrix U are the partial derivatives of the affine transformation matrix with respect to the individual parameters, i.e.

$$U = \begin{pmatrix} 1 & 1 & 1 \\ 1 & 1 & 1 \\ 0 & 0 & 0 \end{pmatrix} \qquad (8)$$

This allows us to recover a set of improved transformation parameters at iteration $n + 1$. Once these are computed, the *a posteriori* measurement probabilities may be updated by applying the Bayes formula to the measurement density function in the expectation step.

3   Spectral Methods for Correspondence Matching

The aim in this paper is to show how the modal structure of point-sets can be used to compute the correspondence probabilities required by the dual-step EM algorithm. The modal approach to correspondence commences by enumerating a point proximity matrix. This is a continuous counterpart of the graph adjacency matrix. Rather than setting the elements to unity or zero depending on whether or not there is a connecting edge between a pair of nodes, the elements of the proximity matrix are weights that reflect the strength of a pairwise adjacency relation. Once the proximity matrix is to hand, then correspondences are located by computing its eigenvectors. The eigenvectors of the proximity matrix become the columns of a transformation matrix which operates on the original point identities. The rows of the transformation matrix represent the components of the original points in the directions of the eigenvectors. We can locate point correspondences by searching for rows of the transformation matrix which have maximal similarity.

Unfortunately there are two drawbacks with the modal method of correspondence. Firstly, there is no clear reason to use Gaussian weighting in favour of possible alternatives. Moreover, the Gaussian weighting may not be the most suitable choice to control the effects of pattern distortion due to point movement under measurement error or deformation under affine or perspective geometry. Secondly, the method proves fragile to structural differences introduced by the addition of clutter or point drop-out.

The aim in this section is to address these two problems. We commence by considering alternatives to Gaussian weighting. Next we suggest how the comparison of the eigenvectors can be effected in a manner which is robust to measurement error and poor ordering of the eigenvalues, The contribution is therefore to show how the correspondence probabilities $\zeta_{i,j}^{(n)}$ can be computed in an efficient and robust manner.

3.1   Point Proximity Matrix

In this section we show how to construct the weighted point-proximity matrix. The role of the weighting function is to model the probability of adjacency relations between points.

The standard way to represent the adjacency relations between points is to use the Gaussian proximity matrix. If i and i' are two data points, then the corresponding element of the proximity matrix at iteration n of the algorithm is given by

$$H_{i,i'}^{(n)} = \exp\left[-\frac{1}{2s^2}|| w_i^{(n)} - w_{i'}^{(n)}||^2\right] \qquad (9)$$

where s is a width parameter.

However, we have investigated alternative weighting functions suggested by the robust statistics literature. One of the most successful has proved to be a continuous variant of Huber's kernel, generated by the hyperbolic tangent function

$$H_{i,i'}^{(n)} = \frac{2}{\pi|| w_i^{(n)} - w_{i'}^{(n)}||} \tanh\left[\frac{\pi}{s}||\boldsymbol{w}_i^{(n)} - w_{i'}^{(n)}||\right] \qquad (10)$$

The modal structure of the point adjacency matrix is found by solving the eigenvalue equation $HE_l = \lambda_l E_l$, where λ_l is the lth eigenvalue of the matrix H and E_l is the corresponding eigenvector. We order the vectors according to the size of the associated eigenvalues. The ordered column-vectors are used to construct a modal matrix $V = (E_1, E_2, E_3, ...)$. The column index of this matrix refers to the order of the eigenvalues while the row-index is the index of the original point-set. This modal decomposition is repeated for both the data and transformed model point-sets to give a data-point modal matrix $V_D^{(n)} = (E_1^D, E_2^D, E_3^D, ..., E_{|\mathcal{D}|}^D)$ and a model-point modal matrix $V_M = l(E_1^M, E_2^M, E_3^M, ..., E_{|\mathcal{M}|}^M)$. Since the two point-sets are potentially of different size, we truncate the modes of the larger point-set. This corresponds to removing the last $||\mathcal{D}| - |\mathcal{M}||$ rows and columns of the larger matrix. The resulting matrix has $o = \min[\mathcal{D}, \mathcal{M}]$ rows and columns.

The modal matrices can be viewed as inducing a linear transformation on the original identities of the point-sets. Each row of the modal matrix represents one of the original points. The column entries in each row measure how the original point identities are distributed among the different eigen-modes.

3.2   Correspondences

With the modal structure of the point-sets to hand, then we can locate correspondences by comparing the rows of the modal matrices. We have investigated three different methods to compute the correspondence probabilities required by the dual-step EM algorithm.

Shapiro and Brady: Based on this eigen-decomposition Shapiro and Brady [ ] find correspondences by comparing the rows of the model matrices V_M and V_D. The decision concerning the correspondences is made on the basis of the similarity of different rows in the modal matrices for the data and the model. The measure of similarity is the Euclidean distance between the elements in the corresponding rows. According to Shapiro and Brady the correspondence probabilities are assigned according to the following binary decision

$$\zeta_{i,j}^{(n)} = \begin{cases} 1 & \text{if } j = \arg\min_{j'} \sum_{l=1}^{o} ||V_D^{(n)}(i,l) - V_M(j',l)||^2 \\ 0 & \text{otherwise} \end{cases} \quad (11)$$

Correspondence Probabilities: Rather than using the binary correspondence pattern of Shapiro and Brady to gate contributions to the expected log-likelihood function, we can use the elements of the two modal matrices to compute the probabilities of correspondence match. This is done by comparing the elements of the two matrices on a row-by-row basis. A simple way of computing the probabilities is to assume that the vectors are subject to Gaussian measurement errors. As a result, the probability that data-point i is in correspondence with model data-point j is equal to

$$\zeta_{i,j}^{(n)} = \frac{\exp\left[-\mu \sum_{l=1}^{o} ||V_D^{(n)}(i,l) - V_M(j,l)||^2\right]}{\sum_{j' \in \mathcal{M}} \exp\left[-\mu \sum_{l=1}^{o} ||V_D^{(n)}(i,l) - V_M(j',l)||^2\right]} \quad (12)$$

where μ is a parameter which is set to control the width of the probability distribution.

Robust Correspondence Probabilities: The shortcoming of this method for computing the correspondence probabilities is the effect of outlier measurement errors. When there is a significant difference between one or more of the components of the eigenvectors, then these errors dominate the argument of the exponentials. This will have the tendency to flatten the distribution and will result in ambiguity and equivocation concerning the pattern of correspondences. One way to make the computation of correspondences robust to outlier measurement error is to accumulate probability on a component by component basis over the eigenvectors. To do this we define the correspondence probability to be

$$
\zeta_{i,j}^{(n)} = \frac{\sum_{l=1}^{o} \exp\left[-\mu || V_D^{(n)}(i,l) - V_M(j,l) ||^2\right]}{\sum_{j' \in \mathcal{M}} \sum_{l=1}^{o} \exp\left[-\mu || V_D^{(n)}(i,l) - V_M(j',l) ||^2\right]}
\tag{13}
$$

In this way large measurement errors contribute insignificantly through the individual exponentials appearing under the summation over the components of the eigenvectors.

4   Sensitivity Study

In this section we investigate the noise sensitivity of the new modal correspondence method reported in this paper. Our experiments are conducted with random point sets. We investigate two sources of error. The first of these is random measurement error or point-position jitter. Here we subject the positions of the points to Gaussian measurement error. The parameter of the noise process is the standard deviation of the point position error. The second source of error is structural. Here we remove random points. This is the most destructive type of error for modal methods.

We compare three different algorithms. The first of these is the standard SVD method of Shapiro and Brady. Here there is no EM iteration. The correspondences are selected using the probabilities defined in Equation (12) so that $f(i) = \arg\max_j \zeta_{i,j}^{(n)}$. The second is the alignment of the point-sets using the standard EM algorithm. This algorithm does not use any information concerning the pattern of correspondences. Contributions to the log-likelihood function are weighted only by the *a posteriori* alignment probabilities $P(z_j | w_i, \Phi^{(n)})$. In other words, we set $\zeta_{i,j}^{(n)} = 1$ for all values of i and j. Finally, we use the correspondence probabilities defined in Equations (13) and (14) to weight contributions to the expected log-likelihood function is the dual-step EM algorithm. We respectively refer to these three algorithms as SVD, EM and EM+SVD.

We commence in Figure 1a by showing the effect of positional jitter on the fraction of correct correspondences. Here we deal with two point-sets of the same size. The positions of the data-points are displaced relative to their counterparts in the model by adding random Gaussian measurement errors. The standard deviation of the Gaussian noise is kept fixed. However, we gradually add more

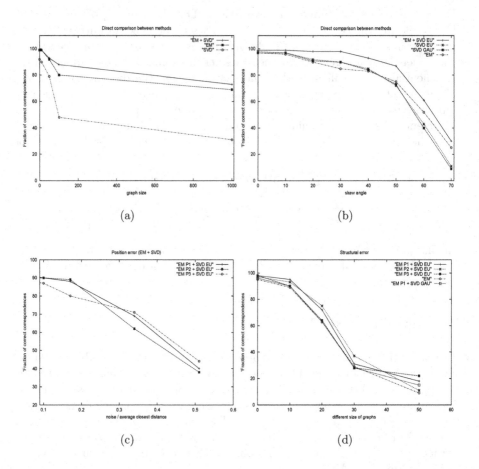

Fig. 1. Effect of a) graph size, b) skew angle, c) measurement error and d) clutter

points to the two point-sets. This has the effect of increasing the point-density, i.e. of decreasing the average inter-point distance. The main effects to note are the following. Firstly, all three methods degrade with the increasing size of the point-sets (i.e. decreasing inter-point distance). The second feature to note is that the new method (i.e. SVD+EM) consistently gives the best results. Moreover, the performance of the pure SVD method degrades rapidly as the relative displacement of the points is increased. Finally, the SVD+EM method outperforms the EM method by a useful margin.

Next we investigate the effect of controlled affine skew of the point-sets. Figure 1b shows the fraction of correct correspondences as a function of the skew angle in degrees. Here we compare the standard EM method, the EM method with a hyperbolic tangent weighting function (EM+SVD+EU), and the use of pure SVD with both a Gaussian weighting function (SVD+GAU) and a hyperbolic tangent weighting function (SVD+EU). Here the use of the dual step EM algorithm with the new proximity weighting function (SVD+EM+EU) offers clear advantages. There is a 10% margin of improvement for all skew angles.

We now turn to the effect of positional jitter. Figure 1c compares the effect of using the three different ways of computing the correspondence probabilities in the dual-step EM algorithm. SVD+EM+P1 refers to the model presented in Equation 12, SVD+EM+P2 to that presented in Equation 13 and SVD+EM+P3 to that presented in Equation 14. Here we add Gaussian measurement errors to the positions of the data points. We report the results as a function of the ratio of the noise standard deviation to the average inter-point distance.

Finally, we study investigate the effects of point-set contamination. Here we investigate the matching of point sets of different sizes. We add increasing fractions of clutter nodes to the data point-set. We commence by noting that the the pure SVD method fails as soon as clutter is added. Hence we can not plot any sensitivity data from the method. Figure 1d shows the fraction of correct correspondences as a function of the fractional difference in the point-set sizes, i.e. the fraction of clutter added to the data point-set. The different curves are for different proximity weighting functions and for different correspondence probability models. The main conclusion to note is that the dual step EM method (i.e. the curves labelled SVD+EM) outperforms the standard EM method by about 5-10%. Also, as the fraction of clutter increases then so the performance degrades.

5   Real World Data

Our final piece of experimental work focusses on real-world data. Here we have matched images from a gesture sequence in which a hand is clenched to form a fist. The feature points in these images are points of locally maximum curvature on the outline of the hand. Figures 2a and 2b respectively show the sequence of correspondence matches obtained with the dual-step EM algorithm and the SVD method of Shapiro and Brady. In each panel the image on the left-hand side is the initial image in the sequence. The images in the right-hand panel are those obtained after 1, 15 and 25 frames have elapsed. Here the sequence is captured at a rate of 10 frames per second. The matches shown are directly from the left-hand frame to the right-hand frame, i.e. no intermediate frames are used. In the case of the dual-step EM algorithm, the matches are all correct in each frame. In the case of the SVD method the method begins to break after 17 frames.

6   Conclusions

In this paper we have described a method for point-set matching which uses the modal structure of the point-proximity matrix to compute correspondence probabilities. These probabilities are used in conjunction with the dual-step EM

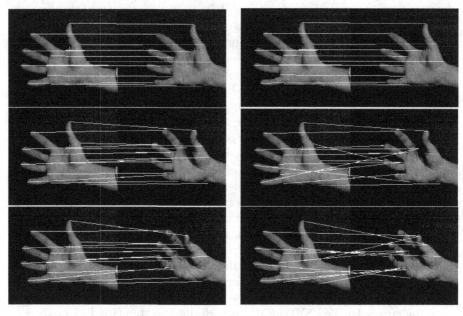

Fig. 2. Matches- dual-step EM+SVD (left) and pure SVD (right)

algorithm of Cross and Hancock [ ] to match point-sets undergoing affine distortion. The method is shown to be effective for gesture tracking in motion sequences.

Our future plans revolve around developing more sophisticated point deformation models. Here there are several possibilities including the use of spline warps and the use of mixture models to capture articulated motion.

References

1. F. R. K. Chung, *Spectral Graph Theory*, CBMS series **92**, AMS Ed., 1997.
2. T.F Cootes, C. J. Taylor, D. H. Cooper and J. Graham, "Active Shape Models - Their Training and Application", *Computer Vision, Graphics and Image Understanding*, **61**, pp. 38–59, 1995.
3. A. D. J. Cross and E. R. Hancock, "Graph matching with a dual step EM algorithm", *IEEE PAMI*, **20**, pp. 1236–1253, 1998.   ,   ,   ,
4. A. P. Dempster, Laird N. M. and Rubin D. B., "Maximum-likelihood from incomplete data via the EM algorithm", *J. Royal Statistical Soc. Ser. B (methodological)*, **39**, pp. 1-38, 1977.
5. M. I. Jordan and R. A. Jacobs, "Hierarchical mixtures of experts and the EM algorithm", *Neural Computation*, **6**, pp. 181-214, 1994.
6. S. Sclaroff and A. P. Pentland, "Modal Matching for Correspondence and Recognition", *IEEE PAMI*, **17**, pp. 545–661, 1995.
7. G. L. Scott and H. C. Longuet-Higgins, "An algorithm for associating the features of 2 images", *Proceedings of the Royal Society of London Series B (Biological)*, **244**, pp. 21–26, 1991.

8. K. Sengupta and K. L.Boyer, "Modelbase partitioning using property matrix spectra", *Computer Vision and Image Understanding*, **70**:2, pp. 177-196, 1998.
9. L. S. Shapiro and J. M. Brady, "Feature-based correspondence - an eigenvector approach", *Image and Vision Computing*, **10**, pp. 283–288, 1992.   ,   ,
10. A. Shokoufandeh, S. J. Dickinson, K. Siddiqi and S. W. Zucker, "Indexing using a spectral encoding of topological structure", *Proc. of the IEEE Conf. on Computer Vision and Pattern Recognition*, pp.491-497, 1999.
11. H. Sossa and R. Horaud, "Model indexing: the graph-hashing approach", *Proc. of the IEEE Conf. on Computer Vision and Pattern Recognition*, pp. 811-815, 1992.

12. S. Umeyama, "An eigen decomposition approach to weighted graph matching problems", *IEEE PAMI*, **10**, pp. 695–703, 1988.
13. R. C. Wilson and E. R. Hancock, "Structural Matching by Discrete Relaxation", *IEEE PAMI*, **19**, pp. 634–648, 1997.

Visualization of Local Movements for Optimal Marker Positioning

R. Boulic[1], M.-C. Silaghi [2], and D. Thalmann[1]

[1] Computer Graphics Lab, Swiss Federal Institute of Technology Lausanne,
CH-1015 Lausanne Switzerland
{Ronan.Boulic,Daniel.Thalmann}@epfl.ch
[2] Artificial Intelligence Lab, Swiss Federal Institute of Technology Lausanne,
CH-1015 Lausanne Switzerland
Marius.Silaghi@epfl.ch

Abstract. Motion Capture has been adopted for the production of highly realistic movements, as well as for the clinical analysis of pathological motions. In both cases, a skeleton model has to be identified to derive the joint motion. The optical technology has gained a large popularity due to the high precision of its marker position measurements. However, when it comes to building the skeleton frames out of the 3D marker positions, significant local skin deformations may penalize the quality of the model reconstruction. In this paper we exploit a local fitting tool to visualize the influence of skin deformation on marker movements. Such a knowledge can in turn improve the layout of optical markers. We illustrate our viewpoint on motions of the upper-torso.

1 Introduction

Various motion capture technologies are used for measuring the movement of human beings either for animating virtual humans or analysing the movement per se (e.g. for sport performance or clinical context). Until now, the most successful technology is optical motion capture. This is due to its high precision measurement of little reflective markers, attached on some relevant body landmarks. In a production context, the movement of an artist is captured with two to eight calibrated cameras. For simple motions, the multiple views of markers allow the automatic reconstruction of their 3D position. Depending on the system, a static posture [1] or a special calibration motion (further referred to as the *gym* motion) is used to build or adjust a skeleton model. The skeleton model helps, in a second phase, to derive the angular trajectories of all the captured motions. In this second phase, the markers are generally assumed to be fixed in the coordinate system of a body segment. This assumption is weak for a body region undergoing large deformations, such as the shoulder. In this paper we exploit a recent tool for the analysis of local marker displacements (i.e. with respect to the un-

H. H. Nagel and F. J. Perales (Eds.): AMDO 2000, LNCS 1899, pp. 133-144, 2000.
© Springer-Verlag Berlin Heidelberg

derlying bones). This tool is designed to provide needed information for the skeleton fitting task, by highlighting marker sites that undergo important relative motion with respect to the underlying bones. It also helps to eliminate redundant markers and identify potentially interesting new marker locations.

The paper focuses first on the problem of skeleton identification for motion capture. Then it recalls our local fitting technique for deriving joint center from relative marker trajectories. The next section illustrates how it can be used to optimize the marker positioning of the upper-torso region. The conclusion summarizes the tradeoffs regarding marker positioning and suggests new research directions.

2   Related Work

Identifying the correct location of human joint center from external information is a difficult problem. The most simple approach is to scale a standard human skeleton to the total height of a given person; needless to say, it requires some adjustments but it is sufficient for entertainment applications [2]. Within the same frame of mind, external anatomic features can be detected and exploited from a static 3D envelop captured by digital cameras [3]. However, the precision of these two approaches is very low.

Other promising techniques emerge from the field of video-based motion analysis [4]. In [5] an arm recorded with a stereo system is being tracked by fitting a model built out of ellipsoids to the data. This way, the skeleton fitting is concomitant to the motion tracking. In the longer term, one should be able to derive a generic model of the skin deformation from such data, thus paving the way to much more precise identification of the underlying skeleton movements.

Presently optical and magnetic systems prevail in motion capture as they offer the best compromise in terms of precision and overall cost (processing and human intervention). It is a standard working hypothesis in the literature to assume that the markers are rigidly linked to the underlying skeleton [6] (it is also reported for magnetic motion capture [7], [8]). However, the rigid body hypothesis causes important errors in the estimation of the joint kinematics. This was reported in [9] for marker-based systems or in [2] for magnetic systems. It is difficult to identify a better model for the local movement of the markers as it results from the combination of the interrelated movements of the bones, muscles, fatty tissues and the skin. Proposed solutions in optical motion capture are: carefully designing marker clusters [10], considering each marker separately [11], or allowing partial freedom of motion between the markers and the associated bones [12]. This latter work proposes a methodology based on an anatomic human model. The human model encompasses a precise anatomic description of the skeleton mobility associated with an approximated envelope. It has a double objective: by ensuring a high precision mechanical model for the performer, the tracking algorithm can predict the 3D location and the visibility of markers. This reduces significantly the human intervention in case of marker occlusion. The work described in the present article exploits the visualization features of a local fitting tool for which we recall the major characteristics in the next section (we refer the reader to [13] for full details).

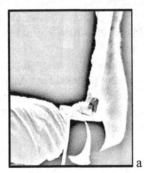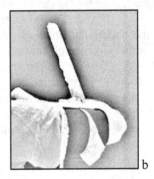

a   b

Fig. 1: Orientation error between a strapped magnetic sensor and the underlying arm during axial rotation. A dedicated approach solving for this problem is proposed in [2] for magnetic motion capture

3   Building Local Frames

When looking for the position of the bones of a person, a first observation is that the relative distance of markers attached to one limb is almost constant. The biggest deviations occur when markers are attached on parts that suffer maximal deformation during the movement, as around the joints or on massive muscles (e.g. on the thigh). Our approach handles this context by decomposing the problem into two tasks: the partitioning of markers into rigid *cliques* and the estimation of joint centers. A *clique* denotes a set of markers where each member remains within a distance tolerance wrt all the other markers of the set. Mastering the partitioning and the joint center estimation allows us to visualize local marker trajectories and thus better understand the skin deformations

3.1   Partitioning Marker into Rigid Segment Set

In the following, we assume that we exploit a motion called the "gym motion", which highlights most of the body mobility with simple movements. The corresponding file of 3D marker locations is the input of the *partitioning* algorithm.

The partitioning algorithm computes the distances between markers at each frame of the gym motion (**Fig. 2**). It selects the biggest cliques for a given distance threshold. This condition defines a rigid segment set. The system may look for the expected number of partitions or the user can interactively tune this threshold (**Fig. 3**). In addition, we define the *attachment weight* of a marker to a segment as a normalized measure of the rigidity of its attachment to that segment. By default, all the attachment weights have a value of 1.0.

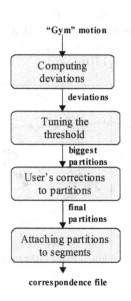

Fig. 2. Partitioning algorithm

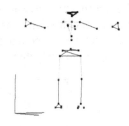

Fig. 3. Partitions after user corrections

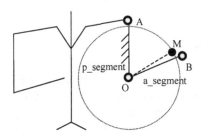

Fig. 4. The trajectory of a marker M around an adjacent segment OA

3.2   Visualizing Relative Trajectories of Markers

If we consider a referential bound to a bone represented by a segment e.g. OA (**Fig. 4**), the markers that are attached on adjacent segments (e.g. OB), theoretically move on a sphere centered on the joint that links the two segments (here joint O). This comes from the hypothesis of constant distance between markers and joints.

The position of a 3D object in space is completely defined by three non-colinear points. Thus, if we have a minimum of three markers on a segment, we can define the position and orientation of that object in space. Afterwards, we compute the movement of the markers on adjacent segments in the referential established by these markers and we estimate their centers of rotation (as in **Fig. 5** and **Fig. 6**). The centers of rotation correspond to the joints. From their position in space, we can approximate the lengths of the body segments as the distances between them. For example, in **Fig. 4** we can compute the position of the joints A and O in space and we get the distance $\|AO\|$.

Due to the deformations undergone by the skin during the motion, the markers attached on a limb change their position with respect to the bone. As long as the deformation is only due to a twisting along the bone segment, it is filtered out by its property of maintaining the distance to the joints. However, a deformation that is changing the distance to the bone (e.g. due to muscles such as biceps) or one that changes the position along the bone induces unknown errors for the joint center computation. Markers suffering such deformation errors are further said to belong to the *noisy class*.

We deal with these errors by introducing a LSQ computation of the center of rotation. We use a modified version of the Levenberg-Marquardt method [14] for all of our least squares computations. Depending on the complexity of the movements, the errors sum up or compensate each other (more details in [13]).

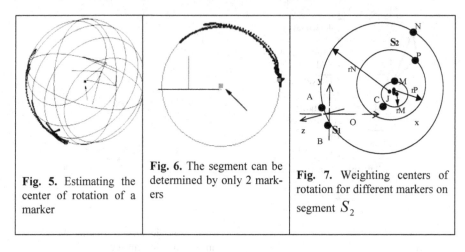

Fig. 5. Estimating the center of rotation of a marker

Fig. 6. The segment can be determined by only 2 markers

Fig. 7. Weighting centers of rotation for different markers on segment S_2

3.3   Estimating the Position of Joints

In the p_segment referential we compute all the centers of rotation for all the markers of an adjacent segment *a_segment* (**Fig. 4**). The center of rotation is estimated as the result of the function:

$$\arg\min_{r,x_0,y_0,z_0 \ trajectory} \sum (d(r,x,y,z) \times weight(r,x,y,z))^2 \qquad (1)$$

corresponding to the LSQ minimization [10] of the function:

$$d(r,x,y,z) \times weight(r,x,y,z) \qquad (2)$$

where:

$$d(r,x,y,z) = \sqrt{(x-x_0)^2 + (y-y_0)^2 + (z-z_0)^2} - r \qquad (3)$$

and the function $weight(r,x,y,z)$ computes the inverse of the density of the trajectory samples in a region of the space. We compute this density by first dividing the space in a set of parallelepipeds in which we count the number of points. First we compute automatically the minimal box containing all the points of the trajectory and we divide it, dividing each direction by a factor of 5 or 10. This increases the importance of poorly populated regions of the space, where the performer stays for very short time.

We then estimate the joint position as the center of mass of the centers of rotation, weighted by the associated marker weight (**Fig. 7**).

$$weight_{center} = weight(mkr, a\_segment)\, factor(mkr, a\_segment) \qquad (4)$$

In our experiments, we found a good value for factor given by:

$$factor(mkr, a\_segment) = \frac{1}{radius(mkr, p\_segment)} \qquad (5)$$

Let us take **Fig. 7** as an example. After defining the system of coordinates bound to S_1, we estimate the center of rotation J of S_2 in this referential. In order to do this, we estimate the center of rotation $\overline{x}_J$ of each of the markers M, N and P. Then we compute the mass center of the centers of rotation for M, N and P using the weights computed with the previous formula:

$$\overline{x}_J = \frac{\sum\limits_{centers} (\overline{x}_{center} \times weight_{center})}{\sum\limits_{centers} weight_{center}} \qquad (6)$$

There is a case where the trajectory of a marker describes a circle and not a sphere, due to reduced degree of freedom for a certain joint (namely the elbow). We project this trajectory in the plan that best contains it. This plan can be found by using a LSQ that minimizes the distance between it and the points on the trajectory (**Fig. 6**).

A certain attention has to be paid to the case where we have less than three attached markers on a segment. This case occurs often in our experiments. Currently, we are satisfied with two markers if the adjacent joints can be acceptably modeled as having only one rotational degree of freedom. In this case we determine the system of coordinates by the plane that contains the two markers of the base segment and the marker whose trajectory is being tracked. The center of rotation is computed in this plane and then mapped back into the global referential. We compute there the center of mass of all the centers of rotation, computed for all the markers on a neighbor segment in order to find an estimate for the position of the joint. Afterwards, we perform as explained before. For example (**Fig. 6**), we compute all the rotation centers of the markers on OA around OB, and all the rotation centers of the markers on OB around OA. Then we compute the center of mass using the weights of the considered markers and the inverse of the radius of the circles or spheres described by them during their motion.

4   Optimizing Marker Position

We propose to exploit the visualization of markers' local trajectories to get more insight into the bone/skin relationship. The tool should allow us to:

> ➢   make decisions relative to the inclusion of a bone in the skeleton model,
> ➢   distinguish between bone movement, muscle mass deformation and skin sliding,
> ➢   discover artifacts due to underlying bone movements,
> ➢   appreciate the correlation between bone configuration and marker position.

We have chosen to illustrate the marker position optimization on a difficult case-study to better stress the interest of the visualization tool. We have retained the up-down (shrugging) and the forward-backward motions of the clavicles. The first part of the study focuses on the relation between partitioning and marker trajectory analysis. The visualization tool allows the assessment of the marker locations with the objective of retaining pertinent ones while eliminating others. The second part of the study highlights the skin sliding in the back region.

4.1   Test-Case Marker Set and Motion

Fig. 8 shows the proposed marker set on the spine and thorax (the image is inverted to remove the black background). All the useful markers have a label according to the following convention. The names of markers on the **back** start with **B**. Those on the spine have a format B_i with i equal 1, 2 (lumbar), 3,4 (thoracic) and 5 (neck base). Two other markers on the thorax are labeled with **BL** (as Low) and **BH** (as High). The names of markers on the **front** start with **F** respectively with **F1** and **F3** on the clavicles joints and **F2**, **F4**, **F5** on the thoracic cage. The distance F4-F5 is approximately 30 cm. Finally the names of markers on the shoulders start with **S** respectively with **SR** for Right side and **SL** for Left side. Compared to standard motion capture practice [1], the present set of makers is deliberately large to explore the local skin deformations.
The motion is performed so as to highlight a single degree of mobility at a time: here the clavicle up-down (schrugging) and forward-backward motions. The motion is repeated a few times for each mobility either independently or simultaneously on both sides. The same initial posture with dangling arms is used for all motion recordings. In addition to being captured, the whole motion capture session has been recorded with a digital video camera. A selection of snapshots has been made from the resulting DVD tape and is presented below.

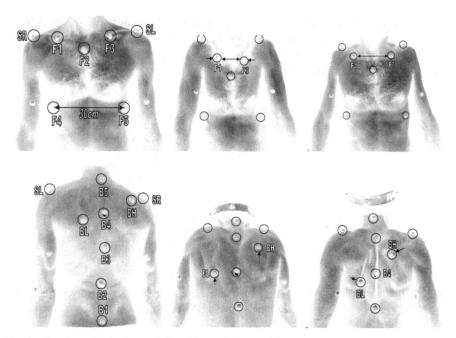

Fig. 8.: Front and back views of the spine and thorax regions

4.2 Retaining Pertinent Markers

The partitioning is the action of grouping markers belonging to the same body segment. This stage is important since it determines the local frames in which marker trajectories are further built and analyzed. Fig. 9 shows the cliques of the upper body. The thorax region is divided into three cliques (marker groups):

* the right clavicle group includes SR, F1 and BH
* the left clavicle group includes SL, F3 and BL

Thorax partition includes all the other (labelled) markers. It is relevant to include also the spine markers into this partition because the studied motion keeps the back straight.

The trajectory displayed on Fig. 10 exhibits a clear rotation behavior of the SL marker during a few shrugging motions. The center of rotation is close to the location of the F3 marker put on the left clavicle joint. Although with a short lever arm, the amplitude of the rotation is about 60°, indicating that a clavicle segment is highly relevant in a skeleton model. The 10cm scale is based on the F4-F5 distance.

When studying the motion of the SL marker, it quickly appeared that the markers on the clavicle joints were suffering strong local displacements due to the clavicle bones underlying motions. The variation of the F1-F3 distance is shown on the images of Fig. 8 and the successive drawings of Fig. 11 (indicated with arrows on (a) and (b)).

In Fig. 11 (top views) we compare the SL marker local trajectory for an alternate thorax partition that excludes the two markers F1 and F3 on the clavicle joints. Although slightly different from the previous partition case, the resulting SL marker trajectory is qualitatively similar, thus justifying the abandon of the F1-F3 markers for the thorax partition. In addition, the removed markers F1 and F3 proved to be a source of difficult 3D reconstruction as illustrated on Fig. 12 with a local rotation artifact during the forward clavicle motion.

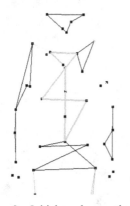

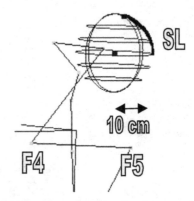

Fig. 9.: Initial marker partioning (front view)

Fig. 10: Front view of the local trajectory of the left shoulder marker SL expressed in the thorax partition frame

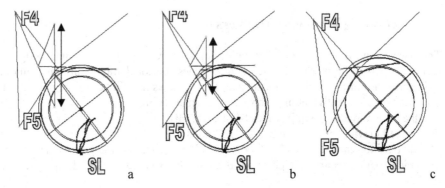

Fig. 11: Top view of the left shoulder marker trajectory with respect to the thorax partitions: initial partition in two postures for high clavicles (a) and low clavicles (b), and alternate partition for (c)

Fig. 12: Local rotation of F1 and F3 due to forward clavicles motion

4.3   Studying Local Skin Deformations

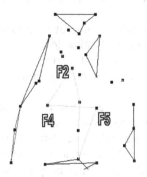

The present section focuses on markers BL and BH that are respectively on the low and high part of the muscular mass associated to the scapula motion. The major aspect in these trajectories is their translational rather than rotational nature. These characteristics have already appeared on **Fig. 8**.

A second alternate thorax partition (without marker B4) had to be defined as this marker could not be tracked during the whole sequence. The marker B4 is subject to severe deformation and pushing of muscular masses (that even led to the loss of this marker and the repetition of this motion).

Fig. 13: Alternate thorax partition (without B4)

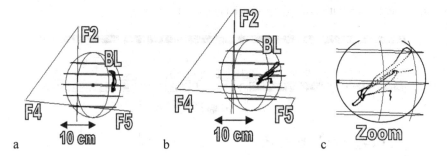

a   b   c

Fig. 14: Front views of marker BL: local trajectories during shrugging (a) and forward-backward motion (b). (c) is an enlargment of (b) trajectory

Fig. 14 explores further the translation characteristics of the markers BL and BH. Their excursion ranges are quantified based on the F4-F5 distance. What is especially noticeable is the regularity of the trajectories highlighting the high correlation between local skin deformation and underlying bone motion. However we have observed sudden displacement of the BH marker in the sagital plane (side view). This artifact possibly comes from the underlying motion of the upper part of the scapula. Unless the scapula motion is of special importance, the region of BH marker should be avoided.

5   Conclusion

This is only one of our first sets of experiences with the analysis of the local trajectories of the markers. The possibility to simultaneously view a movement in several systems of coordinates, makes the decision process clear and efficient (Fig. 15). It provides pertinent feedback on the marker positioning, although highly depending on the quality of the gym motion. Our first conclusion regarding the studied region is that:

❖ Adding more markers (three per segment), definitely helps to improve the local fitting (by selecting and organizing the ones that lead to good estimation),

❖ The scapula joint seems not identifiable with the current optical motion capture methodology. We can however gain a better understanding of the region deformation.

Our results on this type of (i.e. with cyclical movements of independant degrees of mobility) suggest that, in some body regions, there is a strong correlation between skeleton motion and local skin deformation. This is in phase with some observations from Cappozzo in [9]. One approach for the identification of this correlation could be to train a dedicated neural network with the gym motion for each major body region. The result would describe how the marker moves with the skin, as a function of the current posture. Compared with the current assumption of fixed marker w.r.t the underlying bones, we believe such a *marker model* would improve the skeleton identification and the quality of the captured motion. In the near future we plan to focus on the shoulder region with more (and smaller) markers.

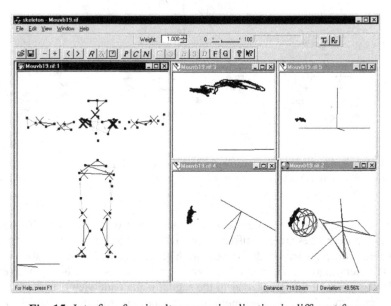

Fig. 15: Interface for simultaneous visualization in different frames

Acknowledgements

We thank our MOCA partner, ACTISYSTEM, for their help in providing test data files as well as our colleagues in LIG for their technical help. The MOCA project was sponsored by the European ESPRIT program. This work is also partly supported by the Swiss Federal Institute of Technology, Lausanne.

References

1. VICON 8: The Manual. Oxford Metrix, January 1999
2. Molet, T., Boulic, R., Thalmann, D.: Human Motion Capture Driven by Orientation Measurements. Presence, MIT, Vol.8, No2, 1999, pp.187-203
3. Gray, S.: Virtual Fashion. IEEE Spectrum, Feb. 98
4. Aggarwal, J. K., and Cai Q.: Human Motion Analysis: A Review. Proceedings, IEEE Nonrigid and Articulated Motion Workshop, June 16,1997, San Juan, Puerto Rico
5. Fua, P., Grün, A., Plänkers, R., D'Apuzzo, N. and Thalmann, D.: Human Body Modeling and Motion Analysis From Video Sequences. International Symposium on Real Time Imaging and Dynamic Analysis, June 2--5, 1998, Hakodate, Japan
6. Veldpaus, F. E., Woltring, H. J., Dortmans, L. J. M. G.: A Least-Square Algorithm for the Equiform transformation from Spatial Marker Co-ordinates. Journal of Biomechanics, 21(1):45-54,1988
7. Bodenheimer, B., Rose, C., Rosenthal, S., Pella, J.: The Process of Motion Capture: Dealing with data. 8th EUROGRAPHICS Int. Workshop on Computer Animation and Simulation'97, Budapest, Hungary, D. Thalmann and M. van de Panne eds., ISBN 3-211-83048-0, Springer-Verlag Wien, pp 3-18
8. O'Brien, J., Bodenheimer, R. E., Brostow, G., Hodgins, J. K.: Automatic Joint Parameter Estimation from Magnetic Motion Capture Data. Proc. of Graphics Interface'2000, pp 53-60, Montreal, Canada
9. Cappozzo, A., Catani, F., Leardini, A., Benedetti, M. G., Della Croce, U.: Position and Orientation in Space of Bones during Movement: Experimental Artefacts. Clinical Biomechanics 11(2), pp 90-100, 1996, Elsevier
10. Cappozzo, A., Cappello, A., Della Croce, U., Pensalfini, F.: Surface-Marker Cluster Design Criteria. IEEE Trans. on Biomedical Engineering 44(12), December 1997
11. Halvorsen, K., Lesser, M., Lundberg, A.: A new Method for Estimating the Axis of Rotation and the Center of Rotation. Technical note, Journal of Biomechanics 32 (1999) 1221-1227, Elsevier
12. Herda, L., Plaenkers, R., Fua, P., Boulic, R., Thalmann, D.: Skeleton-Based Motion Capture for Robust Reconstruction of Human Motion. Proc. of Computer Animation'2000, Philadelphia, May 2000, IEEE Press
13. Silaghi, M-C., Plaenkers, R., Boulic, R., Fua P., Thalmann D.:Local and Global Skeleton Fitting techniques for Optical Motion Capture. (IFIP Workshop on Modelling and Motion Capture Techniques for Virtual Environments) November 26th 1998, Geneva
14. Press, W. H., Flannery, B. P., Teukolsky, S. A., and Vetterling, W. T.: Numerical Recipices, the Art of Scientific Computing. Cambridge U. Press, Cambridge, MA, 1986

Matching a Human Walking Sequence with a VRML Synthetic Model[1]

J. M. Buades, R. Mas and F. J. Perales

Computer Vision & Graphics Group.
Department of Mathematics and Computer Science
University of the Balearic Islands
07071 Palma de Mallorca, Spain
{josemaria,ramon,paco}@anim.uib.es

Abstract - In this paper we present a specific matching technique based on basic motor patterns between two image sequences taken from different view points and a VRML synthetic human model. The criteria used are part of a generic system for the analysis and synthesis of human motion. The system has two phases: an automatic or interactively supervised analysis phase where the motion is interpreted and a synthesis phase where the original motion is applied to a biomechanical model. The main goal of our approach consists of finding a general solution that could be applied to general motor patterns. We define a set of matching conditions and we describe general-purpose criteria in order to reduce the space of search. The complexity of human motion analysis has led researchers to study new approaches and design more robust techniques for human tracking, detection or reconstruction. Whereas mathematical solutions partially solve this problem, the complexity of the algorithms proposed only serve to limit these solutions for real time purposes or general kind of motion types considered. So, we propose more simple, less general approaches but with a low computational cost. In this case the human model information about the kind of movement to be studied is very important in the process of matching between key-frame images. We also try to develop a system that can, at least in part, overcome the limitations of view dependence.

Keywords: detection, tracking and recognition of persons, real and synthetic images, VRML, matching, calibration, graphic and biomechanical model, walking motion.

1   Introduction

Human motion analysis and synthesis are two areas of major interest in a variety of disciplines. Among others we can consider sport analysis, dancer training, choreography, scientific simulation, 3D animation, computer vision, medical rehabilitation, virtual reality and entertainment. There is a great diversity of systems devoted to those disciplines.

---

[1] Supported by the project TIC98-0302 of CICYT

H. H. Nagel and F. J. Perales (Eds.): AMDO 2000, LNCS 1899, pp. 145-158, 2000.

The most largely extended rely on the manual selection of points from the initial sequence of images. The 3D positions, velocities, accelerations and trajectories of the manually selected points are then easily computed. These systems are mainly oriented to capturing the motion parameters. Others systems attach markers - normally semi-spherical markers or infrared sensors - on the human body and they use template matching to automatically detect the positions of the articulations.

In the manual systems, the precision is very dependent on the experience of the user that picks the 2D points. It is an extremely tedious job to pick up points from hundreds or thousands of frames. In the systems that use markers, the inconvenience caused by the small reflectors to the person being tested is obvious. Attaching markers makes it very difficult, if not impossible, to extend the system to applications such as real sport competitions. The systems mentioned above are mostly kinematic. Dynamics-based systems, which deal with torques and forces acting on mass, and hybrid systems that combine kinematics and dynamics [3, 7, 8, 9, 13] are other approaches. We can also find systems that are oriented to modelling motion by using physical laws rather than by capturing the motion parameters.

From a vision view point new approaches have been recently proposed. The temporal-flow models are aimed at learning and estimating temporal flow from image sequences. They use a set of orthogonal temporal-flow bases that are learned using principal component analysis of instantaneous flow measurements. Examples of this kind of models are [14, 15]. Other papers consider a probabilistic decomposition of human dynamics at multiple abstractions, and show how to propagate hypotheses across space, time and abstraction levels. Low-level primitives are areas of coherent motion found by EM clustering, mid-level categories are simple movements represented by dynamic systems, and high-level complex gestures are represented by HMM as successive phases of simple movements. An example of this work is [16]. Based on 3D graphs we can recover and interpret human motion in a scene. This is the case of [12] where a method, based on regular part detection, is presented by which a skeleton is generated. Using 2D regular region, one for each view, with a matching process it is possible to obtain a 3D graph interpretation.

The main goal of our approach consists of finding a general solution that could be applied to motor patterns using specific rules for every kind of pattern. We define a set of matching conditions and we describe general-purpose criteria in order to reduce the space of search.

The system that we propose is based on a kinematic analysis and is non-invasive. The person can move freely without interfering with the system and without the burden imposed by the physical markers. It can be considered to be an automatic, interactive system since it is designed to guide the user in the matching, providing the necessary tools to ease the process and to trace the actual motion of the human body.

To be able to detect the arbitrary motion of objects we restring the problem to just one person without loss of generality. Due to the complexity of the extraction of the motion from a sequence of images, we simplify the problem for our system. Initially we have considered only 3D articulated rigid motion with rotation. But now we present a system that can define matching algorithms for a certain type of motor patterns.

The whole system consists of an analysis part and a synthesis part (Figure 1). The input of the system is a sequence of one or more grey level images taken simultaneously in perspective. The output of the analysis part gives the 3D positions of the body parts at each moment of time from which the trajectories, speeds, accelerations, as well as other parameters of each part are computed. The 3D positions are then visualised with a reconstruction of the human body by the synthesis part. The final output is the synthesised motion of the human body, which should be the same motion represented in the input image. This can be viewed from any viewpoint with all the motion parameters computed for further use. The process of analysis can be done either automatically or manually [5, 12].

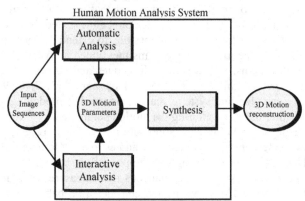

Figure 1. A global view of the human motion analysis system

The main matching job is driven by specific algorithms and with the support of the basic matching conditions of the system to perform the match between the real images and the articulated model. This process is more sophisticated than those used by other systems working with other kinds of entities (points, lines, etc.) on the screen. It has the advantage of working with a higher level entity: a biomechanical model that directly models the human body to be matched.

The interactive analysis part includes a processing-enhancement phase, a modelling phase, a matching phase, and an interpretation phase. Although the processing-enhancement phase in this system is not always necessary but it has to be used in certain cases. The modelling phase lets the user select a biomechanical model from a library of predefined models, or even to define a custom model for the person being tested. All the information measured from the person is stored in the model. Various levels of detail can be defined for visualisation purposes. The goal of the matching phase is to match the projections of the bio mechanic model with the real n-view image sequence (in this case two views). The main strategy is to match the hierarchy of the model as an entity with the image region representing the body position to be detected. The system has full information as to the position and orientation of the 3D-model in each frame of the real image animation [5].

The interpretation phase uses the information from the preceding phases and computes the motion parameters for different parts of the human body. All the information obtained is stored in a database for future use, such as the visualisation of the motion, further analysis of the performance, etc. The synthesis part includes data input and display, which allows the animation and visualisation of the resulting motion. The user has full control over the synthetic camera. Traditional techniques of

Inverse Kinematics and more recent results in Inverse Kinetics [1] can also be used to correct deviations of the resulting postures.

Section 2 briefly introduces the basic ideas of movements founded on basic motor patterns with specific consideration for human walking. Section 3 describes the criteria for walking matching. The application of the criteria of overlapped surface maximisation is in section 4. Finally we use the temporal coherence criterion to recover from a wrong matching (section 5) and we present, in section 6 and 7, the results and new ideas for future work.

2   Motion Founded on Basic Motor Patterns

In the general cases described in [2, 5], the information related to the motion was kinematic, in the sense that we know the approximate displacements of certain segments, but these neither represent a typical movement of the individual nor cause a large displacement of the centre of mass, e.g., a global human body motion. When considering the study of a motion of this type, it becomes necessary to do it on a characteristic movement of the human body. Therefore, walking is considered the most representative basic motor pattern of this kind of movements. Other types of patterns (e.g., running, leaping, throwing, grabbing, hitting, kicking, reaching, etc.) will be studied in future works. We are also very interested in the transition between different movements.

A common characteristic of these motion patterns is the combination of the organised movements according to a specific space-temporal setting. Our goal is to carry out a study of the basic patterns of walking from the analysis of image sequences obtained by a pair of synchronised cameras and a human biomechanical model.

Human walking is a very complex activity. It is a learned activity and is integrated with involuntary actions although it cannot be considered as an automatic activity. Walking undergoes several modifications according to the parameters considered (shoes, ground, load, activity, etc.). For correctness, we will assume that the individual is a western, walking barefoot on a flat floor.

Our objective is centred exclusively on the kinematic analysis of the movement, considering that the person moves its body from one point to another in the space. The body is reduced to a mass point (centre of mass) that is transformed by translations and rotations. The body components define a kinematic pattern which is characteristic of a movement cycle. This cycle is divided into two parts. The stance (foot-floor contact) phase and the swing (foot elevation to create the new step) phase.

Several studies have been carried out on walking, and human movement in general, from different points of view [2, 3, 4, 6]. Several of these studies obtained good results and allowed us to define a new sequence of representative charts and values of the types of trajectories that the different body segments go through during the walking cycle. Unfortunately, these studies, except recent approaches [5, 10, 12, 14], use techniques of data collection based on manual selection - either by digitalisation of points of interest on the film or by the use of measurement equipment (goniometers). Other systems try to model the motion from a synthesis viewpoint, and we have recently seen specific research for concrete motion patterns [7, 8, 13]. Also from a computer vision perspective, we can use colour information [10] or knowledge of person's movement in order to track unconstrained human movement [11]. Recent publications propose the use of contextual knowledge encoded in the higher level models [14],or learned temporal models [15,16].

Our system is aimed at carrying out an automatic adjustment of the defined model using real images that have been previously filmed. Under the context of manual positioning we can obtain motion information in the initial phase of each individual in order to position the first walking cycle.

The first phase will be useful as a control phase and matching with the previous or posterior phases, and will give us specific information on each subject. The obtained values are validated so that the digitalisation process generates point trajectories that agree with the work done by other researchers. The adjustment of basic movement patterns greatly differs from the use on 2D and 3D movements. Conceptually, it is impossible to consider an exhaustive search of the positions in space of all the articulated models. On the other hand, these movements have several occlusions or overlappings that make the process of conventional matching (surface maximisation) difficult.

The proposed alternative considers working with a finite number of N positions of the walking cycle that have been selected by a semiautomatic process from the control cycle defined for each individual. Then, a matching between the model position and the image projections is established, not only based on a possible overlapping of the surfaces but also on the information of the specific characteristics of the movement studied (walking, in this case). This implies that a relationship between the primitives obtained from the images and the biomechanical restrictions of the movement must be established.

The system must be able to allow for oscillations or variations over the basic defined cycle, although these must be relatively small, for the time being. The result will be a objective matching among the N positions of the basic cycle and the considered images.

On the other hand, we present the model graphs overlaid for the cases manually studied in our system. For this manual study we consider a step cycle (right-to-left and left-to-right) and a non-fast natural walking. For the known values, the mean cycle duration is 0.87 seconds with a variation of 0.06 seconds. For normal walking it is 1.06 seconds with a variation of 0.09 seconds. We study a typical value for the natural walking cycle of 1 second. In our case, 36 images (1.44 s.) are studied for one cycle, thus the walking is paused normal.

3   Criteria for Walking Adjustment

This section introduces the criteria needed to carry out an adjustment of the biomechanical model defined on the walking subject projections. The goal is to find a typical parameter sequence for walking, from the image projections that allow us to establish some criteria for discrimination between the model projections and the real images.A first approach to the problem makes us try the same criterion (already used in conventional adjustment, but with different goals) of studying the evolution of the bounding boxes that contain the subject on both views. From the boxes, we could study features of the width, height and area functions on each of them, on the frontal and lateral views. Once these representations are obtained, it is necessary to find the possible relationships or parameters that are important in order to establish a process or pre-selection. The values and charts of these functions are shown in the results section. The frontal view does not allow us to deduce any relationship or dependency among the plots of the studied functions and the key images that we wish to select. When the subject moves towards the camera, its size increases, and therefore so does its height, its width and its area functions. This process hides the possible variations due to the movement, and we can not establish a clear selection process. The lateral view is more meaningful. The distance between the subject and the camera is not significantly modified when walking. So, the variations of the functions considered above are due to the movement pattern itself. If we observe the lateral view (Figure 2a), we can clearly see that there are two minima and three maxima along the studied cycle. The height function is opposite, but the variations are smaller, and they are more error prone. The area function does not give any additional information (it depends on the width function). When we observe the walking cycle images, it is noticed that the swing phase corresponds to the minima of the width function on the lateral view and, similarly, the zones for the stance phase correspond to its maxima.

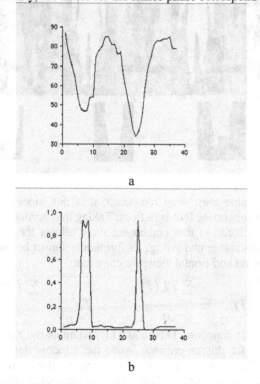

a

b

Figure 2. The lateral view width (a) and maximum swing (b) functions

This first approach to the problem allows us to solve it by reducing it to the initial adjustment of the key images. Then, we want to extend this matching to the sequence remainder using a temporal coherence criterion. By exploiting these special points of the cycle, we see that the subject in the stance phase has his/her both feet in contact with the ground, while in the second phase, a foot swings or moves forward to create a new step. By taking into account this characteristic we could define a function that has a maximum when the feet are in the stance phase and has a minimum when they are in the swing phase. This function computes the transition subject-background from left to right on a window (of N pixels) on the bounding box for the subject from the lateral view. This feature is also useful from the frontal view. The difference with respect to the lateral view resides in that, in this case, the maxima are associated to the swing phase and the minima to the stance phase. Another useful feature of the frontal view that allows us to discriminate the key images more clearly is the vertical pixel height difference between the two legs. In other words, the difference between the minimum value of each leg is larger for the stance phase and smaller for the swing phase (see next examples).

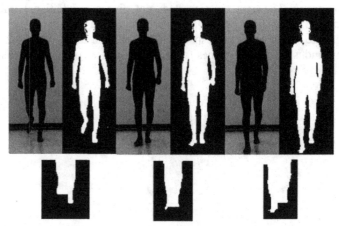

Although this value may seem redundant, it is not, since its sign allows us to distinguish which supporting foot is in front. Taking into account all these parameters, a function was defined, so that combining them allows the discrimination of the points of maximum stance and swing. Its formula is shown below. For the transition function of the lateral and frontal view, we compute:

$$TL = \frac{\sum\limits_{i=1}^{N} TL(i)}{n} \qquad\qquad TF = \frac{\sum\limits_{i=1}^{N} TF(i)}{n}$$

Where the generic functions TF(i) and TL(i) compute the number of background-subject transitions for this co-ordinate inside the window defined in the frontal or lateral view, and N is the number of pixels of the selected window.

A value considered adequate for N is 30 pixels, thus obtaining the following values for the functions defined above.

$$TLn(Maximun) \approx 2 \quad (stance \quad phase) \qquad TL_n(Minimun) \approx 1 \quad (swing \quad phase)$$

$$TF_n(Maximun) \approx 2 \quad (swing \quad phase) \qquad TF_n(Minimun) \approx 1 \quad (stance \quad phase)$$

Similarly, the difference between the minimum of each leg is defined as:

$$DP_{Legs} = (MinVal(PI) - MinVal(PD))$$

Where PI is the minimum co-ordinate calculated in the Y axis for the left leg and PD is the same for the right leg. This value can be positive or negative, its magnitude is used for the discrimination of stances and swings and its sign to know which foot is in front. Based on empirical discriminate tests, we define a suitable function that uses the three parameters described above and that allows for a correct classification of swings and stances:

$$MaxBal_{(TL_N, TF_N, DP_{Legs})} = \left| \left(\frac{TF_N - TL_N}{DP_{Legs}} \right) \right|$$

The function shown in Figure 2b generates two evident maxima that turn these images into candidates as key images for swings. By analogy and based on the same tests, we define a discrimination function for the stance maxima. It is reduced to the following formula:

$$MaxApo_{(TL_N, TF_N, DP_{Legs})} = (TF + TL) \times DP_{Legs}$$

With this function, we do not get as good a selection as in the case above, although we get a not too large sequence of candidate images that will be tested later on by more complex criteria. We should remark that this study is aimed at reducing the number of candidate images for key images. Then, it does not have to yield a unique solution. On the other hand, in the last case the difficulty in finding a discriminatory function can be related to the nature of the movement as it is slower in the stance phase than in the swing phase. This is the reason by which the variations of the studied parameters are also smaller, and therefore, there are more images near the maxima. Figure 3 represents the function of the maximum stances. In this figure, we can also see the minima correspond to the maxima of the swing function.

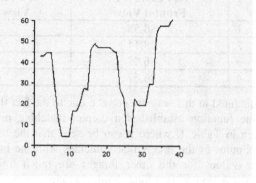

Figure 3. The maximum stance function

4. Application of the Criterion of Overlapped Surface Maximisation

Based on the previous process, the following step implies defining the adjustment criterion using condition C2 (overlapping condition [see 5] for a further explanation) to find the function of maximum overlapping on each view for the model and for its corresponding image. This criterion is applied over all tree nodes, since the motion to study implies a displacement of the centre of mass and, therefore, a motion of almost all nodes in the structure. For each model instance, there must exist an image that implies a very high value of the overlapping function on both views. This function measures the percentage of overlapped area in the image plane for each node, dividing the resulting value by the number of nodes considered. Obviously, the application of this function reduces the candidate images from the previous process.

Initially, we assign to each model its own image as a possible candidate, but the evaluation of the function is extended to the nearest neighbours. As a result, for each model, we must evaluate the overlapping function over the set of candidate images. This should be done for each view and the maximum of the function must be selected. The function to evaluate is

$$MaxSol_{N,I,J} = \frac{\sum_{k=1}^{N} F_I^J(k)}{N}$$

Where N is the number of considered model nodes, I is the instantiation of a model at time t, J is the corresponding candidate image, and represents the function that calculates the common area between the model and the object on the image plane.

For the computed examples and based on the previous plotting, the models are evaluated over a reduced image set (3 or 4), while the number of nodes can vary from 12 (only the most important whose areas are above 100 pixels) until considering all possible ones (24 nodes).

Table 1. Overlapping functions

M	I	%OVERLAPPING Frontal View	%OVERLAPPING View Lateral
1	1	88,58	95,31
1	2	88,14	77,97
1	3	86,47	60,97
1	4	86,57	60,97

The results obtained in this way are correct, due to the fact that the selection of the maximum of the function establishes a correct matching most of the time. One example is given in Table 1, where it can be seen that the overlapping function is evidently a maximum of the image that coincides with the model, from the lateral view, while the values for the other images are much lower. In this table, M represents an instantiation of the biomechanical model, and I represents the candidate image. From the frontal view, this criterion is not useful, and is not applied because the differences, in most of the cases, are very small. The remainder of the tests and results is discussed in the following section.

5   Application of the Temporal Coherence Criterion

Although previous results show that the function can discriminate the images in most cases, there are several situations where it could happen that the selection does not match the model. This means that, for a given model, its image does not have the same order in the sequence. To verify whether this matching is correct or not, the criterion of temporal coherence (C5 condition, see more details in [5]) is used over the sequence. This implies defining a window from the candidate image and evaluating the model instances over such a window under the assumption of the initial matching. This extension implies evaluating the following expression:

$$MaxSol_{T,N,I,J} = \frac{\sum\limits_{l=1}^{T}\sum\limits_{k=1}^{N} H_I^J (F_I^J (k),l)}{N*T}$$

Where $H_I^J (x,y)$ represents the function of temporal coherence and T is a

defined window that in the cases evaluated can vary from 3 to 9 images. If we evaluate those percentages, we see that the coherence is reduced (85 %) when an inadequate selection is made, thus the system selects the second candidate from the previous step, and applies the coherence getting a better value (around 96 %) than before. This process is repeated until an image is found with a coherence that is above an acceptable threshold (typically set to 95%). With this criterion, we make sure that the matching over the key images is the best, rejecting possible incorrect matching from the previous step. These matching are, most of the time, the results of the similarity of some images in the intervals where the movement is slower (stance phase). In Tables 2 and 3 we can see one case of wrong matching and its correction. The initial matching defines a link of model 8 with image 9. On applying the temporal coherence criterion, we see that the percentage drops below the acceptable threshold (95%). Therefore, another image is searched for (image 8) getting the optimal percentage.

Table 2.

M	I	%OVERLAP VF	%OVERLAP VL
8	7	91,61	87,88
8	8	92,79	96,57
8	9	92,42	96,81

Table 3.

M	I	%OVERLAP VL(3)	%OVERLAP VL(5)	%OVERLAP VL(7)	%OVERLAP VL(9)
8	9	86,67	88,77	84,99	85,80
8	8	96,92	96,48	95,95	95,96

The temporal coherence is applied exclusively to the lateral view. As can be deduced, the overlapping percentage is not optimal but it does not drop notoriously when the window is enlarged. This is because the movement is cyclic and symmetrical and some mismatches are balanced. Anyway, in certain images of the temporal window the average percentages are low (around 60 %, and for some segments, 0%) with respect to the optimal (around 95%).

The result of this process is a set of models matched with real images that satisfy the defined conditions on the adjustment criteria. From this matching, the adjustment is extended to the rest of the images in the sequence studied.

6   Results

The experiments have been performed using the C programming language on Silicon Graphics workstations. The first version was more oriented towards solving automatic matching. Now we have a semi-automatic version with a friendly interface. Due to the nature of the users of the system, we designed a friendly, graphical user interface. What is more, for portability purposes we converted our model into a VRML model so we can see the movement on a commercial browser. Here we present a reduced set of images with the corresponding matched model for a walking sequence. The lateral and frontal matched images are presented. Obviously, the recovered matching can be viewed from every point.

7   Conclusions on the Walking Analysis Methodology and Future Work

In this paper we have presented an interactive analysis and synthesis matching system for the detection of human walking motion. The analysis part of the system analyses the sequence of two-view input images to detect the 3D spatial information in each image frame. The process is a supervised matching unit that combines real and synthetic images. As the synthesis part allows for the playback of the detected motion of the human body, it is possible to use the results obtained for further analysis of the motion. We have presented a set of matching conditions and criteria for general purposes.

For specific motor patterns we must define new strategies to reduce the space of search for the matching process. The complexity of a movement which is as sophisticated as human walking forces us to use the adjustment criterion and to focus on the need to use the knowledge and features of the model analyzed. An exhaustive search (as in the 2-dimensional case of simple movements) is obviously impossible, thus an empirical model is introduced that transforms a set of infinite combinations to one of N previously set positions, neither does using 3D-graph matching approximation solve the problem [12] in complex movements. Our system is less robust than those based on learned temporal models [15, 16] but the complexity is also reduced and, for the movements studied, good matching is obtained.

The next goal is to establish a matching between these N positions of the model and the real images based on its parameters that satisfy a set of restrictions. We aim to integrate a balance criteria restriction in order to increase the rate of convergence to the solution. The results obtained are very encouraging, the system is able to carry out the matching on all of the proposed cases. Nevertheless, it does not actually allow a variation of the rotation parameters of each articulation. This would be useful to define a new adaptive system that could adjust to the changes in the rhythms of walking and even to transitions to other movements (walking-running, or vice versa). We are now evaluating these changes and how the matching functions must be modified. We are also working on a possible integration of an analysis-synthesis system that uses physical criteria to extract human motion but with a feedback control system that uses image processing and includes contextual knowledge in order to reduce the search space.

Either way, the system can easily detect a variation if we consider the ability to control the overlapping function. We always require a minimum level of condition satisfaction. What we also wonder is what the criterion to keep such a level could be? Evidently, our results are conditioned to the situation in which segmented images do not have large errors that could notoriously affect the evaluation functions. The criteria applied are also exclusive for the selected views (lateral and frontal), so a change of camera position implies a search for new discriminatory parameters. We must also be careful with occlusion and overlapping of different parts of the body. We have already developed some basic criteria to solve specific cases of overlapping and occlusions but we consider them to be out of the scope of this paper. We are also working with multiple views (3 b/n cameras and 2 colour cameras) and robust estimation using Kalman filtering for tracking blobs as in [14] but using full information at a high level.

On the other hand, it is necessary to somehow validate the results obtained manually, to guarantee their correction. The validation has been done by comparing the results obtained with other works. Plots for the most important nodes analyzed agree with the works mentioned as all of the values are within acceptable limits.

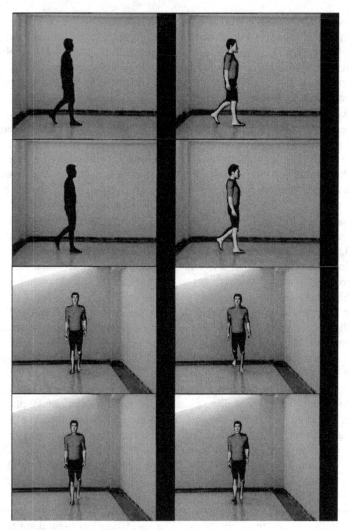

Figure 5. Walking part

References

[1]   Boulic R., Mas R., Thalmann D., Complex Character Positioning Based on a Compatible Flow Model of Multiple Supports, IEEE Transactions on Visualization and Computer Graphics, Vol.3, num.3, pp 245-261, 1997.

[2]   Boulic R., Thalmann N., Thalmman D. A global human walking model with real-time kinematic personification. The Visual Computer, 6, pp.344-358, 1990.

[3]   Boulic R., R. Mas, Inverse Kinetics for Center of Mass Position Control and Posture Optimization, Technical Report N. 94/68, Sep. 1994. Dept. Informatique. Ecole Polytechnique Federale de Lausanne.

[4]   Goddard N., Incremental Model-Based Discrimination of Articulated Movement from Motion Features, IEEE Computer Society Workshop on Motion of Non-Rigid and Articulated Objects, November 11-12, 1994, Austin Texas.

[5]   Perales F., J. Torres, A system for human motion matching between synthetic and real images based ona biomechanical graphical model, IEEE Computer Society Workshop on Motion of Non-Rigid and Articulated Objects, November 11-12, 1994, Austin Texas.

[6]   Van de Panne M. Parameterized Gait Synthesis, IEEE Computer Graphics and Applications. pp. 40-49, March 1996.

[7]   Wooten, W. L., Hodgins J. K., Animation of Human Diving, Computer Graphics Forum, Volume 15, number 1, pp. 3-13, 1996.

[8]   Wooten, W. L., Hodgins J. K., Brogan D., O'Brien , Animating Human Athletics, Siggraph Computer Graphics Proceedings, Annual Conference Series, ACM pp. 71-78, 1995.

[9]   N. Badler, C. Phillips, B. Webber. Simulating Humans. Computer Graphics Animation and Control. Oxford University Press, 1993.

[10]   C. Wren, A. Azarbayejani, T. Darrell, A. Pentland. "Pfinder: Real-Time Tracking of the Human Body". IEEE Transactions on Pattern Analysis and Machine Intelligence, vol. 19, no. 7, pp 780-785.

[11]   D. M. Gravila and L. S. Davis. 3-D model-based tracking of humans in action: A multi-view approach, Computer Vision Laboratory, Proc. CVPR,. Pag 73-80, IEEE, 1996.

[12]   C. Yáñiz, J. Rocha, F. Perales. "3D Part Recognition Method for Human Motion Analysis". CAPTECH '98 Modelling and Motion Capture Techniques for Virtual Environments. pp 41-55.

[13]   Jessica K. Hodgins, Nancy S. Pollard. "Adapting Simulated Behaviors For New Characters". Computer Graphics Proceedings, 1997 pp. 153-162

[14]   Christopher R. Wren, Alex P. Pentland. "Understanding Purposeful Human Motion", Submitted to ICCV 1999

[15]   Y. Yacoob, and L. Davis, Learned Temporal Models of Image Motion ICCV-98,Mumbai, India, 1998, 446-453.

[16]   M. Black and Y. Yacoob, A. Jepson and D. Fleet, Learning Parameterized Models of Image Motion, IEEE CVPR 97, San Juan-PR, 1997, 561-567.

Model Adaptation and Posture Estimation of Moving Articulated Object Using Monocular Camera

N. Shimada[1], Y. Shirai[1], and Y. Kuno[1,2]

[1] Dept. of Computer-Controlled Mechanical Systems, Osaka University
2-1 Yamadaoka, Suita, Osaka, 565-0871, Japan
shimada@mech.eng.osaka-u.ac.jp
[2] Dept. of Information and Computer Sciences, Saitama University
255, Shimo-okubo, Urawa, Saitama 338-8570, Japan

Abstract. This paper presents a method of estimating both 3-D shapes and moving poses of an articulated object from a monocular image sequence. Instead of using direct depth data, prior loose knowledge about the object, such as possible ranges of joint angles, lengths or widths of parts, and some relationships between them, are referred as system constraints. This paper first points out that the estimate by Kalman filter essentially converge to a wrong state for non-linear unobservable systems. Thus the paper proposes an alternative method based on a set-membership-based estimation including dynamics. The method limits the depth ambiguity by considering loose constraint knowledge represented as inequalities and provides the shape recovery of articulated objects. Effectiveness of the framework is shown by experiments.

1 Introduction

In general, the 3-D shape of a non-rigid object cannot be recovered with only one camera even if an image sequence is given. For a certain class of objects like human bodies, however, depth information can be recovered from a monocular camera data if adequate prior knowledge about the shape and structure is available. For example, we can build a structure model of a human body by assuming that its joint motions are related with each other and there are rough correlations between the sizes of body parts. Given such constraints, depth estimation can be broken down into a least squares problem [ ][ ]. Particularly, Kalman filter and its variation for non-linear systems (Extended Kalman filter) are considered to give estimates with good accuracy and popularly applied to estimate an object's shape or pose parameters. If the constraints are rough to be represented by inequalities, this method cannot be applied because the original EKF cannot deal with the inequalities. Shimada et.al [ ] recovered the joint angles and the finger lengths from a monocular image sequence using an EKF variation handling the inequalities by distribution truncation.

In addition, Kalman filter has an essential problem. Although it can give correct estimates only for linear systems and non-linear observable systems, its

H. H. Nagel and F. J. Perales (Eds.): AMDO 2000, LNCS 1899, pp. 159– , 2000.
© Springer-Verlag Berlin Heidelberg 2000

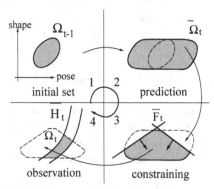

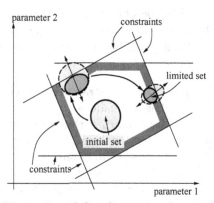

Fig.1. Incremental update of parameter set

Fig.2. Possibility limitation by constraint knowledge

estimate converges to a wrong state due to approximation error in linearization for non-linear unobservable systems. As an alternative way, the paper proposes an estimation method based on *set-membership estimation*. In EKF, the ambiguity of the estimate is described by the estimate covariance In the set-membership methods, a possible parameter set described by its boundary is used for representing the estimate ambiguity, which is represented by the estimate covariance in EKF. In this paper, the combination of the ellipsoidal description[ ][ ] and a rectangular description is proposed. In order to estimate time-varying parameters, the proposed framework introduces an updating scheme by dynamics. Since this method does not calculates probabilistic integration but an intersection set of possible parameters, it can provide more accurate estimation than EKF because it can avoid the accumulation of linearization error. For this ability, loose constraint knowledge such as possible ranges of lengths, widths or joint angles are available to estimate the shape and pose of articulated objects. While the set-membership-based approach has these merits, it is well-known that it has a drawback of the weakness against outliers. Here we concentrate on describing the integration scheme at each time-frame supposing the existence of a outlier rejection method.

In the following sections, the basic idea is first explained and the details are described later. Finally effectiveness of the method is shown by estimation results for an articulated object.

2   Basic Idea

Although monocular imaging systems have unobservability of depth in shape estimation of non-rigid objects, they can estimate depth information if prior knowledge is additionally available. For example, we can recover a human body by approximating it as an articulated object which consists of rigid body parts linked each other and by assuming the following constraints.

(a) Shape parameters (lengths and widths) are constant over an image sequence.
(b) Pose parameters (joint angles and orientation) change continuously.
(c) Each parameter is within a certain range and has relations with other parameters.

Note that these constraints include not only equations but also loose constraints described as inequalities.

Fig. summarizes the basic idea of parameter estimation with these constraints under "unobservable" systems . A vector space of parameters describing shape and pose is first considered and an initial possible parameter set Ω_{t-1} is supposed. Then a predicted set $\tilde{\Omega}_t$ is generated by shifting and diffusing the initial set based on the object's dynamics and its noise. When an observation data is obtained from each image, a parameter set $\bar{H}$ satisfying the observation is considered. Another set $\bar{F}$ satisfying the constraint knowledge is considered as well. Then the updated possible parameter set Ω_t is obtained as an intersection of the three parameter sets. This process is repeated for each image observation. The important point is that the constraint knowledge has an effect to limit unobservable modes as illustrated in Fig. . Until the parameter set intersects with any boundary of the constraints, the system is still unobservable and the ambiguity remains. Once it intersects with a constraint boundary, however, the possible parameter set is limited to only the inside of the boundary. If any parameters are supposed to be constant, such as lengths or widths of rigid parts, the ranges of these parameters should monotonously decrease. As the result of iterative intersection with boundaries during sequential observations, ranges of any parameters including unobservable modes can be limited.

3 Limit of EKF Estimation

3.1 Non-linear Unobservable System

The idea described in the previous section is naturally implemented in a state estimation framework of Kalman filter or its non-linear version (Extended Kalman filter, EKF). Shimada et al. utilized EKF to implement the idea [ ].

Suppose the transition and observation formulas of a system represented as

$$x_{t+1} = Ax_t + Bu_t \tag{1}$$
$$y_t = h(x_t) + w_t \tag{2}$$

where y_t is an observation vector. u_t and w_t are white noises with zero mean and variances U, W. The components of U for time-invariant shape parameters are zeros. If the observation function $h(\cdot)$ is non-linear, the current state $\hat{x}_t$ and variance P_t are approximately estimated by EKF:

---

[1] The term "unobservability" is used in the control theory. It means that there are states which cannot be discriminated by any observation sequences.

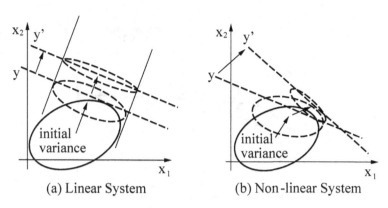

(a) Linear System   (b) Non-linear System

Fig. 3. Linearization error for non-linear unobservable systems

$$\hat{x}_t = \tilde{x}_t + K_t\{y_t - h(\tilde{x}_t)\} \tag{3}$$

$$P_t = (I - K_t h'(\tilde{x}_t))(AP_{t-1}A^T + BUB^T) \tag{4}$$

where K_t is a Kalman gain matrix and $\tilde{x}_t = A\hat{x}_{t-1}$.

EKF is recognized as the estimator to achieve good accuracy. It is correct for linear KF, but not for EKF. Actually the EKF estimate for non-linear unobservable systems essentially converges to a wrong state under a certain condition. Fig.   illustrates the reason. In linear systems, the direction of a hyper-plane satisfying a certain observation y is invariant. Therefore the co-variance ellipsoid decreases only in the observable directions and ambiguity of unobservable modes is properly preserved. In contrast, the direction of the hyper-plane depends on the linearizing point in non-linear systems. Therefore the variance ellipsoid is destined to shrink in any directions even if the system is actually unobservable. When all parameters are time-varying, this is not a serious problem because the erroneous shrinkage is swallowed up by the variance increase in any directions at each time step due to the system transition noise. However, it is fatal for systems including time-invariant parameters such as a length or width of rigid objects. When constant observations only perturbed by noise are obtained, the EKF estimate converges into a wrong state as shown in Fig.   . The vertical bars mean the range of 2 standard deviation. Once the wrong conversion occurs, the estimate is difficult to modify due to too small variance even if observations containing new information are obtained. Then tracking fails as a result. Fig.   shows such a failure example for a 3-link arm in 2-D in which the black circle denotes the fixed origin of the arm and the open circles corresponds to the link-joints or the most proximal tip of the arm.

3.2   Inequality Constraints

The constraints (b) and (c) introduced in section 2 include loose constraints represented as inequalities. Although the equation constraints can be treated as

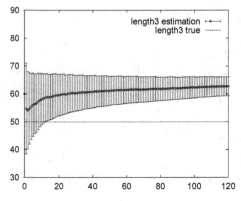

Fig. 4. Wrong conversion

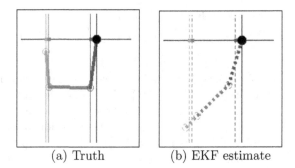

(a) Truth   (b) EKF estimate

Fig. 5. Wrong Estimate by EKF

an observation with a zero variance in the EKF framework, inequalities cannot be dealt in such a simple way. Hel-Or el.al[ ] modified the inequality constraints to quadratic equations with slack variables to linearize them. The linearized constraints, however, are quite different from the original ones. Another way is to introduce the constraints as an initial distribution. It is also inappropriate because the effect of the initial distribution decreases at every frame.

4   Possibility Reduction Based on Set-Membership

4.1   Ellipsoidal Boundary Description

The set-membership methods are known as a way to estimate an unknown system parameters from a sequence of input signals and the corresponding output of the system under bounded signal errors. The methods represent a possible parameter set as intervals of each parameter[ ], a polygon[ ] or an ellipsoid[ ] in

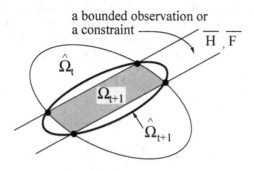

Fig. 6. Update of ellipsoidal set-membership

a high-dimensional vector space. Fogel et al.[ ] formulated a set updating with an ellipsoidal initial set and a linear observation with bounded noise.

Suppose an initial ellipsoid $\widehat{\Omega}_t$ described as

$$(x_t - q_t)^T P_t^{-1}(x_t - q_t) \leq 1 \tag{5}$$

and a parameter set $\bar{H}$ satisfying a noise-bounded observation as

$$|m_i^T x_t - \rho_i| \leq c_i. \tag{6}$$

The latter means the region between two hyper-planes. A parameter set $\bar{F}$ satisfying an inequality constraint is described as well. A certain ellipsoid $\widehat{\Omega}_{t+1}$ covering whole the intersection set Ω_{t+1} between $\widehat{\Omega}_t$ and $\bar{H}(\bar{F})$ (see Fig.   ) can be represented with $\lambda \geq 0$ as

$$(x_t - q_t)^T P_t^{-1}(x_t - q_t) + \lambda(m_i^T x_t - \rho_i)^2 \leq 1 + \lambda c_i^2. \tag{7}$$

which can be reformed to the form of Eq.   . Using a criterion minimizing $\mathrm{tr} P_{t+1}$, λ achieving the smallest ellipsoid is the real root of

$$\beta_1 \lambda^3 + \beta_2 \lambda^2 + \beta_3 \lambda + \beta_4 = 0 \tag{8}$$

where

$$\begin{aligned}
\beta_1 &= G^2 c_i^2 (\mu G - \gamma), \\
\beta_2 &= 3G c_i^2 (\mu G - \gamma), \\
\beta_3 &= G\mu(3c_i^2 - \varepsilon^2) - \gamma\{2(c_i^2 - \varepsilon) + G\}, \\
\beta_4 &= \mu(c_i^2 - \varepsilon^2) - \gamma, \\
\mu &= \mathrm{tr} P_t, \\
\gamma &= m_i^T P_t^2 m_i, \\
G &= m_i^T P_t m_i, \\
\varepsilon &= \rho_i - m_i^T q_t.
\end{aligned} \tag{9}$$

It can be proved that Eq.   always has one real root and two imaginary roots. In addition, if the real root is negative, the minimal $\mathrm{tr}\boldsymbol{P}_{t+1}$ in the domain of $\lambda \geq 0$ is achieved at $\lambda = 0$ (the details of the proof are described in [ ]). Finally, the updated ellipsoid is described in the form of Eq.   by

$$\boldsymbol{q}_{t+1} = \boldsymbol{q}_t + \lambda \boldsymbol{Y} \boldsymbol{m}_i \varepsilon,$$
$$\boldsymbol{P}_{t+1} = z\boldsymbol{Y} \tag{10}$$

where

$$\boldsymbol{Y} = \boldsymbol{P}_t - \lambda \frac{\boldsymbol{P}_t \boldsymbol{m}_i \boldsymbol{m}_i^T \boldsymbol{P}_t^T}{1 + \lambda G},$$
$$z = 1 + \lambda c_i^2 - \frac{\lambda \varepsilon^2}{1 + \lambda G}. \tag{11}$$

Since this method does not calculate a probability variance but a boundary of the intersection, the parameter set should keep its size even if almost the same observations are repeatedly obtained.

4.2   Extension to Dynamic Systems

Most conventional set-membership methods contained no dynamic mechanism [ ] or treated dynamics for low dimensional systems using a simple interval description [ ]. While update by dynamics can be easily introduced into such interval descriptions, it is unable to represent correlations between each parameter. In addition, the set description is inaccurate. The ellipsoidal set-membership can be easily updated in high dimensional systems and has the ability to describe correlations. Thus we introduce a dynamics and prediction phase into the ellipsoid-based method.

Suppose a dynamics of the system is given as Eq.   and the system noise $\boldsymbol{u}_t$ is bounded as

$$\boldsymbol{u}_t^T \boldsymbol{U}^{-1} \boldsymbol{u}_t \leq 1. \tag{12}$$

In the $(\boldsymbol{x}_t, \boldsymbol{u}_t)$ space, a certain ellipsoid including all of the parameters satisfying Eqs.   and   can be represented as

$$(\boldsymbol{x}_t - \boldsymbol{q}_t)^T \boldsymbol{P}_t^{-1} (\boldsymbol{x}_t - \boldsymbol{q}_t) + \lambda \boldsymbol{u}_t^T \boldsymbol{U}^{-1} \boldsymbol{u}_t \leq 1 + \lambda \tag{13}$$

where $\lambda \geq 0$. Combining this and Eq. ,

$$\boldsymbol{q}_{t+1} = \boldsymbol{A}\boldsymbol{q}_t \tag{14}$$
$$\boldsymbol{P}_{t+1} = (1 + \lambda)\boldsymbol{A}\boldsymbol{P}_t\boldsymbol{A}^T + (1 + \frac{1}{\lambda})\boldsymbol{B}\boldsymbol{U}\boldsymbol{B}^T \tag{15}$$

is obtained. See Appendix for details. Here, using a criterion which minimizing $\mathrm{tr}\boldsymbol{P}_{t+1}$, the smallest ellipsoid is given by

$$\lambda = \sqrt{\frac{\mathrm{tr}(\boldsymbol{B}\boldsymbol{U}\boldsymbol{B}^{\mathrm{T}})}{\mathrm{tr}(\boldsymbol{A}\boldsymbol{P}_t\boldsymbol{A}^{\mathrm{T}})}}. \tag{16}$$

After this predictional update, the observations and constraints are integrated in the way described in section 4.1.

4.3   Maximum and Minimum Bounds

In updating by Eq.   , the parameter set can be represented as an small ellipsoid if c_i is small enough compared to the size of the original ellipsoid. Otherwise, the updated ellipsoid tends to include a large region outside the true intersection Ω_t. Fogel et al.[ ] added a pre-process: when any of the two hyper-plane boundaries of Eq.   does not intersect with the ellipsoid to update, ρ_i and c_i are modified so that the non-intersecting hyper-plane is tangent to the ellipsoid. However, if the ellipsoid to update highly sticks out of the hyper-plane boundary, the new ellipsoid simply updated by Eq.   is almost the same as the original ellipsoid.

In our method, the maximum and minimum values of each component of x are calculated by controlling λ in Eq. . The maximum and minimum in direction $n(|n| = 1)$ are obtained by substituting a new criterion minimizing $n^T P_{t+1} n$ for minimizing $\mathrm{tr} P_{t+1}$. λ achieving that criterion is obtained by solving Eq. where

$$\beta_1 = G^2 c_i (GK - L^2)$$
$$\beta_2 = 3Gc_i^2(GK - L^2)$$
$$\beta_3 = GK(3c_i^2 - e^2) + L^2(2e^2 - 2c_i^2 - G)$$
$$\beta_4 = (c_i^2 - e^2)K - L^2$$
$$K = n^T P_t n$$
$$L = m_i^T P_t m_i. \tag{17}$$

The maximum $x_{max}^{(t)}$ and minimum $x_{min}^{(t)}$ are obtained by

$$x_{min}(n) = n^T s - \sqrt{n^T Q n} \tag{18}$$
$$x_{max}(n) = n^T s + \sqrt{n^T Q n} \tag{19}$$
$$s = q_t + \lambda Y m_i \varepsilon \tag{20}$$
$$Q = zY \tag{21}$$

where z and Y are given by Eq. . If x_{max} and x_{min} for any n can be calculated, a convex hull of the true intersection set Ω_{t+1} is obtained. Since systems for articulated objects have much high dimensions, each coordinate axis of the parameter space is used as a representative. Whenever an observation is obtained and the ellipsoid is updated in time t, $x_{min}^{(t)}$ and $x_{max}^{(t)}$ for each parameter are calculated and then max $(x_{min}^{(t)}, x_{min}^{(t-1)})$ and min$(x_{max}^{(t)}, x_{max}^{(t-1)})$ are preserved. At the final stage of each update, a constraint in the form of Eq.   is made from $x_{min}^{(t)}$ and $x_{max}^{(t)}$ and the ellipsoid is updated by the constraint in the way of Eq.   .

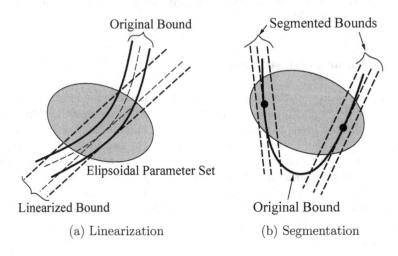

(a) Linearization   (b) Segmentation

Fig. 7. Compensation for non-linearity of bound

4.4   Compensation for Non-linearity of Bounds

In the previous section, we summarize our set-membership-based estimation supposing the observation and constraint formulas are linear as Eq.   . Since they are
actually highly non-linear like Eq.   , they need to be approximated as a linear
form:

$$ \boldsymbol{y}_t = \boldsymbol{h}'(\tilde{\boldsymbol{x}}_t)(\boldsymbol{x}_t - \tilde{\boldsymbol{x}}_t) + \boldsymbol{h}(\tilde{\boldsymbol{x}}_t) + \boldsymbol{w}_t. \tag{22} $$

Since this approximation includes linearization error, ρ and c should be determined so that the parameter set satisfying Eq.   includes one satisfying both
Eq.   and noise bound

$$ \boldsymbol{w}_t \boldsymbol{W}^{-1} \boldsymbol{w}_t \leq 1. \tag{23} $$

First a linearizing point is found by iterative solving of Eq.   with an initial
solution $\tilde{\boldsymbol{x}}_t$. Then Eq.   is linearized and decomposed into each component y_i.
The decomposed $\boldsymbol{h}'_i$ is determined as $\boldsymbol{m}_i$ in Eq.   . Next h_i is sampled in the
predicted ellipsoid and checked whether $w_i = h_i - y_i$ is within its bounds of
Eq.   . ρ_i and c_i are determined from the passed samples as shown in Fig   .
If the passed samples are divided in some divisions like in Fig   , linearization
and sampling are started again for each division and then multiple segmented
bounds are obtained. In such cases, multiple updated ellipsoids are generated.
Each corresponds to a candidate of interpretation.

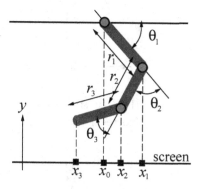

Fig. 8. Representation of an articulated object

Table 1. Object constraints (tight set)

pose constraints	$\|\theta_2 - \theta_3\| \leq \pi/6\text{rad}$, $0\text{rad} \leq \theta_2, \theta_3 \leq \pi/2\text{rad}$,
shape constraints	$0 \leq r_1 - r_2 \leq 15$, $\|r_2 - r_3\| \leq 15$, $65 \leq r_1 \leq 90$, $50 \leq r_2 \leq 75$, $45 \leq r_3 \leq 65$

Table 2. Object constraints (loose set)

pose constraints	$\|\theta_2 - \theta_3\| \leq \pi/6\text{rad}$, $0\text{rad} \leq \theta_2, \theta_3 \leq \pi/2\text{rad}$,
shape constraints	$0 \leq r_1 - r_2 \leq 30$, $\|r_2 - r_3\| \leq 30$, $52.5 \leq r_1 \leq 102.5$, $37.5 \leq r_2 \leq 87.5$, $20 \leq r_3 \leq 80$

5　Experimental Result

5.1　Experimental Setup

We have performed computer simulation experiments to prove the validity of the method. For simplicity, we use a 2-D link object as in Fig.　to estimate its lengths r and joint angles θ. It has a three joints rotating in a $x-y$ plane and its dynamics is unknown – transition matrix A is assumed to be identity. However, all joint angles and the differences between the most proximal joint angle and the second proximal one are constrained within a certain range. Possible ranges of the link lengths are also assumed. As an observation system, only 1-D position x for each joint is observed and the depth y is not available. The transition and observation noise is supposed to be bounded.

5.2　Result of Shape Recovery and Accuracy

In order to verify the estimation accuracy, we show estimation results for the link object. First, the tight constraint set shown in Tab.　is applied. The result

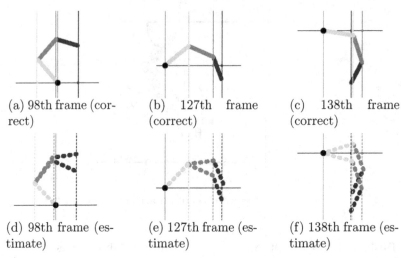

(a) 98th frame (correct)

(b) 127th frame (correct)

(c) 138th frame (correct)

(d) 98th frame (estimate)

(e) 127th frame (estimate)

(f) 138th frame (estimate)

Fig. 9. Multiple estimates

is shown in Fig.   and   . Then another constraint set shown in Tab.   twice times looser than Tab.   is applied. The result is shown in Fig.   . With the tight constraints, the estimated range of r (shown by each vertical bar) is getting small in early time. With the loose constraints in contrast, the range is getting small more slowly but finally converges to the correct value (shown by a straight line). The final range is almost the same as the tight constraints. In Fig.   , there are cases that more than one estimates (shown as circles) are obtained. This means that there are multiple symmetric interpretations due to depth ambiguity (see Figs.   (d)-(f)).

5.3   Dependency on Initial Estimate

Next, in order to verify dependency of the estimate on initial estimates, we show estimation results for the same observation sequence starting from two different initial estimates in Figs.   and   . Regardless of initial estimates, each shape estimate of r_1 finally converges to almost the same correct value. This means that there is no remarkable dependency on initial estimates.

5.4   Identification of Different Shape

In order to verify the ability to identify different shapes, we show estimation results for two objects whose link lengths differ from each other. The estimation for each object starts from the same initial estimate and with the same constraint set. As the experimental result, Fig.   shows the correct, initial, and finally estimated objects extending all joints in order to compare lengths of the

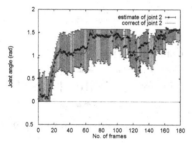

Fig.10. Estimate of joint angle θ_2

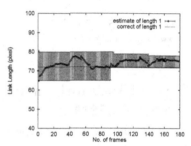

Fig.11. Estimates of the 1st link length r_1

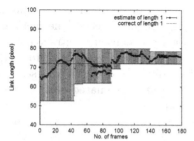

Fig.12. Estimates of the 1st link length r_1 with looser constraints

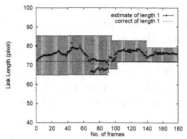

Fig.13. Estimates of the 1st link length r_1 (started from another initial estimate)

corresponding links. Concludingly, Fig.   tells that all link lengths appropriately converge to the correct values for both objects. This means that the system correctly identified the two different shapes.

6   Conclusion and Discussion

This paper has proposed a method which simultaneously estimates a 3-D shape and moving pose of an articulated object from a monocular image sequence.

This paper pointed out a Kalman filter estimate essentially converges to wrong state for non-linear unobservable systems. For an alternative, the paper has proposed a set-membership-based method including dynamics. The method limits the depth ambiguity by considering inequality constraints such as possible ranges of joint angles, lengths or widths of parts. Using these constraints, it provides shape recovery of articulated objects under monocular systems. Effectiveness of the framework has been shown by estimation results for an articulated

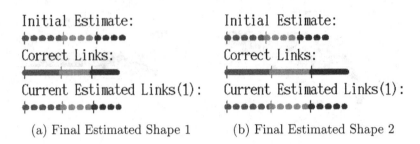

(a) Final Estimated Shape 1   (b) Final Estimated Shape 2

Fig. 14. Object identification

object. Although the system shown in the experiment section adopts an only two-dimensional link object whose joint points can be observed, the proposed method can be applied to cases of three-dimensional objects. The method can use any other observations such as object axes or contours extracted by edge detection or active contour method. A weak point of set-membership methods is an outlier problem. Since bounded noises are supposed, the intersection set may become empty by an outlier noise over the pre-estimated noise bounds. It is a future work to detect and remove outliers.

Appendix: Predictive Update by Dynamics

Here, define a vector z_t as

$$z_t = ((x_t - q_t)^T, u_t^T)^T. \tag{24}$$

With the above equation and Eq. , the following relation

$$z_t^T Q z_t \leq 1 \quad where \quad Q = \begin{pmatrix} (1+\lambda)P_t & O \\ O & (1+\frac{1}{\lambda})U \end{pmatrix}^{-1} \tag{25}$$

is derived and Eqs. and   conclude

$$x_{t+1} = A(x_t - q_t) + Bu_t + Aq_t = (A\ B)z_t + Aq_t. \tag{26}$$

In general, the following relations

$$z^T Q^{-1} z \leq 1, \quad x = Cz + d \tag{27}$$

yield

$$(x - d)^T (CQC^T)^{-1}(x - d) \leq 1 \tag{28}$$

if $m \leq n$ and rank C equals to m where C is a m times n matrix (this condition means that $\{Cz\}$ spans a linear space of m dimensions). Therefore Eq. is rewritten as the form of Eq.   and the followings are derived by substituting $C = (A \; B)$, $d = Aq_t$ and $x = x_{t+1}$ into Eq.   :

$$(x_{t+1} - Aq_t)^T \left\{ (1 + \lambda) A P_t A^T + \left(1 + \frac{1}{\lambda} \right) B U B^T \right\} (x_{t+1} - Aq_t) \leq 1 \quad (29)$$

By comparison of Eq.   with Eq. , Eqs.   and   are derived.

References

1. D. Lowe. "Fitting Parameterized Three Dimentional Models to Images". *IEEE Trans., Pattern Anal. Machine Intell.,vol.13,No.5*, pp. 441–450, 1991.
2. R. J. Holt, A. N. Netravali, T. Huang, and Richard J. Qian. "Determining Articulated Motion from Perspective Views: A Decomposition Approach". In *Proc. of Workshop on Motion of Non-Rigid and Ariticulated Objects '94*, pp. 126–137. IEEE, 1994.
3. N. Shimada, Y. Shirai, Y. Kuno, and J. Miura. "Hand Gesture Estimation and Model Refinement using Monocular Camera – Ambiguity Limitation by Inequality Constraints". In *Proc. of 3rd Int. Conf. on Automatic Face and Gesture Recognition*, pp. 268–273, 1998.   ,
4. F. C. Schweppe. "Recursive State Estimation: Unknown but Bounded Errors and System Inputs". *IEEE Trans. on Automatic Control, vol.AC-13, No.1*, pp. 22–28, 1968.   ,
5. E. Fogel and Y. F. Huang. "On the Value of Information in System Identification – Bounded Noise Case". *Automatica, vol.18, No.2*, pp. 229–238, 1982.   ,   ,
   ,
6. Y. Hel-Or and M. Werman. "Recognition and Localization of Articulated Objects". In *Proc. of Workshop on Motion of Non-Rigid and Ariticulated Objects '94*, pp. 116–123. IEEE, 1994.
7. S. P. Engelson G. D. Hager and S. Atiya. "On Comparing Sastistical and Set Based Methods in Sensor Data Fusion". *Proc. IEEE Int. Conf. on Robotics and Automation '93*, pp. 352–358, 1993.   ,
8. L. Chisci, A. Grulli, and G. Zappa. "Recursive State Bounding by Parallelotopes". *Automatica, Vol. 32 No.7*, pp. 1049–1055, 1996.
9. R. E. Ellis. "Geometric Uncertainties in Polyhedral Object Recognition". *IEEE Trans. on Robotics and Automation, vol.7, No.3*, pp. 361–371, 1991.

Automatic Selection of *Keyframes* for Activity Recognition

X. Varona, J. Gonzàlez, F. X. Roca, and J. J. Villanueva

Computer Vision Center & Dept. de Informàtica, Universitat Autònoma de Barcelona
Edifici O, 08193 Bellaterra(Barcelona), Spain
xaviv@cvc.uab.es, poal@cvc.uab.es
http://www.cvc.uab.es

Abstract. Recognizing activities in image sequences is an open problem in computer vision. In this paper we present a method to extract the most significant frames from an activity sequence. We name these frames as the *keyframes*. Moreover, we describe a pre-processing stage in order to build a robust representation for different human movements. Using this representation, we build an activity eigenspace that is used to obtain a probability measure. We use this measure to develop a method to select the activity *keyframes* automatically.

1   Introduction

Humans use a lot of languages to communication. One of them is body language which can give different types of information such as emotions and warnings. The basis of body language are the human movements and activities. The parts of the human body can move in quite independent ways. Human movements, such as walking, running, kicking, etc., are very constrained by factors including motion symmetries or dynamics. A sequence of human movements is a human activity.

Recognizing human activities is not a new task in computer vision [, ,]. There are two basics approaches: physics or appearance based. The physics based approach might involve locating and tracking the limbs and extremities of the body under control of a mechanism that optimizes the tracking with respect to known physical contraints embedded in a body model. This appoach requires a controlled environment due to the difficulties of identifying body parts in natural video imagery. Also, it is difficult to develop efficient computational methods for modeling and enforcing such physical constraints.

The alternative approach is to use appearance based models for human motion. The main challenges to such models are viewpoint dependence, dealing with appearance variability (changes in clothing, shadows, body size and proportions between individuals), recognition in the presence of occlusion, etc. These challenges involves that the domain of such methods is still very constrained, i.e., stationary or controlled background. Our work is based on this approach.

Consider the frame shown in Fig. . Even with only one frame you can recognize the activity as someone running. Such capability argues for recognizing

H. H. Nagel and F. J. Perales (Eds.): AMDO 2000, LNCS 1899, pp. 173–   , 2000.

Fig. 1. Eadweard Muybridge, The Human Figure in Motion, frame extracted from Plate 23: Man running. [ ]

an activity only by selecting few frames from the entire sequence. These frames correspond to the most distinctive movements of the activity. We will call them the *keyframes* of an activity. This paper addresses the problem of automatic selection of these characteristic frames. With these frames, we have a representation of the entire activity. By detecting these keyframes in an on-line sequence, we should be able to describe the activity which is being performed.

The method presented here is based on appearance methods. Therefore, we need to use a description of human body that is invariant to changes in environment and in human clothing. In section 2 we describe this process. In section 3, we present an automatic algorithm for the extraction of *keyframes* following a probabilistic scheme. Experiments are showed in order to validate our method. Lastly, conclusions and further work will also be presented.

2   Human Body Description

Before extracting the *keyframes* from an activity sequence, some pre-processing operations are required. An activity recognition system involves, first of all, the segmentation of the actors in order to detect them. To achieve such a segmentation, we have followed the method described by Oliver et al., the *EigenBackground* [ ].

This method of background subtraction copes with lighting changes if objects of interest are small because it is possible to adapt the model during the extraction process. In our case, we do not adapt the model after the learning stage due to size of the actors. Therefore, it is necessary a previous stage in order to correct the effects of lighting. The global variation of lighting in a sequence is found and removed from the input images.

The description details of the lighting correction process can be found in [ ]. Once a set of background images $\{B^1(x,y), B^2(x,y), \cdots, B^L(x,y)\}$ has been acquired, the reference background image $M(x,y) = (M_R(x,y), M_G(x,y), M_B(x,y))$ is computed as its average. The effects of illumination changes are assumed to be isotropic and to act as an independent contrast factor for each color channel. That is to say, a background image $B^i(x, y)$ can be expressed as:

$$B^i(x, y) = M(x, y) \begin{pmatrix} k_R & 0 & 0 \\ 0 & k_G & 0 \\ 0 & 0 & k_B \end{pmatrix} + \varepsilon(x, y) \tag{1}$$

where $\varepsilon(x, y) = (\varepsilon_R(x, y), \varepsilon_G(x, y), \varepsilon_B(x, y))$ is a zero mean noise term and k_R, k_G and k_B are the parameters that must be determined in order to correct the illumination. An estimation of the k factors (k_R, k_G and k_B) could be found by minimum squared errors.

In order to perform the background modeling, we compute the mean background image, μ_b, and its covariance matrix, Σ_b. After applying dimensionality reduction using Principal Component Analysis (PCA), the background model is represented by a set of eigenvectors corresponding to the biggest eigenvalues. Small movements of the camera and the background are well described in this eigenspace model, so a more robust segmentation is achieved.

When an image from the activity sequence is processed, after the ligthting correction is applied, it is projected onto the eigenspace of the background model. By reconstructing the image, pixels corresponding to foreground regions will dissappear, due to the fact that they have no contribution to the background model. After, subtracting the reconstructed image from the original image gives the set of pixels corresponding to foreground objects. A thresholding operation is performed in order to generate clean silhouettes of the foreground objects. We can see the results of the segmentation process in Fig. .

Fig. 2. Example of the segmentation process. Left: Original frame. Right: Actor segmented

In other related works such as [, ,] the blob-like representation is suficient to achieve activity recognition. However, they are based on 2D models of humans and simple blob statistics. These features are not enough to extract the most distinctive frames from an activity. Kovàcs et al. suggested a concise representation of visual shape based on skeletal representations [ ]. In their work, they computed a function based on an equidistance metric. Thus, a grey-level non-uniform skeleton is found. Peaks represent the largest amount of edge information. Based on their work, we apply the transform map onto the segmented image. This representation is local, compact and suitable to perform multi-scale analysis. Also it is highly affected by changes in shape. This is a very desiderable characteristic because we seek, in fact, changes in shape in order to select the most distinctive ones.

Fig. 3. Human description used for the *keyframe* extraction method

For our purpose, this representation has also another great benefit : it is independent of the appearance. That is, it doesn't mind, for example, if actors wear different clothes. We don't use the pixel values of the original frame. Applying the distance map involves that only the shape of the actor is relevant to perform the *keyframe* analysis. In Fig.   it is shown the final image of the complete preprocessing stage.

3   The Method for *Keyframes* Selection

In a sequence, the most distinctive frames of a human activity, the *keyframes*, correspond to the less probable ones. That means, in an activity we can found quite a few repetitive frames. The less repetitive frames corresponds to extreme motions, and they are those which distinguish between different activities. Our goal is to find these frames.

Using different example activity sequences, we build an eigenspace in order to represent an activity as a set of points, each one corresponding to a frame of the sequences. The method for human description described before is applied to obtain the movement description for each frame of the sequence. The descriptions extracted from different image sequences of the same activity are used to model the activity eigenspace.

Using the activity eigenspace we can use a likelihood measure, described by Mogghaddam and Pentland in [ ]. This method uses a Gaussian density in order to model the eigenspace. Therefore, it is possible to compute the probability that a pattern, $\mathbf{x}$, i.e. a frame, belongs to the eigenspace. Moreover, if the dimensionality reduction is applied, the authors present a distance definition as a sufficent statistic for characterizing the likelihood,

$$\hat{d}(\mathbf{x}) = \sum_{i=1}^{M} \frac{y_i^2}{\lambda_i} + \frac{\epsilon^2(\mathbf{x})}{\rho} \qquad (2)$$

where $\mathbf{y}$ are the frame projection in the activity eigenspace, λ_i are the eigenvalues, and M is the number of dimensions of the reduced eigenspace. $\epsilon^2(\mathbf{x})$ is the distance from feature space (DFFS) and it is computed as

$$\epsilon^2(\mathbf{x}) = \sum_{i=M+1}^{N} y_i^2 = \| \tilde{\mathbf{x}} \|^2 - \sum_{i=1}^{M} y_i^2 \tag{3}$$

where $\tilde{\mathbf{x}}$ is the frame $\mathbf{x}$ (image pixels in lexicographic order) mean normalized (by subtracting the mean), and N is the original dimension of the image space. Finally, ρ is a weight that is found by minimizing a cost function (see [ ]),

$$\rho = \frac{1}{N - M} \sum_{i=M+1}^{N} \lambda_i. \tag{4}$$

Using $\hat{d}(\mathbf{x})$ we have a distance measurement for each frame. Applying a temporal ordering to each distance of an activity sequence we obtain a graphic distance vs time that is used to find the *keyframes*. For example, in Fig.   it can be seen the graphic for an activity sequence. Peaks of Fig.   correspond to less likely frames. These less likely frames can be thought as the frames that contains more information (the entropy is the inverse of probability). Therefore, these frames are considered as the *keyframes* of the activity sequence. Moreover, temporal ordering makes suitable to use a difference operator in order to obtain the *keyframes*. The graphic of Fig.   has been calculated from the sequence shows in Fig.   .

The method interpretation is that extreme motions correspond to the most distinctive frames from an activity sequence. The rest of movements are repetitive and they occur to arrive to the extreme movement. From a probability point of view, extreme movements are the less probable in an entire activity sequence. This fact is simply a consequence of the number of frames where the movement appears (less than the repetitive movements).

4   The Experimental Results

The complete process to obtain the *keyframes* for an activity are:

1. To obtain a sufficient number of example sequences for an activity.
2. To normalize the activity sequences using the preprocessing stage to compute a robust description for the human movements.
3. To build the activity eigenspace applying PCA to the normalized sequence.
4. To compute the frame distances for each sequence.
5. To use a voting scheme to select the keyframes.

The voting scheme consists of obtaining the *keyframe* candidates for each activity sequence of the sequence data set used to build the activity eigenspace. Candidates that appear in most sequences are selected as *keyframes*. In Fig.

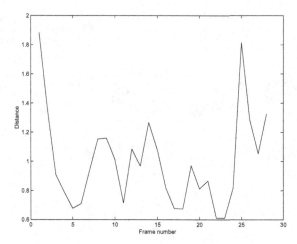

Fig. 4. This graphic shows the distance values, $\hat{d}$, for each activity frame in temporal order

Fig. 5. Sequence used to draw the graphic of Fig.   . The frames are ordered in lexicographic order. From Fig.   the maximum values correspond to frames 9, 14, 19 and 25th. These are the *keyframe* candidates

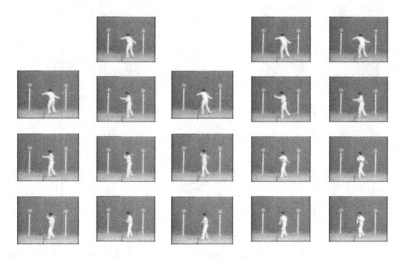

Fig. 6. *Keyframe* candidates : each column represents the keyframe candidates for each of five sequences of the same activity

we show the candidates of different sequences corresponding to the same tennis activity.

In order to evaluate the algorithm we took sequences as shown in Fig. . We took four different tennis activities, and five different sequences for each activity. Fig. , , and   show the *keyframes* generated for each activity. One can easily guess which kind of activity is being represented by each set of *keyframes*.

Fig. 7. *Keyframe* set for first tennis activity

5   Conclusions and Further Work

We have defined *keyframes* like the most representative frames from an activity sequence. To obtain these frames, we preprocess the image frames to obtain a suitable representation for human movements. Using this representation, we build an activity eigenspace and we use a likelihood measure to select automatically the *keyframes* for an activity.

Fig. 8. *Keyframe* set for second tennis activity

Fig. 9. *Keyframe* set for third tennis activity

Fig. 10. *Keyframe* set for fourth tennis activity

The natural extension of our work is test the activity *keyframes* in real sequences of simple human movements. Our method can be used in an on-line manner to known the human activities when a *keyframe* appears.

References

1. J. Aggarwal and Q. Cai. Human motion analysis: A review. *Computer Vision and Image Understanding*, 73(3):428–440, 1999.
2. A. F. Bobick. Movement, activity, and action: The role of knowledge in the perception of motion. Technical Report 413, M.I.T. Media Laboratory Perceptual Computing Section, 1997.
3. A. F. Bobick and J. Davis. An appearence-based representation of action. In *Proceedings of International Conference on Pattern Recognition (ICPR'96)*, 1996.
4. D. Gavrilla. The visual analysis of human movement: A survey. *Computer Vision and Image Understanding*, 73(1):82–98, 1999.
5. I. Haritaoglu, D. Harwood, and L. S. Davis. W4: Who? when? where? what? a real time system for detecting and tracking people. In *Proceedings of Third International Conference on Automatic Face and Gesture Recognition*, pages 222–227, Nara, Japan, 1998.
6. I. Kovacs, A. Feher, and B. Julesz. Medial-point description of shape: a representation for action coding and its psychophysical correlates. *Vision Research*, 38(15-16):2323–2333, 1998.

7. B. Moghaddam and A. Pentland. Probabilistic visual learning for object represen- tation. *IEEE Trans. Pattern Analysis and Machine Intelligence*, 19(7):696–710, 1997.   ,

8. E. Muybridge. *The Human Figure in Motion*. Dover Publications, 1955.

9. N. Oliver, B. Rosario, and A. Pentland. A bayesian computer vision system for modeling human interactions. In *Proceedings of Intl. Conference on Vision Systems (ICVS'99)*, 1999.

10. A. Pujol, F. Lumbreras, X. Varona, and J. Villanueva. Locating people in indoor scenes for real applications. In *Proceedings of International Conference on Pattern Recognition (ICPR 2000)*, Barcelona, Spain, 2000.

11. C. R. Wren, A. Azarbayejani, T. Darrell, and A. P. Pentland. Pfinder: Real- time tracking of the human body. *IEEE Trans. Pattern Analysis and Machine Intelligence*, 19(7):780–785, 1997.

Author Index

Lecture Notes in Computer Science

For information about Vols. 1–1804
please contact your bookseller or Springer-Verlag